The Quality and Productivity Equation

The Quality and Productivity Equation

American Corporate Strategies for the 1990s

Ross E. Robson
Editor-in-Chief
Associate Dean for Business Relations and Director,
Partners in Business Program, College of Business
Utah State University

Productivity Press
Cambridge, Massachusetts   Norwalk, Connecticut

658.4
Q1

Productivity Press
P.O. Box 3007
Cambridge, Massachusetts 02140
United States of America
telephone: (617) 497-5146
telefax: (617) 868-3524

ISBN: 0-915299-71-2

Jacket design by Joyce C. Weston
Text design by Caroline Kutil
Typeset by Rudra Press, Cambridge, Massachusetts
Printed and bound by The Maple-Vail Book Manufacturing Group
Printed in the United States of America

Grateful acknowledgement is made to the National Academy of Engineering for permission to reprint "Turning Ideas into Products" by Ralph E. Gomory, originally published in the Spring 1988 journal *The Bridge*, Vol. 18, No. 1.

Library of Congress Cataloging-in-Publication Data

The quality and productivity equation: American corporate strategies for the 1990s/Ross E. Robson, editor-in-chief: foreword by John Young.
    p.   cm.
    ISBN 0-915299-71-2
    1. Industrial management — United States.   2. Industrial productivity — United States.   3. Quality of products — United States.
4. Competition, International.   I. Robson, Ross E.
HD70.U5Q35   1980   89-70204
658.5 — dc20   CIP

90 91 92   10 9 8 7 6 5 4 3 2 1

Contents

A Note from the Publisher

American manufacturing is being challenged today by an extraordinary increase in world productivity. This challenge comes particularly from Japan and other Pacific Rim nations, and it will soon be joined by "Europe 1992." Without hesitation I can say that Utah State University's Partners in Business seminars help educate students and businesspeople alike to what is happening in the United States today — in both good and "needs work" areas.

When I first went to Japan in the early 1980s, the Japanese were criticized regularly for being copiers, not creators. Everybody said, "All they do is copy us; they don't do anything original." I became a little confused by the criticism after seeing shop windows filled with advanced tape recorders, cameras, and video cassette recorders. In their plants, I saw the widespread use of clever mistake-proofing devices that prevented defects. More and more, Japan looked like a very creative society.

I am told that Japan has made very few breakthroughs in basic science. There is evidence, in fact, that the situation might not change. A recent survey by the Japan Management Association polled companies about issues in research and development. Companies said that the second most important R & D issue was spending more money on applied rather than basic research. (The most important issue was that any new field a company entered had to be an extension of an existing technology.)

In 1988, Kenichi Fukui, a Japanese Nobel Prize winner, criticized Japanese industry for this over-emphasis on applied research at the expense of basic scientific inquiry. Japan couldn't hold it's head up as a nation if it left basic research to others, he argued. Japan had a "moral obligation" to support basic research because it benefitted from that done in other countries. Japan had to sow as well as reap.

Every country reaps the benefits of research done in other countries. We all copy, to a degree, because every original idea is built on the ideas of others. It was a British scientist who discovered electrons in the late 19th century. Does that make the entire U.S. electronic industry a bunch of copycats? No. Americans built on the original work that occurred in Britain, and added a lot of their own along the way. But I'll bet 50 or 60 years ago, people in Britain criticized the United States for being a nation of copiers, taking the fruits of British research to build a prosperous industry.

The real keys to creativity are our willingness to question and struggle. Without a questioning mind, one that is always looking for improvement, we will never be creative because questioning is hard. Most people never do it.

The danger in writing off the Japanese as a nation of copiers is that we lull ourselves into a false sense of security. If they are copiers, then we don't have to worry about them competing with us in basic science. That attitude is dangerous. Once, we thought they could never compete with us in electronics or automobile manufacturing.

Mr. Fukui, who won the Nobel Prize in chemistry in 1981, made another important point about creativity. Only one American won a Nobel Prize, not counting the Peace Prize, in the first 20 years after the award was established in 1901. Europe dominated the arts and sciences. Now the United States dominates. Between 1960 and 1980, two-thirds of the winners were Americans. But who would have guessed in 1901?

This is the second book Productivity Press has published of material coming out of the Utah State business seminars. In this volume, you will read about creativity in America today. You will learn about different techniques that successful U.S. companies are using to compete in today's global environment. You will read words of wisdom and promise from some contributors, while others balance their remarks with realism and caution. We need to hear all sides. To be aware in today's business world is to be conscious of the many aspects influencing our existence.

Ours is an age of rapid change. We cannot afford to fear the uncertainty of our challenges. To survive, we must promote innovation and creativity in every area of our enterprises, from top to bottom and from bottom to top. To succeed, individual corporate leaders as well as top and middle managers must become entrepreneurial and innovative. While trying to produce the highest quality goods or services at the lowest cost, we must simultaneously explore new areas of endeavor. This challenge will not end.

It is imperative that the kind of information in this volume be available to the manufacturing world. We have a lot to learn from each other and it is a special thing when people come together, as they do via these seminars, to discuss ideas, divulge success stories, and compare experiences.

As the publisher, I wish to thank everyone who contributed to this project. Utah State University's College of Business has sponsored yet another series of progressive seminars on primary topics addressed by today's leaders in corporate and academic America. I am exceedingly grateful to those contributors who speak out in praise as well as in reproof. Every one of us in business needs to expand our awareness. We should all be grateful for having another opportunity to learn.

I personally wish to acknowledge the persistence of the Productivity Press staff involved in this project, particularly Cheryl Rosen, project editor; our production staff of David Lennon and Esmé McTighe; and Steven Ott, vice president and acquisitions. Gayle Joyce and Michele Seery of Rudra Press achieved their usual high quality design and composition as did freelance cover designer, Joyce C. Weston.

Norman Bodek
Publisher

Foreword

Creating a successful quality and productivity equation with an eye toward profitability is an immense challenge for any business. But as the corporate challenges and strategies outlined in this seventh volume covering Utah State University's Partners in Business seminars conclude, the challenge *must* be met for businesses to remain competitive in the global marketplace.

The global challenge can be met by ensuring an educated and trained workforce and by recognizing and addressing the everchanging need to innovate and reorganize our management systems to meet the needs of today's customers.

Many American firms are striving to meet the challenges of the rapidly-changing environment, and this volume chronicles their efforts. The bottom-line message of U.S.U.'s seminar proceedings is that businesses must meet both quality and productivity standards or prepare for a declining share of the market, if not extinction. The chapters of this book present attainable methods and strategies to meet the challenges of the future. I commend this book to anyone seeking an understanding of the quality and productivity challenge facing worldwide business.

The enviable Partners in Business program of the College of Business at Utah State University is celebrating its twentieth year of "building an academic/corporate America" capable of competing in our global marketplace. The Partners in Business is a program to be commended for its efforts to improve the condition of American competitiveness. Today's challenges require the interaction of the best minds in business and academia for the betterment of training for the future.

John A. Young
President & CEO, Hewlett-Packard, and
Chairman, The Council on Competitiveness

Acknowledgements

This is the seventh volume of the proceedings of the Partners in Business seminars held annually at Utah State University. The previous volumes were edited by Professors Y.K. Shetty and Vernon M. Buehler, who have paved the way for this volume.

The best company practices and research reported herein primarily represent the proceedings of three of seven seminars conducted by the student-staffed Partners in Business program, which is now in its 20th year. Executive visits to the campus of Utah State University not only enhance the student and faculty experience at that institution, but also benefit the nearly 600 business and governmental partners who subscribe to the program. The 32 chapters in this volume were selected from over 100 presentations by business and governmental executives and academics from across the United States. Over 17,000 partners and approximately 3,000 to 5,000 students benefitted from the 1989 presentations by executives and academicians from the following organizations:

3COM, Santa Clara, California
Adolph Coors Company, Golden, Colorado
Allen, Nelson, Hardy & Evans, Salt Lake City, Utah
American Express, Salt Lake City, Utah
American Transtech, Jacksonville, Florida
Arthur Andersen, Chicago, Illinois
Ask Computers, Los Altos, California
Bank of America, San Francisco, California
Bartel Software, Midvale, Utah
Baxter Healthcare Corporation, Deerfield, Illinois
Baxter Travenol Laboratories, Deerfield, Illinois

Bechtel Group, San Francisco, California
Beehive Machinery, Sandy, Utah
BellSouth, Atlanta, Georgia
Bethlehem Steel, Bethlehem, Pennsylvania
Boeing Company, Seattle, Washington
Brigham Young University, Provo, Utah
Canadian Consulate General, San Francisco, California
Cargo Link International, Salt Lake City, Utah
Carnegie Endowment for International Peace, Washington, DC
Cedarapids Inc., Eugene, Oregon
Centers of Excellence, Salt Lake City, Utah
Chemical Bank, New York, New York
Chicken Soup Inc., Minneapolis, Minnesota
Cirris Systems Corporation, Salt Lake City, Utah
Columbia University, New York, New York
ConAgra Inc., Omaha, Nebraska
Conway Quality Inc., Nashua, New Hampshire
Copeland Griggs, San Francisco, California
Council on Competitiveness, Washington, DC
The Diebold Group, New York, New York
Eaton Corporation, Cleveland, OH
Excel Industries, Elkhart, Indiana
Farmers Group Inc., Los Angeles, California
Federal Express, Memphis, Tennessee
First Interstate Bank, Salt Lake City, Utah
Florida Power & Light, Miami, Florida
Forbes Inc., New York, New York
GTE Communications, Phoenix, Arizona
General Dynamics, Fort Worth, Texas
General Signal, Stamford, Connecticut
Geneva Steel, Provo, Utah
George Washington University, Washington, DC
Georgetown University, Washington, DC
Granville-Phillips, Boulder, Colorado
Gullian/Craig & Associates, San Francisco, California
Harvard University, Cambridge, Massachusetts
Hewlett-Packard, Palo Alto, California
* Hill Air Force Base, Utah
Hughes Aircraft, Fullerton, California
* IBM, Armonk, New York
Index Technology, Cambridge, Massachusetts
Information Ideas Inc., Oakland, California
Infoworld, Menlo Park, California
Ingersoll Engineers, Rockford, Illinois
Intel, Santa Clara, California
Intertek Services, Rolling Hills, California

* Johnson & Johnson, New Brunswick, New Jersey
Kellogg Company, Battle Creek, Michigan
Krishna Copy Center, San Francisco, California
Litton Industries, Woodland Hills, California
MCI, Arlington, Virginia
MSU System Services, New Orleans, Louisiana
McDermott Inc., New Orleans, Louisiana
Morrison & Foerster, Washington, DC
* Motorola, Schaumburg, Illinois
Mrs. Fields Inc., Park City, Utah
Mutual Benefit Life, Newark, New Jersey
National Science Foundation, Washington, DC
Novell, Provo, Utah
Peat, Marwick & Main, Salt Lake City, Utah
Perkin-Elmer, Norwalk, Connecticut
Perot & Associates, Dallas, Texas
Pinchot & Company, New Haven, Connecticut
Rohm & Hass, Philadelphia, Pennsylvania
Ryder System, Miami, Florida
SJS Advanced Strategy, Washington, DC
Santa Clara University, Santa Clara, California
Security Pacific Corporation, Los Angeles, California
SmithKline Beckman Corporation, Philadelphia, Pennsylvania
Suitter Axland Armstrong, Salt Lake City, Utah
TRW Inc., Cleveland, Ohio
Tandem Computers, Cupertino, California
Terralab Engineering, Salt Lake City, Utah
Texaco, Houston, Texas
Texas Instruments, Dallas, Texas
U.S. Consulate General, Calgary, Alberta, Canada
U.S. Chamber of Commerce, Washington, DC
Unisys, Salt Lake City, Utah
United Auto Workers, Detroit, Michigan
United Auto Workers Local 974, East Peoria, Illinois
United HealthCare, Baltimore, Maryland
United SteelWorkers, Salt Lake City, Utah
University of Southern California, Los Angeles, California
University of Michigan, Ann Arbor, Michigan
University of North Carolina, Chapel Hill, North Carolina
Utah International Trade Development Office, Salt Lake City, Utah
Utah State University, Logan, Utah
Utah Transit Authority, Murray, Utah
Wal-Mart, Bentonville, Arkansas
Walt Disney Company, Burbank, California
Weirton Steel Corporation, Weirton, West Virginia
XICOM Incorporated, Tuxedo, New York
Xerox, Stamford, Connecticut

* indicates multiple visits

In addition, we acknowledge the considerable assistance of a number of state and national professional associations in support of both the Partners in Business program and the Shingo Prizes for Excellence in Manufacturing, which Utah State University administers.

Special recognition is due to Karen S. Richards for her outstanding editorial review of each chapter, and to Cheryl Berling Rosen, project editor for Productivity Press.

The Partners in Business student staff assisted in numerous ways, with Walter Young providing timely assistance and support in all facets of the production process, Jay Ward recording and collecting original manuscripts, and the remainder of the staff assisting in all facets of the seminars. These staffers include:

Roger Anderson, David Bland, Rebecca Brown, Darin Bushman, Julie Duersch, Mike Humberstone, Brad Kartchner, Jill Layton, Mark Merrill, Glenn Morris, Jill Robinson, David Ward, Jennifer Ward, and Laurica Winn. Thanks are also extended to Dixie Lee Jenson, who recently joined Partners in Business as administrative assistant.

Without the generous support and assistance of David B. Stephens, Dean of the College of Business; President Stanford Cazier; Provost Karen W. Morse; Vice Presidents Val R. Christensen, Bartell C. Jensen, William F. Lye, and Evan N. Stevenson; and the College of Business faculty, the scope and quality of the program could not be assured.

Lastly, to my wife, DaNece Newey Robson, and my children, Kyle, Kimberly, Trent, and Travis, who share their husband and father in his professional pursuits, I give my love and thanks.

The Quality and
Productivity Equation

PART I

The Equation

1

Corporate Strategies for the Quality and Productivity Equation

Karen S. Richards and Ross E. Robson

The importance of aiming for ever-increasing levels of quality and productivity to ensure American competitiveness in the global marketplace has been recognized for years. To be successful, American firms must adapt to the new, increasingly competitive global business environment. This elusive goal will undoubtedly continue to be stressed well into the 21st century.

The productivity and quality equation, like any equation, is made up of variables and constants. Starting with the premise that all enterprises share certain constants — capital, a production process, information and records, and the human element, for instance — the variables in the equation can be defined as how policies are formulated and applied to these constants to optimize quality and performance. While the variables involved in quality and productivity are difficult to quantify, they are, nonetheless, often identifiable. Of course, each individual enterprise must ultimately develop its own equation for enhancing quality and productivity which is specifically tailored to its particular product or service, markets, technologies, and work force.

The M.I.T. Commission on Industrial Productivity in its book *Made In America: Regaining the Productivity Edge* (M.I.T. Press, 1989) suggests looking to "best practice" firms — those that are responding successfully to opportunities and constraints of a new environment in making significant simultaneous progress in quality, cost, and speed — to help identify strategies that can be applied to improving productive performance.

The Commission suggests examining the situation on a case-by-case basis and building from specific observations to more general conclusions regarding the crucial elements of productive performance. They have found that although there is a lack of consensus concerning what matters most in this equation, patterns and similarities have emerged in the successful firms that they have studied.

The Commission suggests that the similarities in most effective firms include the following:

1. Simultaneous improvement in quality, cost, delivery, human resources, and MIS. These firms strive to be the *best* in their respective industries, and are constantly monitoring and comparing themselves to other industries throughout the world.
2. The firms foster close relations with both the customer — by being aware of and responding to the market and the end user; and with suppliers — by emphasizing close coordination in cutting inventories and costs, reducing defects, and speeding the flow of products.
3. Using technologies for strategic advantage. Best-practice firms have integrated technology choices into the rest of their business planning, including strategies for manufacturing, marketing, and human resources. Technology ultimately must help meet customers' needs.
4. Best-practice firms tend to evolve flatter and less compartmentalized organizational structures. These new, nonhierarchical structures require a basic change in company culture, which can be a wrenching and difficult process. The potential benefits, however, are great: increased employee participation, teamwork, communication and cooperation among departments, and decision making at lower levels in the organization.
5. Innovative human resource policies that promote participation, teamwork, trust, on-the-job education to develop firm-specific skills, job security, profit sharing, and investments in training. These kinds of strategies help focus employee attention on long-term organizational goals.

The distinguished participants in the Partners in Business seminars represent the successful, state-of-the-art application of a rich cross-section of "best-practice" principles in a wide range of industrial, service, consulting, educational, and governmental settings, and provide real and concrete examples of what can be accomplished.

Although it is undoubtedly impossible to achieve a perfect synthesis of opinion regarding what constitutes "best practice" in achieving optimal quality and productivity, the thoughtful reader will certainly discover many recurring themes throughout this record of 1989 seminar proceedings.

While the productivity and quality equation remains something of a nebulous mystery, the results of its successful application are not. Improved productivity and quality are ultimately evident in increased profits, an enhanced standard of living, and the assurance of continued long-term viability and competitiveness. As Kevin F.F. Quigley of the Carnegie Endowment for International Peace points out, "Rising productivity is the key to economic growth, which in turns provides for a rising standard of living." Alan Magazine of the Council on Competitiveness echoes this philosophy: "That is what competitiveness is about: being able to produce goods and services that assure a rising standard of living for Americans."

The speakers at the three Utah State University Partners in Business Program seminars address all of the closely interrelated themes mentioned by the M.I.T. Commission report. A brief overview of some of the predominant issues of the quality and productivity equation follows.

Simultaneous Improvement. One theme that consistently emerges is the concept that productive change must be deeply rooted in the entire fundamental organizational culture and have unconditional management support at all levels of the organization. A piecemeal "cure-all" approach simply will not work. Truly successful companies are those that strive to be "best in their class" in all quality and performance categories, and which try to make sure that all aspects of their business strategies are mutually reinforcing.

Florida Power & Light Company was recently announced as a Deming Award winner. Joe Collier, a participant in the 1989 seminars, played a major role in FP&L's successful quality improvement efforts, which used four basic principles in its push for quality: (1) focusing on the customer, (2) continuous improvement, (3) management by fact, and (4) respect for people.

Mr. Collier recommends organizational flattening, facilitated by cross-functional teams, and an emphasis on quality in daily work. He states:

> We teach our people that if you achieve quality, productivity will fol-
> low. We don't have to sell quality to our customers, we just have to
> create it. The customers will buy it. We think that quality is first and
> foremost a management process. If managers will just get out of the
> way and let their people perform, they can solve a lot of problems. We
> know that employees want to do the right thing... The role of man-
> agement then is to provide the environment, training, tools, and
> leadership and then get out of the way. Let your people do a good job.

Xerox was recently honored as a recipient of the Baldridge Quality Award. Paul A. Allaire, president of Xerox, makes the following
observations about quality, which demonstrate the philosophy and
attitude that earned Xerox this recognition:

> The quality process is continuous. That's because as we improve, two
> highly dynamic forces are at work. First, as we get better, so does our
> competition. Second, as we meet the requirements of our customers,
> their expectations of Xerox also increase. What we see is an upward
> and never-ending spiral of increased competition and heightened cus-
> tomer expectations.

University of Southern California Professor Jay R. Galbraith
highlights another aspect of Xerox's success: a much tighter coupling
with their suppliers, the number of which has decreased in recent
years from 3,000 to 300, allowing Xerox to become more competitive
through longer-term relationships, guaranteed high volume, and
elimination of intermediate activities such as incoming inspection.
The close relationship with suppliers is further strengthened by the
fact that Xerox shares gains with them.

Close Relations with Customers and Suppliers. M. Anthony Burns,
president of Ryder System, believes that relationships with suppliers and customers must be based on establishing a mutual bond of
trust through consistently conducting business in a highly ethical
way, which, he says, is "not only the moral thing; it's also very good
business."

Several speakers point to the use of information technology systems in providing an ongoing link with rapidly-changing customer

preferences, which facilitates better satisfying customer needs. Customer needs must drive every design effort — thus, it follows that direct customer contact is essential.

Innovative companies like Benetton, Reebok, and Nike are noted for their incredibly effective use of information technology in staying on top of customer demand, as well as their evolution as what Professor Galbraith calls "network organizations" — notable for their close ties with suppliers — which he defines as follows:

> Network organizations are really flexible networks of organizations. There is a hub firm that is a broker for the entire network. It establishes sets of relationships between these companies and looks out for the good of the order. All they are is marketing outfits. Everything else is subcontracted out to other people, but they control the brand, the advertising, and the financing for the entire network. They do not see these people as competitors. They look at margins for the entire network.

Technology for Strategic Advantage. Strategic information management represents one of the most important and promising applications of technology in meeting business goals. As Mylle Bell of BellSouth succinctly expressed: "Information is power."

Alan Magazine focuses on several advantages of effective information utilization:

> Information that is quickly channeled from the marketplace to the corporation speeds product development, spurs innovation, and promotes diversity as each customer's needs are assessed and filled. High-quality information management also allows the sophisticated coordination of production flows required for new techniques, such as just-in-time inventory management.

The importance of the role of research and development in the quality and productivity equation cannot be overstated. New technology is making many innovative approaches possible that will be vital to a firm's economic survival: incremental product improvements, flexibility in customizing products to individual customers, and speeding the entire production and delivery process.

Spencer Hutchens, Jr., chairman of the American Society for Quality Control, points out that:

> In business, research and development activities are undertaken for only one reason: pursuit of profit. Defining "strategic design" is simple. It means aligning the customer's needs — quality, reliability,

value, and timely delivery — with the company's goals — productivity and earning a profit.

Technology that is closely coordinated with manufacturing and human resource policies will work far better. Continuous on-the-job education of employees will enable them to maximize the potential of new technology.

Flatter and Less Compartmentalized Organizations. The hierarchical organization that still predominates in most American companies will not be adequate for the environment toward which we are rapidly moving. Mr. Magazine contends that:

> Today, progressive corporations understand that competitive advantage is built and sustained around four components: speed, innovation, diversity, and information. All are anathema to the old organization ... The old ways are just too slow and cumbersome for today's global, technology-driven economy.

Management observers view employees as members of a "symphony" more than a vertical hierarchy, with everyone responding to one CEO as the conductor keeping everyone on the same beat.

Flatter, less compartmentalized organizations have been demonstrated to promote greater speed in product development and greater responsiveness to changing markets by dismantling functional barriers, encouraging flexibility, and making direct, ongoing communication with customers more feasible.

Innovative Human Resource Policies. Human resources are at the very heart of competitiveness. More and more companies are recognizing that productivity, technology, and profits ultimately depend on a motivated, flexible, skilled work force. In the "old" organizational structure, human resources are not used to the fullest extent possible. Critical thinking, creative problem solving, analytical skills, innovation, team work, and meaningful communication are fundamentals in the quality and productivity equation, and require new approaches to reach fruition.

To tap into the full productive potential of our human resources, Terril N. Hurst, visiting scholar at Hewlett-Packard's Stanford Science

Center, points out that "people can't simply be ordered to be productive; they must be in control of their own environment and participate in any decisions which alter it." In short, progressive companies must work toward achieving a partnership with their employees.

James Whaley, vice president of Bank of America, addresses this issue:

> Lower profitability and sometimes failure wait around the corner for companies who don't build a partnership with their employees. Employee involvement reflects the basic understanding that people who feel involved with their jobs and their company do better work day-in and day-out than employees who are treated like cogs in a wheel.

Other issues in human resources include training, managing cultural diversity, and union-management teamwork.

Quality and Productivity Awards. The aim of three quality and productivity awards is to recognize and publicize North American business excellence, as well as to encourage other businesses to improve quality and productivity strategies.

The Malcolm Baldridge National Quality Award was established in 1987 by the U.S. Government (Public Law 100-107) with the stated purposes to:

- Promote quality awareness.
- Recognize quality achievements of U.S. companies.
- Publicize successful quality strategies.

Recipients of the award in the manufacturing and producers category have included Motorola, the Commercial Nuclear Fuel Division, Westinghouse Electric, Xerox, and Milliken & Company. The only recipient thus far in the small business category has been Globe Metallurgical. In addition to the promotion of quality in business, the broader goal of the Baldridge Award is to call attention to the importance of quality in all facets of business and society, including the incorporation of quality courses in educational curricula.

The NASA Excellence Award for Quality and Productivity was established in 1985 to recognize the highest standards of performance among NASA's aerospace industry contractors, subcontractors, and

suppliers. In the words of James C. Fletcher, former NASA administrator, "Quality enhancement is a precursor to productivity improvement." The NASA Excellence Award's three primary goals are to:

1. Recognize outstanding achievements in quality and productivity
   among NASA contractors.
2. Promote transfer of superior methods and ideas within the aerospace community.
3. Enhance public awareness of the importance of quality and productivity to the nation.

Only four NASA Excellence Awards have been given to date.
Recipients have included IBM Federal Systems Division, Martin
Marietta Manned Space Systems, Rocketdyne Division of Rockwell
International, and Lockheed Engineering & Scientists Company.
One criterion for application is that a "candidate must achieve a high
level of customer satisfaction and have sustained excellence and out-
standing achievements in quality and productivity for a minimum of
three years" prior to application.

The Shingo Prizes for Excellence in Manufacturing for businesses
located and operated in North America, as well as for academic research, was established in 1988. The award is named in honor of Dr.
Shigeo Shingo, whose profound insights and lifelong dedication
have resulted in vast improvements in quality and productivity not
only in Japan, but around the world. Dr. Shingo is recognized as the
primary genius behind the Toyota production system and just-in-
time. His contributions also include single-minute exchange of die
(SMED), zero quality control through the *poka-yoke* system, and key
strategies for plant-wide improvement.

Up to three business awards may be given in two categories —
large businesses and small businesses — with the dividing point
being 500 employees. Academic awards are also given in two categories:
students, both graduates and undergraduates; and professional researchers, including university faculty and commercial researchers.
The only 1989 business award winner was Globe Metallurgical. The
Van Dyke Plant of Ford Motor Company and United Electric Controls
were finalists. Academic awards were received by individuals from
Kean College, Stanford University, Auburn University, Penn State
University, University of Utah, State University of New York, University of Rhode Island, Bryant College, and Utah State University. The

purposes of the Shingo Prizes are to (1) recognize and foster excellence in manufacturing and (2) encourage further research and publication of Shingo-related manufacturing techniques. The common goal of the three U.S. awards, in addition to Japan's Deming Award, is to identify the best company practices and, in the case of the Shingo Prizes, research efforts that clarify and document the quality and productivity equation. Unfortunately, the equation remains a mystery to too many U.S. businesses.

Conclusion. Assuming that these observations are valid, the quality and productivity equation might be depicted as follows:

Simultaneous Improvements
+ Close Relations with Customers and Suppliers
+ Technology for Strategic Advantage
+ Flatter Organizations
+ Innovative Human Resource Policies
= Quality and Productivity

Best company practices, as called to our attention by Tom Peters and amplified by the quality and productivity awards, are aimed at documenting and verifying the equation.

It is toward this end, the elucidation of the quality and productivity equation, that this book is directed, by outlining appropriate American strategies for the 1990s.

PART II

The Global Challenge
and Equation

2

How Now and What Next?
The Global Challenge

Malcolm S. Forbes, Editor-in-Chief, Forbes Magazine

I cannot resist telling you a little anecdote about a couple of girls, just to put into perspective the fact that today, I think, people have more depth of awareness than these girls did in the Roaring Twenties. They had graduated from high school together in the 1920s. In the early thirties the Depression set in, and they happened to get together again. The Depression had wreaked havoc with their respective family finances. The one girl said to the other that things had been so tough that she had resorted to the world's oldest profession, prostitution. Her friend said, "Oh, before I'd do that, I'd dip into capital."

The depth of perception that people used to obtain at some educational institutions was limited. I don't think that is generally applicable anymore, but I do think that we are not yet fully aware of what a turning point we are at.

Two very epic things are happening simultaneously. These will go beyond the term of the new president and on for quite awhile. For the last several decades since World War II, the military confrontation — whether it was a cold war or a hot war in different areas of the globe at one time or another — has been real and has been in a mostly military posture. It has been a war in the sense of either piling up the hardware, or piling up the capabilities of the superpowers to destroy the globe more quickly than some of the less atomically armed nations could. It has been military.

Economics have been largely tailored to a structure of providing what is needed to preserve the free world. The economics of Russia and her allies have been tailored to what they felt they needed to stand off a hostile free world. This has changed dramatically. What we are going to face in the next decade is a very tough war. It may not be bloody, except there might be a few upheavals in domestic economies in countries that are going to be in economic trouble, but the confrontation is shifting.

Communism, as an *ism*, has not had any appeal for a very long time. It was military power that made Russia a very consequential reality as an opponent. The collapse of communism as an economic system is quite total. For us to debate whether Mr. Gorbachev is to be trusted or whether he is moved by concern for the rest of the world is irrelevant. His motivations are simple — there is very little on the shelves of Russian stores. Russia's problems lie in the collapse of its economic system and in the great epic development of this computer age. It cannot be a factor in the world today as a superpower if it does not have a grass-roots understanding and awareness of this high-tech computer age.

You cannot cut people off from information. Glasnost did not come about because Gorbachev had a vision to suddenly say, "Well, maybe we can report plane crashes now, maybe we can report things that happen both within Russia and the world that are not the way we want them to happen." Glasnost did not come about because he is an idealistically inclined reformer. It came about because of the most powerful necessity of all — economic necessity. You cannot develop a grass-roots, meaningful economy in the computer age unless information is widely accessible and shared. We cannot even keep enterprising young wizards out of the computers of the Pentagon.

Russia does not have that kind of resource bank. They do not have young people who are tuned-in and aware of how to use the age of technology of which they are a part. This economic confrontation, our big confrontation, will not be with Russia. In the decades ahead, it is going to be with the Common Market. That decade begins in about three years. It is not going to be overnight, but the reality of it is pretty tough. We have already engaged in little skirmishes with what will be the Common Market of Europe.

The reality of that has not fully set in, in either this country or in Japan and the Pacific Basin. Japan has some problems with its extraordinary progress. Korea is doing to Japan, to a degree, what Japan has done to us for the last twenty years. The development that is occurring throughout the whole Asian Basin — Taiwan, Singapore, Hong Kong, and especially Thailand — is creating new economic powers of great consequence. In this country we have what is still the most vast, homogenous, single economic market in the world. But there is the European Common Market, which in many respects is going to be far larger and stronger.

This will not happen on a set date. It will not suddenly be a situation of total unity, with all the tariff barriers gone and a common currency in circulation. Unfortunately, what is going to help keep the members of the European Common Market together in the critical beginning stages is a confrontational crisis with the United States. It is like an era when you have internal problems that are so deep that you divert the attention of your people by calling on their patriotism. They are then confronted with an enemy from without. If you don't have an enemy, you create one so as to be able to call upon your people to make sacrifices in the name of patriotism. The members of the European Common Market draw together most quickly in response to the menace of the American invasion of their markets. Many American companies are just waking up to the fact that having plants within the borders of the European Common Market will not suffice. It depends on how much of the plant's production comes from the United States and the degree of domestic content.

It is an extraordinary confrontation that does not have to be a confrontation. Wiser heads must prevail. We picked very flimsy ground for our first little skirmish — hormones in beef. I've heard of hormones in a lot of things, but the Europeans think it is a health risk, so they have said, "No hormones in your beef." In this little skirmish, they have banned our beef until we guarantee that it contains no hormones. We have, in turn, banned a number of their products, and now the situation could escalate.

What we are going to need in this shift from a military to an economic confrontation is not just muscle, but brain power. That plays enormously to the strengths of this country. Our strength lies in leadership, negotiation, and in those who will do the negotiating. The fact that in this new administration we have some people who are pragmatic, who are negotiators, is a strength. It is in the best interest of the free world that the Third World and Russia become viable markets. Even China is now developing the sinew to be a marketplace.

In the Third World, particularly South America, we have to deal with the problems of indebtedness. However, there is so much that can turn out positively in this new arena that I think the economic and moral future of this area is very exciting.

Another element of America's strength is high-tech development. This is reflected in the innovative software that makes technology so useful, usable, applicable, and cross-applicable, to medicine, chemistry, and the marriage with biology. All these things have value in terms of instantaneous information. Japan has not developed software capabilities. What they do is latch quickly onto ours as it is developed. We have been too quick to license, to give away, to get some revenue from this technology before it gets ripped-off or copied. America is still and will continue to be the most innovative country in the world.

The geniuses of software were not much older than many of the students on this campus when they developed existing software. The innovation, exploration, and application in this area is constant and almost explosive. We are on the verge of the results of this high-tech age.

For example, people are going to be living longer as a result of the ability to compress so much medical research with the use of computers, such as the ability to structure and restructure genes on-screen and to multiply incalculable calculations instantaneously. What a shortcut this is compared to fiddling around with fragile mice and seeing what happens. The result is that people are living, and will be living, considerably longer. I must say that the prospect does not enthuse my children. This has an extraordinary impact on people when they are wearing out, not "diseasing out." The progress will be very appreciable. When you add 5 or 6 years to the average lifespan in less than a generation, you have created a whole new economic equation. It is just as well, because the generation of my children has had fewer children than my generation did.

We have a manpower shortage in most areas of the United States. Because of this, older people are being urged either to go back to work or stay at work. It is quite a new factor in life. When people do live longer, they have greater, but different, needs.

The shift is exciting and can be positive. There have not been more entrepreneurs, on a percentage basis, in any other period in American history. It is that entrepreneurial strength that has been the spark plug of our economic engine. This is demonstrated by the fact that many people would rather work for themselves, have their own shop, or pursue their own thing, than work for somebody else eight hours a day. They are often willing to work 25 hours a day for themselves for less money than they could pay anyone else to work for them. It is crazy, but it works. There are enough people who feel and act that way that it creates an adrenaline injection of entrepreneurship.

In World War I, one of our great strengths was that so many young Americans had tinkered with Model T Fords and engines that they were aware of what was then beginning to be a very important battlefield factor: the ability to fix. Engines intrigued, attracted, and challenged. We have that same kind of thing flourishing on a far more difficult and meaningful scale. In the high-tech age, we are not behind the parade. We are ahead of the parade and will continue to be, because it challenges the imagination.

Russia's problem is that it does not have the structure to be part of the high-tech age. It does not know how to distribute, to disburse, or to determine instantly what each factory actually needs and what has been allocated. The allocation is arrived at by a formula that is five years ancient in relation to the market-place and consumer demand. Should we be for Gorbachev or against him? I think we should be for him, because the man has an almost hopeless job. He is trying to turn around and develop an entire monolithic bureaucracy. The Russian system of aristocracy is so imbedded that every privilege goes to the party boss. Their system is just aristocracy by another name. It takes ability and innovativeness to relate output to what people need in the stores.

So we have this tremendous challenge with our old enemy. I do not mean we have to trust each other and let our guard down, but the real, fundamental relationship has changed. What we have to do now is learn how we can best and most nimbly cope with this new confrontation. We have to be careful that it does not become too much of a battle with the Common Market of Europe, Japan, and the growing markets of the Pacific Basin. These are exciting prospects. If the structure can be developed, computers and high-tech-age productivity can be harnessed to require much less physical effort. We are on the verge of immense applications.

All these things are to our advantage in the economic warfare that is replacing military confrontation. That is real. Now we are going to find the world regrouping. The emphasis will be on what you put in the pool, how you distribute it, how you earn market share, how you innovate, how you finance. These are all areas where our know-how is useful and will come to the forefront.

It is exciting to be part of this period in history. I think we are a vital part of it, and on the eve of something that is enormously alive and exciting. We enter with tremendous advantages.

3

Competitiveness in Today's Global Economy

Alan H. Magazine, President, Council on Competitiveness

Today I'm going to talk about our nation's competitiveness — its ability to compete in world markets — but in doing so I am going to focus on the role of human resources. It may seem surprising to this audience, but it has only been in the last few years that our economic performance has even been linked to human resources or to the performance of people.

There are many other dimensions to America's ability to compete in world markets, that tend to draw more interest than human resources. Technology is a big attention getter. So is trade. And believe it or not, so is fiscal policy. We constantly see articles in papers and magazines trying to figure out who is ahead in the race to develop superconductors. Or what the potential is for an all-out trade war with Europe. Or even how the latest budget battle is shaping up between the president and Congress. Those are all interesting and critically important issues, and they all relate to our competitive ability, but when you get right down to the heart of competitiveness, it is human resources — the American people — that matter the most.

Without world-class scientists, there would be no superconductivity research. Without hard-working people to scour the world for sales opportunities, there would not be much trade.

Yet oddly enough, people are the forgotten component of competitiveness. And it is not just the public debates that have ignored human resources. For years, many companies have left consideration of human resources out of fundamental discussions of corporate strategy and planning.

Companies around the country are now beginning to remember that people do matter; that productivity, technology, and growth depend on a skilled, motivated, and flexible work force. But for a long time — most of our industrial history, in fact — we operated as if people were an afterthought. We treated labor as a commodity and individuals as expendable. A friend and colleague of mine, TRW economist Pat Choate, refers to this period as the era of the "throwaway worker."

Our industrial system was even designed to minimize the things people do best, like think critically, solve problems, communicate, and work in teams. People were basically taken out of the production equation. The plants we designed were large and complicated, but all the workers had to do was stand on the assembly line and tighten a bolt for eight to twelve hours a day.

Today, labor is no longer a commodity. Work is being transformed by technology (invented by people, of course) and by fundamental changes in the structure and operation of our economy. The new emphasis is on brainpower. Individuals have to solve problems, make decisions, and analyze data in a hotly contested international marketplace. To do that, they have to have skills.

Unfortunately, our human resource development has not kept pace with our new found recognition of the importance of people to competitiveness. If we continue to undereducate Americans, our standard of living will ultimately suffer. That is what competitiveness is about: being able to produce goods and services that assure a rising standard of living for Americans.   Before I address the way that we educate and train our work force, I would like to take a minute to look at some of the changes within our economy that are overhauling the role of labor. The American workplace is in the midst of one of the fastest and most dramatic periods of change in history, surpassing even the changes that took place when the economy shifted from an agricultural base to an industrial one.

To fully appreciate the change, consider for the sake of comparison how work was organized in the assembly-line era. In that period, companies were hierarchical, centrally planned, bureaucratic, and generally authoritarian. The pathway to success was to cover your tracks and not stir up a fuss. The prevailing principle was "if it ain't broke, don't fix it."

Today, progressive corporations understand that competitive advantage is built and sustained around four components: speed, innovation, diversity, and information. All are anathema to the old organization. Companies that emphasize these components are changing the way we work.

Let's look at each of these components, starting with speed. Not too long ago, companies could afford to take their time bringing new products to market. Now, foreign competition from Japan, Europe, and the newly industrialized countries is forcing companies to move faster in developing and introducing products. Technology must be rapidly capitalized upon. For instance, IBM has cut its development time for mainframe computers from three years to 18 months. Ford has knocked a year off its product development time and is aiming to cut much more. Technology is playing a critical role. The use of computer simulators has allowed many companies to race through product development stages that were once painstakingly slow.

Once products are developed, companies have to penetrate as many markets as possible as fast as possible in order to recoup investments. That means nimble and fast-moving marketing staffs must prepare to seed markets with new products even while the product is still in the conceptual stage. Without speedy product development, companies quickly become technological laggards.

Closely related to speed is the need for constant innovation. With shorter product life cycles, companies have to develop a steady flow of new products to maintain growth and profitability. Moreover, companies are finding ways to continuously improve existing products through incremental changes in design, engineering, or manufacturing. New technologies offer the opportunity to constantly upgrade products. Because of the ongoing development of new products as well as constant incremental changes to old ones, product lines are being revamped much more quickly than in the past. At 3M, more than a quarter of last year's sales were generated by products less than 5 years old. One of Monsanto's top executives points out that in today's competitive environment, "the name of the game is to keep putting things through the pipelines." In other words, in today's economy, you assume that it *is* broke and you work to fix it — again and again and again. And if your goal is just to cover your tracks, it means you are not doing your job.

Each product that is introduced today must be adapted to fit the specific needs of different customers. In manufacturing and in services, companies are running from standardization and toward diversity, the third component of competitive advantage. The Model T was the archetype of the assembly-line era: one color, one model. Today, if you order a Japanese car, you pick from several hundred options or modifications.

American companies are playing the game, too. A Whirlpool plant in Ohio changes washer models every hour. That is diversity. A Cross and Trecker machine-tool part facility in Kentucky uses only six machining centers to produce almost an infinite variety of parts, depending on customer orders. That is a far cry from the Model T assembly line.

Information utilization is the fourth characteristic of the new corporation, and it is the glue that holds the others together. Information that is quickly channeled from the marketplace to the corporation speeds product development, spurs innovation, and promotes diversity as each customer's needs are assessed and filled.

High-quality information management also allows the sophisticated coordination of production flows required for new techniques, such as just-in-time inventory management. Information allows companies to cut costs by tying up less working capital to stock up for production.

Manufacturing is not the only domain where information management is making a difference. Information is one of the main weapons in the arsenals of retailers like Wal-Mart, Mrs. Field's Cookies, and The Limited. Each day The Limited collects information from every cash register in its 3,200 stores across the United States and transmits it to factories in the Pacific Rim. The next day the factories begin cutting cloth to replace goods that have been sold, or produce more of an especially popular item. A couple of days after that, 747s leave Hong Kong for the United States with the newly manufactured products. Less than a week from sale to replacement, with an ocean between the factory and the store.

Speed, innovation, diversity, and information. Compare these approaches to the hallmarks of the old corporation. That corporation emphasized steadiness, predictability, standardization, and bureaucratic planning.

Harvard economist Robert Reich observes that in the past, "The goal was high-volume, standardized production in which large numbers of identical items could be produced over long runs. Every step along the production process was to be simple and predictable, so that it could be synchronized with every other step." Not any longer. From the factory floor to the corner office, the work process in America is being overhauled.

Bureaucracy is giving way to teamwork. Central planning is succumbing to front-line decision making. And the mind-numbing repetition of factory work is yielding to shop floor workers who must work with computers and robots to solve complex problems. To work in such an environment, workers must have different skills from those they needed in the assembly-line era.

In an automated factory, a worker does not tighten bolts. A worker operates a computer console controlling millions of dollars worth of complex machinery. That makes the individual worker central to the whole production process. As one manufacturing manager at Lockheed observes about his company's high-tech production, "This system really brings the employee back into the manufacturing equation."

The white-collar work force is also being transformed, and the introduction of advanced technology into the office is a major reason for the change. Between 1990 and the year 2000, the number of PCs in offices will double, rising from 23 million to 46 million. One in three white collar workers will be using a PC, compared to just one in five today. Even executives will be relying on computers to do their jobs. According to one estimate, only 10 to 15 percent of executives have computers today. Only about half use them properly. I am in the other half. But by the mid-1990s, about 70 percent of executives will need to be proficient with computers to survive.

In today's workplace labor and management add value by brainpower, by having the literacy and numeric skills to properly use technology, by working in teams, and by making on-the-spot decisions. There is no time to wait for reports to filter up to top management and decisions to trickle back down to the line. Companies will also be drawing upon a wealth of information: all in the name of speed, innovation, and diversity. So much for compartmentalization, bureaucracy, and central planning. The old ways are just too slow and cumbersome for today's global, technology-driven economy.

Of course, the success of this transformation depends on workers who can work in teams, make decisions, and solve problems. What are the prospects that the work force will be up to the challenge? To answer that question, we must examine where our future workers are coming from and what kind of education they are receiving.

First, we have to recognize that no matter where our future workers are coming from, there are going to be fewer new workers than in the past. The labor force is growing more slowly than at any time since the 1930s. During the 1970s, the labor force grew by almost 3 percent per year. Over the next several decades, the labor force is projected to expand by about 1 percent per year, and maybe even slower. At the same time, job growth in the American economy will continue at an astonishing pace. Since 1972, the United States has created 31 million new jobs. By the end of the century another 21 million jobs will need to be filled. Most of these new jobs will require high levels of math, reasoning, and communication skills. One study found that between 1984 and the year 2000, more than half of all new jobs will require some education beyond high school and a third will require a college education.

A slowing rate of labor force growth when job availability is expanding rapidly means employers will have a smaller pool of potential employees to choose from. Employers will have to take who they can get, so it is essential that the available workers be qualified for the complex jobs companies are creating.

Also, the composition of our slow-growing labor force is radically different from the existing labor force. Today's work force is predominantly white and male. In fact, nearly half of all workers today fall into this category. Only 17 percent of today's workers are minorities. In contrast, over the next two decades only 15 percent of the entrants into the work force will be white males. Some 85 percent will be women and minorities; 42 percent will either be from a minority or an immigrant group.

On the one hand, this is a positive development. The enhanced demand for workers means that immigrants, minorities, and women will be given opportunities to enter fields that have been closed to them in the past and to become part of the economic mainstream. Success is not guaranteed by the numbers, however, because the sad fact remains that our nation has done a poor job of educating those who are not already in the economic mainstream. This is not to suggest that minorities or immigrants are uniformly disadvantaged. That is not correct. However, they are disproportionately disadvantaged.

In 1986, the overall poverty rate was about 13 percent. But more than 31 percent of blacks and more than 27 percent of Hispanics lived below the poverty line. Only about 70 percent of black teens graduate from high school, while less than 60 percent of Hispanics do. In 1986, just one black in all of America received a doctorate in computer science. But poor development of our children's nascent abilities is not a problem reserved for minorities. America is ignoring most of its children at a time when it needs to pay the most attention to them.

Today, the high school class of the year 2000 is seven years old. In about a decade, those of you who are employers will be hiring many of these kids, and many others will attend colleges like Utah State. Of these children, 35 percent are already at risk of never entering the economic mainstream. They are either poor, handicapped, or cannot speak English. Another 24 percent of these kids live below the poverty line. That means they probably do not have proper nutrition or medical care, which are absolutely critical to intellectual and physical development. Many come from broken families.

We have an ideal of family life in America shaped by the suburban lifestyles exemplified by "Leave it to Beaver" or "Father Knows Best." Even Archie Bunker was married and owned a home. Today 12 percent of all children are born out of wedlock. Half of those have teenage mothers. In fact, each day in America, 40 teenage girls give birth to their third child. A social worker in the Bronx reports that he has worked with families who have grandmothers under the age of 30.

Another 40 percent of kids will live in a single-parent home before reaching age 18, and an increasing number of children have no home at all. In Washington, DC, more than 800 children attend public schools but do not even have a home to return to at night. Across the country, 500,000 children are homeless. Even briefly overlooking the moral imperative of helping children who have no roof over their heads, from a strictly economic perspective it is essential that we address the needs of these children. Our labor force is growing slowly and we need every person we can get, but if we do not act fast, we may as well write off the 500,000 homeless kids.

It is extraordinarily difficult for schools to provide an education when children's basic needs are not met. And the problem of inadequate basic support and nurturance is not confined to the homeless. In America's inner cities, the problems schools face are already acute. In the past educators grappled with problems such as talking in class, chewing gum, and passing notes. In inner city schools today, they deal with muggings, rape, carrying concealed weapons, and drug addiction.

The fact is, we are running the risk of leaving a generation of inner-city kids behind. We are doing that at precisely the time when we need their talents and productive abilities the most. Many of these disadvantaged kids will end up as workers stuck in low-paying service jobs, earning the minimum wage, because they won't be able to find a place in the technology-intensive factory of the future. More likely, they will discover that, with mainstream economic opportunities foreclosed, crime really does pay.

It costs society $24,000 per year to keep someone in prison. On the other hand, if you live in Utah and go to school at Utah State, tuition costs you $1,380. For $24,000 you could spend a year in prison or go to school here for 17 years. I know that is an oversimplification, but I think you get the picture: it is cheaper to educate and train early in life than to penalize later in life.

I have focused on the problems faced by minorities and inner-city youth so far. But there is another story to tell about our children that is equally alarming. That is the story of the general educational performance of all American students.

Consider some of the indicators of school performance. Each year, more than a million high school students give up on school altogether. Of the 2.5 million students who do graduate from high school each year, about a quarter cannot read at the eighth-grade level. In other words, of more than 3 million kids who should graduate, almost half either drop out or have the reading skills of a 14-year-old. SAT scores for all students are well below what their average levels were in the 1960s.

But the most distressing signals of our educational deficiencies show up in the area of science and math results. In a recent comparison of science and math skills, the United States finished at or near the bottom in every subject. In biology, we finished dead last. In algebra, we were twelfth out of 13. The only country that turned in lower results was Thailand. Math and science are the foundations of technology. Robert Solow, an economist from M.I.T., recently won the Nobel prize for economics by showing that technological progress is more important to an industrialized country's growth than labor force size in new factories. But technology is driven by people with the skills to innovate. Without scientists and engineers, how will companies innovate to stay competitive? How will the economy grow?

Of course, not all American students are doing poorly. The fact is, America produces some of the top minds in the world. But we don't do nearly well enough in science and math. In fact, the average Japanese student outperforms all but the top 1 percent of American students in math.

The poor preparation of students in science and math at the elementary and secondary level causes problems that extend into higher education. The percentage of students choosing science and engineering is not increasing, and in some disciplines it is falling. Set against a backdrop of decreasing numbers of college-age students, a declining percentage in technical fields means that the total number of science and engineering students is falling. A growing percentage of the students choosing to remain in these areas is foreign-born. In other words, the United States, a nation of more than 240 million people, for some reason cannot prepare enough of its youth to pursue science and math degrees in college and must rely instead on students from other countries.

These educational problems are not divorced from our economic competitiveness. Already the poor preparation of our students is having a dramatic effect on the private sector. A survey last month by the Battelle Memorial Institute of corporate R&D plans for the upcoming year found companies tailoring back R&D. One of the main reasons cited was a shortage of chemists, physicists, and biologists. There has also been a persistent shortage of university professors to teach science and engineering to the next generation of workers. According to the National Science Foundation, there are approximately 1,300 engineering school teaching vacancies for which universities cannot find candidates. So students are taught in larger classes, or some classes are not taught at all.

The problem of finding skilled employees extends beyond the search for scientists and into entry-level ranks. NYNEX, one of the Baby Bell companies, had to administer tests to 60,000 applicants for entry level jobs to find 3,000 who could perform simple, routine functions. That is a 95-percent failure rate. Chemical Bank in New York had to interview more than 40 people to find even one who had the potential to be trained as a teller — a 98-percent failure rate.

Once businesses do manage to assemble a work force, they often spend huge amounts of money to teach workers the basics, such as reading and writing. One-third of Polaroid's hourly workers are enrolled in a company-sponsored elementary reading and writing program.

David Kearns, the CEO of Xerox, calls this type of training "doing the schools' product-recall work." It is expensive and time-consuming. Most important, it channels resources into training that just repeats an earlier educational process, rather than providing funds for job-specific training. Wouldn't it be better to educate our kids in school so that as adults they can be trained in the workplace?

We have seen that work is changing dramatically. Higher levels of skills are needed to stay competitive. We have also seen that education and training have not kept pace. We have a supply-and-demand imbalance, but because we need higher skills and not just more hired hands, we cannot solve our problems by opening the borders to immigration, as we did in the past. Correcting this imbalance requires cultivating and nurturing our human resources through improved education. America has learned to utilize many of its once-abundant natural resources more wisely. It must now do the same with its people.

Given the complexities of our education system, what can we do? I will just mention five starting points today, five components for an effective human resource strategy for the 1990s.

First, we need to hire good help. We need to begin to make the teaching profession more attractive to our best and brightest. Right now, we are spending more and more money in the schools for administrative and support staff. There are almost as many nonteaching staff members in our school systems as teachers. In addition, teachers may spend up to half their time on non-teaching functions. About one-quarter of the hours we pay for in education are teaching hours. Because of such high staff levels, schools have less to spend on teachers' salaries. On average, teachers earn slightly more than airline ticket agents but less than mail carriers. Engineers earn 70 percent more than teachers. With low pay and often difficult conditions, teaching quality suffers. According to the National Science Foundation, an estimated 60,000 science and math teachers in American public schools are not qualified to teach their subjects. And over the next five years, we will need to attract 200,000 science and math teachers to fill vacancies created by retiring teachers. You can see the problem we are going to have. Labor markets are growing tighter. Businesses need lots of people with science and math literacy. And teacher salaries are low. Without some new incentives, it is unclear where we will find the people to fill these jobs. The allure of business will be too great.

Second, we need to give the disadvantaged a fair shake. We need to pay more attention to the problems of inner-city schools. One of the main problems is finding the money to fund these schools, since it cannot be done through the local tax base. In Detroit, for example, one suburban school teaches its students science in state-of-the-art labs. By contrast, the inner-city school a few miles away with 600 students has an annual science budget of $800. That is $1.33 per student — less than a penny per day. At that rate, students cannot even afford to turn on the Bunsen burners.

Third, we need to start earlier. We need to start meeting the basic needs of the disadvantaged when they are very young. Currently, less than one in five eligible children participate in programs like Head Start, although such programs have been shown to reduce later incidence rates of delinquency, dropouts, and crime. Early intervention through education, health care, and nutritional assistance can lay the foundations for improved education later in life.

Fourth, business needs to team up with education. If business can adopt one strategy for human resources in the 1990s, it should be to get involved with education now. Business can participate in the business of education by adopting schools, providing internships, and letting the schools know what types of skills workers will need. Many businesses are already expanding their links to the education community. General Electric and Hewlett-Packard operate programs to improve science and math teacher training. In Boston, more than 300 firms have joined the Boston Compact, which provides employment incentives for local students. In Atlanta, more than 350 companies formed a business partnership to support the public school system. Employees from ARCO help teach students at an elementary school in Los Angeles. Honeywell sponsors a summer teachers' academy in Minnesota. There are hundreds of ways business can get involved in education. But clearly, the first step is to recognize that the performance of the school is linked to the performance of the corporation.

Fifth, national leadership must promote the types of changes needed in our educational system. Educational responsibility has traditionally rested with state and local governments, but if we are to assure that the American people are prepared for the challenges of the new workplace, leadership at the national level will be required.

The president is in a unique position to offer leadership to the goal of educational improvement. President Bush has said that he wants to become the "education president." Given the many problems in our education system, the timing is certainly right for a more assertive presidential role. Education is too central to the nation's future for the federal government to be a passive bystander when it comes to identifying educational needs and priorities, and helping to develop strategies to make sure the American people are better prepared for the workplace of the future.

I have outlined the changes in the workplace that are transforming work, the changes in the work force that are confronting businesses, and a brief strategy for making sure the work force is actually prepared for the workplace. A big job faces America. What are the chances we will respond to our human resources crisis in time to properly educate young Americans for the workplace that awaits them? Based on our history, I think they are very good indeed. Our nation has a habit of taking its rich resources for granted until a crisis of some sort provokes a more careful cultivation of what once seemed an endless bounty. The Dust Bowl of the 1930s taught us the dangers of reckless farming, and we responded with crop rotation, proper irrigation, and soil management.

The long lines at the gas pumps in the 1970s taught us to conserve oil. We may be forgetting the lesson, but for a while we were building and driving smaller cars, and our industries became much more energy-efficient.

The pollution of our air and water is leading us to find ways to lessen harm to the environment and clean up the mess we have made. The same ingenuity and energy that Americans have brought to these problems will no doubt be brought to the problems of education as well. But it will take time and tireless effort. Our economic competitiveness and very standard of living are at stake. We can do no less than try our hardest to make sure young Americans get the education they, as individuals, deserve, and the education we, as a nation, must have to thrive in today's global economy. As current and future leaders, that is one of the challenges facing each of you.

4

Economic Policies in a
Changing Global Society

Sidney L. Jones, Professor of Public Policy,
Georgetown University, The Brookings Institution

As I try to distill the last 20 years that I have served in Washington, DC, it seems to me that the United States has three fundamental economic problems. I will briefly describe two of those and then spend a little more time on the third one. I will then suggest the solution to those three problems. Fortunately, the solution is the same for all three problems, and my analysis, at least, suggests that there is no other solution, so this is sort of the golden strike.

Our Declining Growth Rate. The first problem I see is that there has been a very significant slowdown in economic growth. In the 1950s, economic growth expanded by 38 percent, or about 3.7 percent per year compounded. During the 1960s it accelerated and grew 45 percent, well over a 4 percent compounded growth rate. During the 1970s we had a variety of difficult experiences — the oil embargo, worldwide droughts, and a significant slowdown in the economic activity of many countries — and the growth rate decreased to 32 percent. From 1980 to 1988, we had a 25 percent growth rate. If we are able to avoid an economic recession in the near term, we will complete this decade with about a 30 percent increase, making it the slowest period of economic growth of any postwar decade.

The reason this is so important is that it has created a gridlock in the public policy environment. During the 1950s and 1960s, public policy officials could distribute the economic growth to the claims of society, and while not every claim got the same share, there was the expectation of improving conditions. We call that the politics of distribution. During the late 1970s and much of the 1980s, the slowdown of economic growth has created an environment of redistribution. If you want to give something more to someone, you must take it away from someone else, and that creates a very ugly, confrontational, and difficult environment.

Competing in an Integrated World Economy. The second problem is that we have to prepare to compete in an integrated world economy. I realize that is a platitude that every speaker, every professor, every TV commentator is obliged to articulate. But what is really amazing about it is that it is true. I have traveled to 50 countries, and I am truly impressed with what is happening out there. Every country in the world is rapidly moving toward the same economic or production model. Even Russia, the most backward and pathetic of major nations, has realized that if they don't do something significant relatively quickly, they will be a fifth-rate economic power by the end of the next decade, lagging far behind the United States, Japan, Europe '92, and the People's Republic of China. The Chinese changed their agricultural system in the 1970s because it was an inefficient system. They changed their services system in the early 1980s. A group of young economists in Beijing is currently developing a program to begin to modify the nationalized manufacturing sector. The Chinese have recognized the importance of making economic adjustments, and they are doing so. Under Gorbachev, the Russians are at least beginning to talk about it.

Trade: When I arrived in Washington in 1969, world exports were approximately $200 billion. Last year they were $2.52 trillion, with another $500 billion of services. We're talking about a $3 trillion world export market that will grow very rapidly in the future, more rapidly than overall production.

Finance: A decade ago Bank of America was the world's largest bank. Today you would have to go far down the list to find CitiCorp. The ten largest banks are Japanese. The others are French, Canadian, British, German. There are reasons for that. We have 15,000 banks; they have a few national banks. But in essence, the world has changed. A large American bank typically has only a few billion dollars of capital. The large Japanese banks usually have much larger capital positions. The same pattern applies to investment banking. We think of U.S. investment banks and brokerage firms as powerful institutions. But the comparable Japanese firms are much larger and are rapidly moving into international markets.

What about raw materials? It is obvious that no nation is independent — not the United States, not Brazil, not Russia, not China. No one can go it alone. We must share natural resources and coordinate our economic policies. The United States, after many years of ignoring other national policies, is now in favor of having the seven major industrial nations cooperate in setting exchange rates. We must coordinate foreign aid.

The per capita gross national product in America is currently about $17,000. In Japan it's about $19,000 per person. By the year 2050, our projections are that the per capita gross national product in Japan, in the United States, and in Europe '92 will be at least $100,000 per person, and that is at a fairly moderate growth rate.

The outlook is much different in the poorest nations of the world. Among the worst examples, the average of the poorest countries was only $700 in 1984. These same projections indicate that by 2050 that figure will change by $66. Not $66 per year; $66. Now it doesn't take much expertise to figure out that if a handful of countries are living at $100,000 per person per year and the vast majority of countries are living at a few hundred dollars per year, then the international system won't work. We must get the world on track, and that will take the economic leadership of the United States, Japan, and Europe, and increasingly of China and India.

Technology, the Most Important Variable. But more important than any of these variables — indeed probably as important as all of the others combined in leading the world to an integrated system — is technology. Since resigning as Undersecretary of Economic Affairs in late 1985, I have given approximately 300 speeches to diverse audiences. In every single lecture I have asked the same question: "Is there anything that your company does that cannot be taken anywhere else in the world and be reproduced within six to twelve months?" Not one single time has anyone challenged that assertion. Technology is perfectly portable.

Three years ago I went to the People's Republic of China. I watched them building oceangoing cargo liners using the most advanced technology in the world. Canton will soon become one of the dominant industrial centers of the world. India has appeared on the scene. It is clearly the most exciting period of my personal career to watch this international development.

The problem is that the Americans are about 40 years behind in their perception of the international economic changes. We remember 1950, when we produced 80 percent of the world's automobiles and 48 percent of the world's steel, and when the U.S. dollar was the only significant currency in the world. That America is gone. We must learn to compete against people in China, whose wage rate is $1 per day. Or Korea, where workers are paid $2.31 an hour in the Hyundai automobile plant, and they use the most advanced steel in the world. Or Japan, where the industrial wage rates are $9 and $11 an hour. Compare those figures to the wages of workers in America.

But even more egregious, compare executive salaries. I had dinner the other evening with the chairman of a large Japanese company with many subsidiaries, including automobiles, construction, chemical, and manufacturing operations. His salary is $100,000 per year. Most of my students at Georgetown expect that much as a merger and acquisition specialist one or two years out of school. There is a tremendous disparity.

Squaring the Population Pyramid. The third challenge is perhaps the most interesting of all. I'm convinced that demographic trends are now the number one variable in the U.S. economy, and for that matter the world economy.

Figure 4.1 indicates the overall population expansion. During the 1950s the population increased about 13 percent, or about 1.2 percent per year; the next decade about 1 percent per year; in the current decade less than 1 percent per year. In the 1990s we anticipate a 7.5 percent increase in the population. Among the white majority, that figure is decelerating rapidly. During the 1990s the white majority will increase about 3 percent. This group has basically opted out of society through their birthrate decisions. The minorities are growing more rapidly — two to three times as fast — but are also beginning to slow down. In the 1990s the black population will grow about 14 percent. Hispanics will become the second-largest population group, growing about 17 percent.

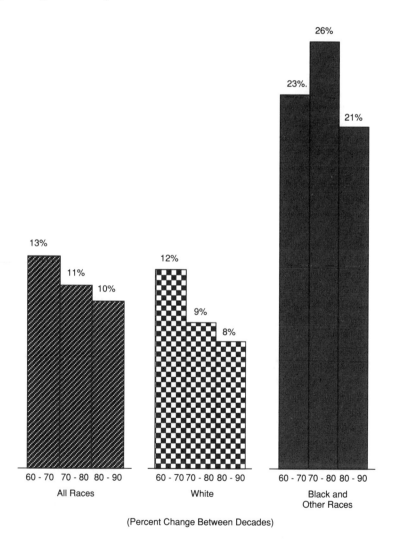

(Percent Change Between Decades)

Figure 4.1 Population Growth in the U.S.

As Figure 4.2 demonstrates, future demographic patterns will square the population pyramid. In 1900, there was a traditional population distribution. As the average woman gave birth to four children, the fertility rate was four. The average person, at birth, could expect to live to 47 years of age. A handful of people — 5 or 6 percent of the total population — would live to be over 65, and would spend about 3 percent of their life in retirement.

Almost all of our public policies are based on the concept of a pyramid. The older generation, and those who can no longer produce and contribute to production, are then supported by an ever-growing young labor force, because the population fits into a triangle or a pyramid pattern.

In the early 1900s we also had a very rapid immigration rate — about 1 million people per year, approximately double the immigration rates of today. That immigration accounted for about 30 percent of the changing population. This influx of people was an important part of America's great success. America became the melting pot, drawing in many of the best people, ideas, and cultures from around the world. That generation is now retired. About 12 percent of the total population is now over 65 years of age. The next generation — the people born during the 1920s and 1930s — was a "not-born" generation. The Great Depression shifted the fertility rates, so that the average fell to 2.3 births per woman. So my generation was not born. There are a relatively small number of us, and we will be retiring over the next 20 years or so. The prospective retirement income system will work very well, because there aren't many of us.

By 2050 we anticipate the population distribution will become square. We will literally have more people over 60 years of age than we have children under 20 years of age. The other two population groups — 20 to 40 and 40 to 60 — will be about equal. That will cause a fundamental change in public policy. We cannot anticipate an ever-growing population to fill in that population support level. The pace of births has been below the replacement fertility rate since 1972. It is currently about 1.85 births per woman. Every industrial nation in the world has the same characteristic — a non-replacement birthrate.

In Figure 4.3 you can see the effects of the baby boom on the total population. Whatever age the baby boom is — the 80 million people born between 1946 and 1964 — that is society, because this group represents one-third of the entire population. One out of three Americans

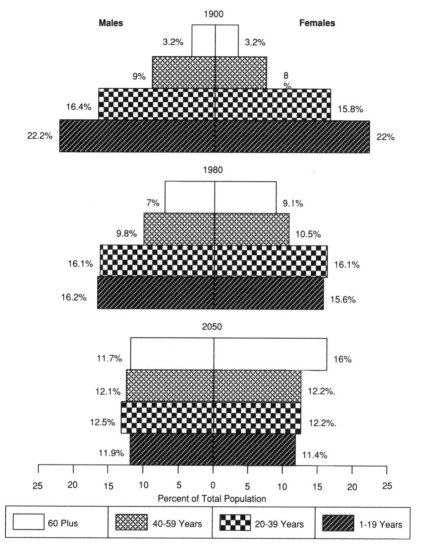

Note: Projections are middle series

Source: U.S. Bureau of the Census, Decennial Censuses of Population, 1900 - 1980, and
Projections of the Population of the United States, 1982 to 2050; Current Population
Reports, Series P-25, No. 922, October, 1982.

Figure 4.2 Actual and Projected Change in Population Distribution, 1900 - 2050

alive today was born during the baby boom. The earliest vanguard of that group passed their 40th birthday last year. The youngest are about 25. By the end of this century the large baby-boom group will move up into their forties and fifties, and we will have a different kind of society — a society of services, medical care, travel, entertainment, and less emphasis on consumer durable goods and housing.

Figure 4.4 shows what economists call the dependency ratio. You will notice in 1900 that for every hundred people in the labor force we had about 84 dependents. About 76 of those dependents were children, and 6 or 7 of them were older people. During subsequent years that dependency ratio began to decline. By 1960 it was down to about 60 dependents for every 100 workers. Then there was

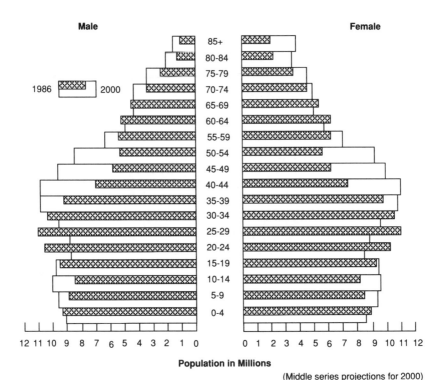

Figure 4.3 Population by Age and Sex, 1986 - 2000

(Number of Persons Per 100 Aged 18 to 64 Years)

	1900	1920	1940	1960	1980	1982[1]	1990	2000	2025	2050
Total support ratio (under 18 and 65 and over)	83.65	75.69	62.84	81.95	64.39	62.86	62.57	61.86	71.00	74.46
Aged support ratio (65 years and over)	7.35	7.99	10.90	16.84	18.59	18.82	20.70	21.16	33.31	37.85
Young support ratio (under 18)	76.30	67.70	51.94	65.11	45.80	44.04	41.87	40.70	37.69	36.61

[1]Based on estimates

Source: U.S. Bureau of the Census, Projections of the Population of the United States, 1982 to 2050 (Advance Report), Series P-25, No. 922, and Estimates of the Population of the United States by Single Years of Age, Color, and Sex, 1900 to 1959, Series P-25, No. 311, July 2, 1965. Projections are the middle series.

Figure 4.4 Total Support Ratio, Aged Support Ratio, and Young Support Ratio Actual and Projected, 1900-2050.

a bubble as the baby boom occurred, and now we have settled back down to having 60 dependents for every 100 workers. As the baby-boom generation begins to retire, that dependency ratio will begin to rise slowly back into the seventies. Nevertheless, the overall ratio never again goes back to the level we had at the beginning of this century. The significant point is, however, that the balance of old and young dependents is reversed. The dependent group used to be dominated by young people. Spending money on young people represents investment in the future. The mix of dependents will increasingly become older people, so that public spending will represent more consumption. The two lines will criss-cross about 2030, and we will begin to see a different kind of America.

In summary, America faces three major economic challenges. As a nation we need to increase our economic growth rate into the 3 to 4 percent zone in order to include everybody in the system and to achieve our potential. The second challenge is we must prepare to compete in an integrated world economy. The third category will become crucial about 20 years from now when the baby-boom generation begins to retire, and we must fill in for the missing labor force created by the mixture of the smaller baby-dearth generation born since 1965. I believe that there is only one solution for increasing economic growth on a sustained basis, being able to compete with disparate wage rates around the world, and filling in for the missing labor force — and that is productivity.

Productivity: The Solution. Productivity is the only solution I can think of. What used to be a 3 percent growth of productivity in the early postwar period, from 1948 to 1960, decelerated to a growth rate of about 2 percent from 1966 to 1973, 1 percent from 1973 to 1978, and then to nothing between 1978 and 1982, before returning to an annual average pace of about 1.5 percent during the cyclical expansion of 1982 to date.

Productivity has something to do with capital investment — how much you are putting into plant and equipment. It has something to do with technology — how much you are putting into research and development. And it has something to do with human resource development.

Where do we stand on those three issues — capital investment, technology, and human resource development? Compared with the capital investment rates reported by industrial nations, we have been at the bottom of the list since the early 1960s. We invest about 10 percent of our gross national product in plants and equipment. The Japanese invest approximately 20 percent in new business assets. The rest of the industrial nations are somewhere in between.

Where do we stand on technology? Well, the United States used to put about 3 percent of its GNP into technology. That figure is gradually being eroded. The national figures for 1986 indicate that America allocated about 2.8 percent of its GNP, about $120 billion, to research and development. The Germans committed an equal amount — about 2.8 percent of their GNP — to technology, about $36 billion. And the Japanese spent about 2.7 percent, or about $76 billion, on research and development. However, almost all of the Japanese and German investment goes into private-sector technology. One-half of our technology goes into defense activities.

The number one recipient of patents from the United States Patent Office in 1987 was Japan. Now you may say, "But Japan can only copy. They've received only four Nobel prizes. How can they be a great technical society?" The Nobel prize is awarded for something you did as a graduate student 30 years ago. It is not a good measure of current spending on new technologies. If one cares to look at state-of-the-art engineering and science, particularly in the manufacturing sector, one can well look to our Japanese friends.

The Education Gap. How do we stand on education? When our children go to what we call school, they go for 180 days per year. Japanese students go to school for 240 days a year, and then they study every afternoon and weekend for their examinations. When Japanese students graduate from high school, they are the equivalent of a college graduate. Most of my students are studying to be merger and acquisition specialists. Who's studying the hard stuff — engineering, science, and mathematics? A large share of the students, particularly in technical subjects, come from foreign countries. Many of them stay in the United States after graduation and we receive the benefit of their intelligence and creative capabilities, but America needs to emphasize the importance of these technical disciplines.

Reallocating National Resources. America must reallocate its national resources. Ninety percent of the federal budget in this country is spent on consumption. Ten percent is spent on roads and dams and bridges and a few other capital investments. We must reallocate our resources to investment in plant and equipment, technology, and the development of our people, that is, health, education, training, and organization.

That transition is already underway, and will not be that difficult to accomplish. Indeed, if one looks at the GNP in real terms for the last five quarters, you will see what the America of the 1990s will look like. Eighty percent of the current economic growth is coming from export increases and investment in the plants and equipment needed to produce those exports. The rest of the U.S. economy for five quarters has grown at a 1 percent compound real growth rate, and that signals what the future will look like. We're going to have to produce in the 1990s to pay for the national consumption of the 1970s and 1980s.

The thing that worries me, however, is the political adjustment. The economic policy adjustments will be worked out by the marketplace, but the political adjustment will be excruciating, because sometime in the 1990s some very brave politician is going to have to come to the American people and tell them, "You're going to have to take a hit."

The familiar rhetorical question I often ask my audience is: "When is the last time that anyone ever asked you to do anything?" and I've only gotten two answers: Winston Churchill in 1940 and John F. Kennedy in 1960. I can assure you that in the 1990s our political leaders will have to ask for some national sacrifices.

The Savings Rate and the Budget Deficit. America has the lowest domestic savings rate in the world. We are consumers. We spend about 91 percent of our personal disposable income on ourselves. For over a hundred years — before taxes, after taxes, during recessions, after recessions — Americans have saved about 6.5 percent of their personal disposable income. The other 2.5 percent has been used for interest and transfer payments.

State and local governments are in surplus at the moment — not because of how they're operating, but because they're collecting huge pension fund contributions.

Those in the business sector also tend to be slight savers. When you combine the savings of individuals, businesses, and the pension funds of state and local governments, during the 1950s the private savings rate was about 8.5 percent; during the 1960s it was 9.5 percent; and during the 1970s it was almost 10 percent. In other words, the domestic savings rate for 30 years was very stable, averaging somewhere between 8.5 to 10 percent.

Government deficits are an offset to the private savings of individuals, businesses, and state and local government pensions. The federal budget has reported a deficit in 27 of the last 28 years. During the period from 1950 to 1980, the federal budget deficit was relatively stable, averaging about 1 to 2 percent of the GNP in most years. While the deficit was serious, it was not the end of the world, because it could be financed out of domestic private savings. During the 1980s, however, some very interesting things happened. Spending exploded in the defense sector, in the entitlement sectors (Social Security and government pension), and in health care — Medicare and Medicaid. Those three programs — defense, income security, and health care — plus interest on the national debt now comprise about 85 percent of the budget.

Fiscal policies were changed in 1981 to provide the large personal and business tax reductions promised during the elections. The combination of rising federal spending and large tax rate cuts caused federal revenues to level off at about 18 percent of the GNP, while federal spending rose to about 24 percent of the total national output. The federal budget deficit opened up a 5 to 6 percent gap, which had to be financed through savings. As this fiscal gap increased, however, personal savings declined as the baby boomers moved through the spending phase of their lives. The resulting $200 billion deficits each year added $1.8 trillion to the national debt during the last eight years.

Possible Actions to Reduce Prospective Budget Deficits. Most analysts agree that chronic federal budget deficits have created serious economic and political distortions and that they should be reduced to avoid massive borrowing from domestic and foreign financial markets. A strong argument also can be made that budget surpluses during periods of strong economic growth are needed to encourage private investment to improve future productivity results. There is little agreement, however, about which fiscal-policy actions should be used to achieve the desired budget-deficit reductions. Reform suggestions are controversial because fiscal policies create benefits for some interest groups and sacrifices for others. There is no "magic bullet" available to correct budget-deficit problems quickly or painlessly. Therefore, specific proposals will have to become part of an eclectic package designed to create maximum political support and minimum economic costs. The following list indicates the range of possible actions.

- *Rely on faster economic growth to increase potential tax revenues.* This suggestion is popular because it avoids the risks and pain of changing spending and tax policies. The major problem with this "rosy scenario" is the difficulty of figuring out how to create the incremental growth and then sustain it for more than a few months. The prime labor force — workers in the 25- to 55-year-old age bracket — currently is growing rapidly, but long-term demographic trends eventually will constrain the future pace unless immigration trends accelerate. The long-term trends of the average number of hours worked and the level of unemployment are stable at this time. This analysis suggests that productivity gains are the most likely source of incremental economic growth. Increasing investments in plants and equipment, technology, and the development of human resources would improve the long-term prospects, but the results are likely to be evolutionary rather than revolutionary. Sustaining moderate growth and avoiding serious recessions will be a difficult challenge most of the time.
- *Eliminate fraud, waste, and abuse from government budgets.* Some critics claim the egregious examples of inappropriate government opera-

tions, such as the current Pentagon purchasing scandals, prove that budget deficits could be reduced significantly by enforcing better management practices. Eliminating inefficiency and fraud are desirable goals, but the amounts of potential savings are uncertain and likely to be relatively small compared with the total deficit reductions needed.

- *Increase the fees charged for government services and facilities.* User fees can help to improve the analysis of priorities by assigning part of the costs of government services and facilities to those who receive the actual benefits. It is unrealistic, however, to assume that user fees will change government spending burdens or raise much revenue compared with the size of prospective budget deficits.
- *Increase the sale of government assets.* The public sale of redundant, or unnecessary, government assets is a useful strategy for improving efficiency and raising modest amounts of revenue. Once an asset is sold, however, it obviously cannot be sold again or used to produce future government operating revenues, so such one-shot transactions do not provide sustained budget-deficit relief.
- *Make small reductions in the big government-spending programs.* Spending for national defense, income security, and health care, plus net-interest payments on the national debt, represent approximately 85 percent of the federal budget outlays. It is logical, therefore, to assume that these three major programs provide the most promising targets for necessary spending restraint. Existing budget priorities suggest that this familiar assumption is not realistic. Future defense spending already has been restricted by recent congressional appropriations decisions; Social Security and government pension payments are acknowledged sacred cows; popular Medicare outlays continue to dominate the health-care category; and interest obligations must be honored. These three program categories are large because they have been assigned the highest national priorities by the political process.
- *Make big reductions in the small government-spending programs.* The protected status of the three big spending categories forces budget planners to concentrate most of their restraint efforts on the many small budget programs that make up the residual 15 percent of total outlays. Most of these programs provide specific benefits to powerful interest groups and they typically have active political advocates in the Congress and Executive Branch. It is a rare event when any existing program is eliminated, although a few may be modestly reduced or frozen at existing spending levels. The budget plans prepared for the Executive Office of the President typically have a list of the "usual suspects" targeted for elimination or reduced funding, but these paper savings have a way of disappearing when Congress prepares the actual appropriations.

- *Raise marginal income-tax rates for individuals.* An increase in personal tax rates, particularly for high-income taxpayers, has been suggested as the most direct approach to raising more revenues to close the deficit gap. The option would utilize the existing tax system, and it can be argued that most taxpayers still would have lower personal income-tax rates than they did under the old rate schedule in place before the tax-relief actions of 1981 and 1986. Any attempt to raise personal income taxes would create a political fight, however, and would reverse the important effort to improve incentives by reducing the marginal tax rates on personal incomes. The large personal income tax rate reductions in 1981 and 1986 have been popular, and it would require an act of extraordinary political courage to recommend an increase in personal taxes.
- *Raise marginal income-tax rates for corporations.* This proposal would avoid the political-backlash risks linked to proposals to increase personal income-tax rates, but it probably would not raise much incremental revenue. Many analysts are concerned already by the tendency to increase business taxes without giving enough emphasis to the importance of increasing investment incentives by improving the after-tax rate of return on business activities.
- *Amend, or repeal, the indexation of the income-tax schedules.* The decision in 1981 to index the income-tax system — to recognize the effects of inflation pushing taxpayers into higher marginal tax brackets — eliminated most of the traditional fiscal strategy of financing future budget outlays with revenues created by the automatic effects of bracket creep caused by inflation, without the political risk or pain of raising tax rates. The 1986 tax reform legislation cut the number of personal income-tax brackets to two levels, 15 and 28 percent, plus a surtax on some taxpayers. Indexation rules have considerable political and theoretical support.
- *Increase excise taxes on selected consumer goods and services.* Excise taxes have been used to raise revenues and discourage some types of consumption. Increasing taxes on purchases of cigarettes, alcoholic beverages, recreation activities, and other goods and services has been proposed, but the potential revenues are limited and some analysts question this particular use of the tax system.
- *Increase the alternative minimum tax.* The 1986 tax reform legislation made significant changes in the alternative minimum tax for individuals and corporations. Some analysts have recommended even higher minimum rates and tighter rules.
- *Increase taxes on energy commodities and services.* A variety of energy-related taxes have been proposed to increase revenues and promote conservation, including a general tax on energy consumption, oil-import fees, and excise taxes on gasoline purchases. These suggestions are controversial because the tax burdens would be concentrated on specific users of energy, particularly in certain geographic areas of

the country. Critics also emphasize the inflationary risks, competitive problems linked to domestic production costs, and the cost burdens placed on low-income people.

* *Restrict the exemptions and deductions permitted ("tax more income less").* Some analysts believe that incentives could be improved by lowering tax rates in exchange for elimination of existing deductions and exemptions available to some taxpayers. They believe that revenues would be increased by expanding the income subject to taxation as an offset to the lower rates. The 1986 tax reform legislation did make many important adjustments combining these two tax actions.

* *Impose a national consumption tax.* The imposition of a national consumption tax, such as the value-added tax used in many European nations, would create a major change in the U.S. tax system, which traditionally has relied on personal and business income taxes for most of the revenue collected (payroll-tax collections are a third major source). Advocates of the consumption tax emphasize the potential revenues that could be raised. They also argue that it would improve our competitive position in foreign trade because such taxes can be rebated to exporters, and would add an important incentive to encourage investment. Critics argue that consumption taxes are regressive, that the burden of a flat-rate tax is heavier for low-income people, and that a federal tax on consumption would usurp part of the tax sources used by state and local governments to raise revenues through sales taxes. Others attack the consumption tax by claiming that it would lead to increased government spending, because the revenues raised would be used to increase public programs rather than to reduce the deficit gap. Political controversy has prevented a serious national debate on the consumption-tax option, but concern about the large federal-budget deficits may force the issue onto the public-policy agenda.

Summary and Prospects. The 50-year sequence of vending-machine responses to interest-group demands for increased spending and tax relief to sustain public and personal consumption has created budget deficits. The public-policy agenda has become more sensitive to fiscal constraints as the decelerating pace of economic activity and increasing international competition have limited current revenues, but spending has been sustained by substituting government borrowing, particularly from foreign investors, for the missing tax revenues. There is universal criticism of the real and alleged distortions attributed to the budget deficits, but no definitive commitment has led to specific solutions.

The current debate suggests the familiar paradox of an irresistible force (the need for more investment to increase productivity) meeting an immovable object (the chronic budget deficits). This intense conflict eventually will determine the next fiscal-policy rule, one that will be based on investment needs rather than current spending and tax priorities. The United States will have no choice because we must reorient national priorities toward investment to meet three fundamental challenges: increase in the pace of economic growth; adjustment to international economic competition; and the approaching demographic twist that will result when the huge baby-boom generation begins to retire and the smaller baby-dearth generation must provide the prime labor force. These three challenges can be met by improving national productivity.

Therefore, prospective federal-budget deficits should be reduced gradually to a level that will not interfere with the necessary allocation of capital into new plants and equipment, technology, and the development of human resources. While the economic necessity of this realignment of national priorities is compelling, the political realities of attempting to get the general population to shift from immediate consumption goals to long-term investment requirements will be excruciating. Competitive forces eventually will force the adjustment to be made, but the political transition will not be pleasant. Fiscal policies must create much smaller deficits, or even occasional surpluses, so that more national resources can be invested to enhance future productivity. The current budget deficit is a symbol of our national preference for immediate consumption. A significant reduction in future deficits will become a symbol of our willingness to prepare to compete in a future world economy that will be dramatically different.

5

Human Progress through Economic Progress

Richard L. Lesher, President, U.S. Chamber of Commerce

My topic is human progress through economic progress. That topic recognizes that budget policy, tax policy, trade policy, and regulation impact corporations of all sizes, large and small.

It seems to me that humankind has lived throughout history with two overriding fears. First, the fear of poverty; and secondly, the fear of war. That, of course, was predicted by the scriptures. Unfortunately, both predictions have come true throughout most of history. My thesis and conviction is that we have done more in the last eight years to eliminate those two fears than has been done in any similar period in history.

Today peace is replacing warfare throughout the world. Governments are turning away from failed, centrally controlled economies, and are turning toward market economics and democratic capitalism. Now don't misunderstand; the threat of war will probably never be abrogated. We cannot eliminate wars with "great wars;" we ought to have learned that by now. I think we have also learned that peace cannot come without a war on poverty. Peace will come only with the prospect of continued prosperity. I would argue that more progress toward worldwide prosperity has taken place in this decade than at any time in history. And that, to me, is what clearly makes the period we live in the most exciting period in history.

Some time ago a London economist published some historical economic research that suggested that worldwide income two thousand years ago, at the time Christ walked on earth, was two hundred dollars per person per year. Now, that is roughly the per capita income today in many of the underdeveloped Third World nations. In other words, two thousand years ago everyone, with very few exceptions, lived in poverty. When this nation was founded more than seventeen hundred years later, that statistic had not changed. Income per capita at the time of the writing of the Constitution was still two hundred dollars per person per year. People still lived in poverty. Life in the colonies and everywhere else in the world was difficult. We tend to forget that there were trade wars among the colonies. There were tariff barriers between the colonies. That was one of the major reasons there was not more trade and investment flowing among the colonies, as well as from Europe.

Then something wonderful happened, called America: a simple notion that government should be "of the people" rather than "to the people." The Constitution put limitations on government. Government could only do a few isolated things. The Constitution also embodied the commerce clause, which did away with barriers to trade and investment among the colonies. It created, in my terminology, the world's first common market. Think about that. It accelerated trade and investment flows among the States, did away with the tariffs on the waterways — the Chesapeake Bay, the rivers, and the canals — and encouraged trade and investment. The basis of that noble idea was very, very simple: allow the people to govern themselves and reward their industry and initiative. For most of the next two hundred years this fledgling nation did extremely well. We had some recessions, we even had a couple of depressions, but we accelerated after World War II to become the strongest lending nation in the world. The United States continued to prosper in the 1950s, 1960s, and 1970s, but some difficulties began to creep in. We began to let things slide.

Government grew dramatically. It became fashionable to throw a government program at every problem, real or perceived. There were problems everywhere and plenty of blame to go around. Companies where fat and complacent. Many American corporations forgot about quality control and allowed competitors from Asia and Europe to come in and steal away large chunk of their market. By the end of the 1970s, the American economy was in grave difficulty. It was marked by the energy crisis. Many businesses were in extreme difficulty. The economy was heading for true disaster, driven by the highest rate of inflation in our country's history, 13 percent. The Fed responded to that by driving up interest rates to over 20 percent. Unemployment was high. By the late 1970s, the pessimists were predicting that America would become a second-class citizen of the world.

But all around the world there was a discovery that socialism and communism were not delivering, nor was any other form of centralized or planned economy. Some people forecast major institutional changes for the 1980s.

Ronald Reagan came into office with big dreams of freedom, private enterprise, and placing limitations on big government. He had dreams of a new Federalism and pushing public policy decisions back to the grass roots as much as possible. Those were some of his ideas. But the two most important ideas were peace through strength and lifting the heavy hand of government regulation and taxation to keep our economy aloft. He believed that you cannot negotiate if you don't hold any of the cards. He wanted to rebuild the defense establishment so we could move to a point where we could sit down with the Russians and negotiate from a position of strength.

Two years ago the U.S. Chamber of Commerce celebrated its seventy-fifth birthday, and we tried to put things into a historical perspective. We looked back at the period of 1912-1920 to see what was bothering the business community at that time. You might be interested to know that the top issues at time were: (1) over-taxation of business; (2) the over-regulation of business; (3) runaway government spending; (4) immigration problems; and (5) trade policy. Tomorrow's business leaders must understand that George Washington was right when he said, "It's the natural order of things for the government to grow and for liberty to yield." If regulation and taxation get out of hand, free markets are doomed.

After World War II, many Asian countries began adopting some of our market principals. That was part of the "deal" of the American occupation. Earlier in this decade, this trend began to spread throughout Latin America, Europe, and Australia. Great Britain is returning to the principles of privatization and private markets. Australia and New Zealand are throwing off the shackles of socialism and turning toward market incentives. Three months ago Sweden introduced supply side economics with major tax reductions into their socialistic economy. Why? Because their markets were not working.

The cost of running the system was out of control and their young people were leaving in droves. Their tennis players and musicians were not going home because they had to pay 80 percent taxes on their income. All of that is truly amazing and remarkable, making this a very, very exciting age to live in.

But far more dramatic than this are the developments in the Communist bloc. China is already making great progress. I visited China about nine years ago and gave lectures on democratic capitalism that would have landed me in jail two years earlier. I will never forget sitting with the Vice-Premier of China as he made a long speech that I could summarize in a just few phrases. He said, "America is rich and China is poor, and you must help us." I responded with one question: "How is it that the greatest country on earth in terms of population and land mass; a country with a great history of inventiveness; a country with oil, gas, coal, and many other natural resources; a country with a good transportation system and a good climate, keeps its very industrious and hard-working one billion people in poverty?" Of course, you could have heard a pin drop as the Chinese sat and thought about that. I then suggested that the system did not work because it did not provide incentives to those one billion people.

In a few weeks, I am going back to China. My friends who have been there tell me that enormous progress is being made there. Entrepreneurs have come out of the woodwork. Some who were thrown in jail are back running major enterprises. They are running as fast as they can away from communism and socialism, and toward market economics. They are even selling stock in Communist China.

The Soviets are trying to travel the same course. Every day there is a new announcement. It seems to me that the Soviet Union will have a much tougher time getting to a private market mechanism than the Chinese. Former Chief Justice Warren Burger of the Supreme Court remarked on the likelihood of the Soviet Union achieving a dynamic economy. He said that, in his opinion, they will have a much more difficult task ahead of them than anyone else, because they have no tradition of private-sector decision making. That is true because the Czars ruled the country before the revolution. The Chinese, on the other hand, have a long history of private enterprise, inventiveness, and incentives. But throughout the Eastern bloc, they are hungry for everything they find out about market incentives. They are very busily putting free enterprise back to work.

Now in my view, these things did not come about by accident. Peace though strength forced the hand of the Soviet Union. I have suggested that they are more intimidated by the economics of "Star Wars" than by its technical aspects. Their system was already beginning to crumble. Their people were very unhappy with the alcoholism rate and the other social problems. A major weapons system buildup was the last thing they wanted, so they decided to try and move in a different direction.

Looking ahead to the future, I would suggest that we are poised to enter the best period economically, and perhaps in terms of freedom, that the world has ever known. Secretary Baker said that America can make a difference for peace and freedom throughout the world. I believe that we already have. It is easy to predict that critics will continue to harp. The unions will continue to try to stem their long-term decline in membership by trying to get some things through Congress that might save their hides. But I suspect that Congress will turn away from corporate socialism, because they see what it has done in Europe.

I do not mean to assert that we will never again have problems. We do have some problems, some big problems. But we have the spirit to deal with those problems. The drug problem is not going to go away. President George Bush has said that the drug problem is the single highest priority in his administration.

We will have our problems, but our economy is back and peace through strength works. The United States is strong and getting stronger, and will continue to lead the way in today's global economy.

We do indeed live in a very exciting age. There is realistic hope for lasting peace and continuing progress toward the goal of eliminating poverty from the face of the earth.

6

Roles Within Organizations — Implications for Competitiveness

Edward H. Northrop, Chairman, XICOM Incorporated

In November 1987 I participated in the seventy-fourth American Assembly sponsored by Columbia University. The topic of the conference was "Running Out of Time: Reversing America's Declining Competitiveness." That conference was one of the most rewarding experiences that I've ever had, and yet it was also one of the most frustrating.

The rewarding side had to do with the exchange of ideas about competitiveness issues. Basically, the tone of the conference was that America's economy is growing more slowly than it has in the past, more slowly than it needs to, and more slowly than the economies of our competitors. We're consuming more than we produce. Our prosperity is threatened, as is our capacity to provide world leadership. We cannot long continue on this path without profound consequences.

American companies have lost command of markets to international competitors. Customers' wants and needs have too often been subjugated to short-term goals. American management has neglected the opportunity to mobilize the knowledge of its own work force.

During the course of the conference, we examined the Japanese model and focused on their criteria for success, quality, low-cost production, employee involvement, and being customer-driven providers of goods and services. We concluded that we are gambling recklessly with our destiny.

The frustrating part of the conference was that we did not discuss what to do about this issue of competitiveness. I was looking for some action steps to take home with me. Lou Gerstner of American Express recognized the balance that is needed between the conceptual approach and implementation. He said, "It is my absolute conviction that you can out-manage your competition by having brilliant strategies, and that brilliant strategies have to be executed brilliantly." To be competitive, you must have both.

Roles Within Organizations. The point of departure that I've chosen is roles within organizations. From an organizational point of view, how can we bring out the best in people who are in our organizations? And, from an individual point of view, how do I position myself in an organization so I can bring out the best in myself? This issue of role can be a first step toward translating the concepts of competitiveness into action, to having people add greater value, and to being more competitive.

The first step is to develop a common language about roles; second, to describe roles within organizations; and third, to identify the implications, particularly as roles relate to power and control within organizations.

One caution: This is not a "quick fix" or a simple solution to the issues of competitiveness. There's a tendency, particularly when dealing with human relations issues, to latch on to an idea and pursue it with blinders on. H.L. Mencken made a great observation, "There is always an easy solution to every human problem: neat, plausible, and wrong." So, rather than provide a quick fix, my focus will be to identify options and alternatives for managing roles within organizations.

We have identified nine roles that must be present for an organization to get work done over a period of time. There are two points to keep in mind as we go through these roles. First, there is no intrinsic value associated with these roles. One role is not more valuable, better, or worse than another role. They all need to be present over a period of time for work to get done. Second, it is natural for people to try to imagine themselves in various roles and ask the questions, "What am I good at?", "What do I do well?", or "What don't I do so well?" Don't worry about trying to be "superperson" or about being good at all of the roles. If we're lucky, we each probably have real strengths in three of these roles at the most.

In addition to providing a description of the roles, I'm going to use some images to develop some texture and feeling about the roles, so that you can relate them to your individual experience base.

The Diagnoser. The first role that needs to be present within organizations is that of the *Diagnoser*. Diagnosers are analyzers. They analyze and clarify forces that are present in organizations. They look at issues. They look at resources that are available within organizations. They analyze potential problems. They are able to assess downside risks, payoffs, and contingencies. They are able to look at alternatives. Diagnosers are skilled observers. They need to get "out there" and observe firsthand. Diagnosers are often the people in organizations that manage by "wandering around." Diagnosers are good lateral thinkers. In other words, they're able to take a concept, relate it to other observations, and identify its implications. Organizational literature identifies three skills: conceptual, technical, and human. The Diagnoser has an abundance of conceptual skills. An example of the Diagnoser would be the physician. These people are trained in the "differential diagnosis" model. They take the patient's presenting complaint, examine it, and arrive at a diagnosis through a process of elimination.

Roger Ailes, George Bush's media consultant, made some diagnostic observations about what it takes to get attention during a political campaign. He said, "You've got to understand that the media has no interest in substance. There are three ways to get on the air: pictures, attacks, and mistakes. So, what you do is spend your time avoiding mistakes, staying on the attack, and giving them pictures. You do that and you're guaranteed to get a lead story on the evening news." A simple, clear, diagnostic statement.

One way of getting a clearer understanding of these roles is to ask, "What happens if we take one of these roles to excess?" If the diagnostic role is taken to excess, an organization becomes a "think-tank" environment, with a great deal of conceptualizing but not much being accomplished by way of task orientation.

The Monitor. The next role is that of the *Monitor*. Monitors are controllers. They monitor findings and report progress. They are masters of control, supported by two other roles that we will describe later, the Expert and the Detailer. They are measurers and analyzers. If we remember our early school days, the street-crossing guard or hall monitor functioned in this role. Air traffic controllers have a strong monitoring role in terms of controlling air space. And all of us have a new outside partner in our organizations who may not have been as present 15 or 20 years ago. These are the government regulatory agencies that monitor various aspects of our business and educational institutions.

The monitoring role, when taken to excess, may be destructive to an organization. It has the potential to generate turf wars as people try to exert control over resources.

The Documenter. The third role is that of the *Documenter*. These are people who record and report results. Sometimes they're historians. Sometimes they're responsible for pulling the facts together. Their role is to preserve a written record for purposes of continuity. If you walk into a meeting and the chairman asks you to take the minutes, one of your roles becomes that of the Documenter. You may have a variety of other roles and you may have arrived with other expectations, but one of your roles in the meeting is that of Documenter. It will both limit what you can do at the meeting and at the same time provide opportunities for influencing future action depending on how events are recorded.

Going back to physicians, once they have completed a diagnosis, they have to generate a medical record. At that point the physician's role shifts from that of Diagnoser to that of Documenter.

From this example of the physician emerges the concept that we take on a variety of roles within organizations at different times. The trick is to become conscious of the various role options and how they can be used to accomplish the task at hand.

Taking the role of Documenter to excess is best exemplified in sales organizations where the call report becomes more important than making the sale. As a result, the salesperson becomes activity-driven instead of results-oriented.

The Detailer. The next role is that of the *Detailer*. Detailers are logistical coordinators or microplanners. They get involved in the nitty-gritty details of a program or project. They are concerned with accuracy, and at times they're accused of being nit-pickers. Detailers are present in situations where two-person control is required. For instance, when a second signature is required to make a financial transaction, the second person is functioning as a Detailer to insure the accuracy of the transaction. Sometimes the role of detailer is performed by technology; "spell check" on a computer is an example. It frees a person from the detailing role of having to look up words in the dictionary. As a result we can add greater value in other roles. Other examples of the detailing role would include people in technical fields checking their data or calculations. Auditors and accountants spend a great amount of time as Detailers.

If this role is taken to excess, people in organizations lose the ability to see the forest for the trees. With their mental blinders on, they tend to look only at the details and often miss the big picture. The risk of looking at a problem from a Detailer's perspective is that the context of the analysis can be distorted.

The Integrator. The next role is that of the *Integrator*. Integrators are linkers. These people mobilize organizational resources to accomplish a task. At times they have to deal with conflict. They are skilled in the science of human and group dynamics. They are skilled in the art of cooperation and collaboration. They bring together different parts of an organization to achieve synergies. In terms of organizational roles (conceptual, technical, and human), these people have an abundance of human skills. They are skilled in arbitration, and oftentimes function as humanistic politicians. During World War II General Eisenhower's function was not that of a battlefield commander. His function was to be an Integrator in terms of mobilizing and coordinating resources to accomplish a strategic objective.

If this role is taken to excess, the Integrator becomes a networker and views networking as an end unto itself at the expense of accomplishing the task. This leads to great networking, but very little substantive accomplishment. Sometimes it turns out to be one great big happiness trip: "I'll scratch your back and you scratch mine."

The Expert. The next role is that of the *Expert*. Experts possess special knowledge, skills, or training. This role is undergoing great change. We used to be able to master the knowledge within a field or discipline. However, with the explosion of knowledge in the last 25 years, it's become impossible to know everything about a specialized area. So the definition of the Expert is changing. It's no longer just knowing and mastering a subject; it's also knowing how to access and retrieve information about that subject. Experts are often authorities or technical specialists within a given subject area. In terms of organizational skills (conceptual, human, and technical), this person relies on technical skills. For these people, knowledge is power. Those with Ph.D.'s are Experts. They have pursued a very rigorous, disciplined program in terms of knowing a subject in great depth. People who have gained certification are Experts. Going back to the physicians, once they have made a diagnosis, they function as Experts in prescribing a course of treatment.

If this role is taken to excess it is possible to wind up with "know-it-alls." Sometimes the Expert tries to control situations based on his or her expertise. People with expertise are often the worst teachers.

The Inventor. The next role is that of the *Inventor*. Inventors discover new knowledge or new ways to use existing knowledge. There's a great emphasis on lateral thinking. Sometimes they are experimenters. Other times they devise new ways to look at issues and solve problems. Many times they're just tinkerers. Thomas Edison, of course, comes to mind as a great Inventor. Or the person at 3M who invented the Post-It note. He took existing technology and persevered until he was able to perfect a new application. Edison's comment is worth noting: "Success in this area is 1 percent inspiration and 99 percent perspiration."

What happens when the role of Inventor is taken to excess? Inventors often just want to keep tinkering with an idea or a project until it's perfected. They get extremely protective about their intellectual property.

The role of the Inventor is hard to appreciate and is often undervalued in traditional learning situations.

The tough issue with Inventors is how to nurture creativity. It's an important question if we are trying to bring out the best in people in order to become competitive. But the everyday systems around us emphasize order, structure, and organization, and tend to stifle creativity. In order to be successful, inventors are often dependent on having Integrators as mentors.

The Initiator. The next role is that of the *Initiator*. When initiators see something that needs to be accomplished, they wade in and get things started. Just by taking the initiative, these people often define what the outcome will be. They're like a bull in a china shop; they just lower their head and away they go. The Initiator's view of the world often divides people into three categories: those who make things happen, those who watch things happen, and those who wonder what happened. Initiators want results yesterday. Somebody once commented that 90 percent of life is just showing up. Sometimes, it's enough just to be at a meeting or to be present when a process is getting started; the initiator doesn't have to make any contribution; they define the outcome just by taking the initiative to be present.

General Patton had strong Initiator characteristics. At times he outran his supply lines and his resource support: very different from General Eisenhower, who was performing the Integrative role. Entrepreneurs are strong Initiators. They've got the initiative to get started, often with very limited resources.

What happens if this role is taken to excess? The Initiators shoot themselves in the foot, or they shoot first and ask questions later. One person with high Initiative skills made this statement: "When the other person does something without being told, he's overstepping his bounds; when I do it, that's initiative."

The Leader. The final role is that of the *Leader*, and this is probably the most difficult to define. There are countless courses and seminars being given and books being written on the subject every day. Companies and organizations spend millions of dollars to develop leadership skills. We hold leadership up on a pedestal, yet we still don't have a definitive answer as to what leadership is. A Leader is, among other things, an integrator of the eight preceding roles. They are probably strongest in initiation, integration, and diagnosing, and as a result they tend to be at ease with power. Leaders usually generate some feeling of trust from those around them. Leaders tend to be pretty good judges of trade-offs. Somebody once said that a good Leader finds north without a compass. And of course, they represent the phrase that we all know, "The buck stops here." These are some of the images of leadership.

I just came from Minnesota, where they had a hundred-mile dog sled race. The lead dog is obviously a Leader and a very highly valued member of the team. In that case, the pace of the Leader determines the speed of the pack. The same thing can often be said about organizations. It's difficult to examine the role of Leader without becoming overwhelmed by value judgments. As an example, Bismarck and Hitler had different values as to what extent "the end justifies the means." Yet both occupied leadership positions and had a significant impact on history.

A recent article in *Fortune* that focused on the downside of leadership was entitled, "A Case Against Leaders: They Manipulate People, Get Too Much Credit, and Sometimes Take Organizations Over the Edge. How Necessary Are They?" The article made several points.

> Leaders really make far less difference than we give them credit for. A leader is only as good as the situation in which he himself. Leaders manipulate people. Unchecked, leaders can run off the rails, taking organizations with them. They don't inspire baby boomers. As management becomes more participatory, are leaders really necessary?

And then, of course, the great mystery: "Even if we do want leaders, we don't know how to produce them."

All nine of these roles need to be present for an organization to get work done over time. How do we use these concepts and start to translate them into action?

First, let's look at it from an organizational point of view. As a mini-case study I'd like to examine a situation in which an organization developed a mission statement and then used it to identify the roles that the trustees and executive director would play in accomplishing the goals of the organization. The Orange County Citizen's Foundation is a not-for-profit organization, founded in the early 1970s to look at issues of growth and planning in Orange County, New York, which is about 50 miles north of New York City. In the mid-1970s they developed a mission statement to deal with the trade-off between environmental concerns and economic growth issues.

The next step was to identify the jobs necessary to fulfill the mission. The foundation identified about twelve of them; probably pretty standard guidelines for a not-for-profit organization.

What the organization did next was unique. Once the mission statement was designed and the jobs that were necessary to accomplish the mission were identified, the Citizen's Foundation focused on the *roles* needed to achieve the various jobs. As an example, the job of "deciding which issues the foundation should be involved in" requires heavy diagnostic skills and some expertise. "Raising money" requires many roles: diagnosing, monitoring, document-ing, detailing, integrating, and initiative. The foundation identified the roles needed to achieve each job.

From Mission Statement to Action. Getting from mission statement to action is a five-step process:

1. Make sure that the purposes of the organization is clearly stated (mission statement).
2. Identify the jobs needed to accomplish that mission.
3. Identify the roles necessary to accomplish those jobs.
4. Decide who's going to do what jobs. In the case of the foundation, the trustees decided which jobs they were going to take on and which jobs they were going to ask the executive director to do. These decisions were made largely as a result of the roles required to accomplish the job.
5. Recruit people into the organization on the basis of who can fulfill the roles that will be required to accomplish the job successfully.

This is one way that the concept of roles can be used within organizations to focus the energy of the organization and get people to do what they're best at from an organizational perspective.

Let's take another look at how to use this concept from an organizational point of view. In this simulated organization we've identified twelve people. On the basis of managing them, we have made some assumptions about their strengths. Sue, for example, has demonstrated very strong initiative-taking in her work, as well as integrative and diagnostic capabilities. The other people's strengths are identified as well. This has implications for the organization. Do we have the right people to accomplish our organizational goals? In this case the organization is pretty thin on Integrators. That may be good or bad. Remember, there's no value attached to the roles. And there's no identified Leader. That may be good or bad; we don't know. It depends on the purpose of the organization and the tasks that need to be accomplished to get the work done.

The role identification process can be used to evaluate an organization in the same way an investment portfolio is used. What are people good at? What are their strengths? Are the people's role skills appropriate to accomplish the tasks of the organization?

Another way to look at this is from the perspective of the individual. I will use myself as an example and focus on what I like doing best.

I like history because of the focus on people and impact on events. I liked my behavioral science courses in graduate school. In terms of our company activities, I prefer to spend time on management-consulting projects as opposed to administration. In terms of outside activities, I like community and volunteer work. And for recreation and free time I enjoy athletics, triathalons, and cross-country skiing.

If I identify the roles involved in the activities, I find that I like situations where I have to use diagnostic skills, where I have to mobilize resources, and where I have to take some initiative. This also tells me that I'm probably not going to do very well if you put me in an office with four walls and expect me to perform a lot of detailing, documenting, and control functions. That's probably why I wasn't very happy during my early years in the banking business, where my job entailed a great deal of credit analysis and number-crunching. I need to be in situations where I can play off my strengths.

Now that we have identified some of the ways to use the concept, what are some of the implications? Within organizations people have traditionally been evaluated on the basis of their expertise, because it is neat and easy to measure. We can look at transcripts, grade-point averages, and work experience. We can identify a person's area of expertise. It is easy to put on a resume. Next, if we can document a person's expertise, we can then make some assessment as to whether they can master details.

Finally, if they're experts and they can pay attention to the details, can they maintain control? The combination of those skills — expert, detailer, monitor — was the criteria for success in organizations until the mid-1970s.

Well, where did that lead us? Three industries provide good examples:

1. In the early 1950s, the management of the *automobile industry* seriously underestimated the threat of foreign competition. Up until that time the industry was run on the basis of predicting market share. The primary producers made a "guesstimate" as to market share for the coming year and then ran the assembly lines to meet that estimated demand. This was fine as long as there was a stable environment of domestic players. Once the foreign competition emerged, the rules of the game changed completely.
2. In the *airline industry,* management — which for years had managed in a regulated environment — was not able to deal with rapid deregulation.

3. And finally, there is the classic example of *the railroads,* which saw themselves as being in the railroad business instead of the transportation business.

These three industries — which managed by control, Experts, Detailers, and Monitors — have all been seriously affected by not keeping up with changing conditions. So what's the alternative?

- In today's world, a diagnostic presence is needed more than ever in organizations to ask questions like: What's going on in the environment? Who's the emerging competition? What's happening in our organization? What are the forces at play that are going to affect us as an organization, or me as an individual?"
- Once the Diagnoser has assessed these questions, then he or she must have the skills to do something — to take initiative. The world abounds with ideas, but somebody has to take the initiative to translate them into action.
- And finally, if someone has good diagnostic skills and is a good initiator, then he or she must be able to mobilize the resources within the organization to achieve synergies.

The presence of people with these skills — diagnostic, initiative, and integrative — would have helped the automobile, railroad, and airline industries avoid the traps and pitfalls that beset them. Individuals within organizations would have had the potential to manage competitively by assessing what's going on in the environment, making informed decisions, and by mobilizing resources to avoid becoming obsolete in an age of rapid technological development.

The combination of the Diagnoser, Initiator, and Integrator is a *power* model, as opposed to the *control* model of the Expert, Detailer, and Monitor. The power model has the potential to retain or regain the competitive edge that we are in danger of losing. That model gives us a chance to focus on quality, to be consumer-driven, and to generate employee involvement. It is a model that tends to invite people's involvement and to empower those within organizations. It is a means for us, as managers, to gain leverage within the organization. Most important, by enlisting people's help, involvement, and participation, we are focusing on value added.

What are the implications for those in organizations with responsibility for hiring? In the selection and interview process, look beyond expertise or experience on a resume and search for other qualities and potential. Look beyond "what is" to "what might be."

For those of you in this room who are students searching out your first job, you're in a Catch-22 situation. Without experience there's no job, and without a job there's no experience. Ask yourself if there are activities or other work that you have done in which you have demonstrated initiative-taking, diagnostic, integrative, or other role-oriented skills. This allows you to move beyond experience and demonstrate your potential to add value.

Well, where does all of this leave us? The easiest part of a conference like this is attending and exchanging ideas. The hard part is *doing* something to translate those ideas into action. If we leave with a sense that roles are a critical ingredient in managing competitiveness and in helping people do what they do best, we won't be running out of time as organizations and individuals — we will be having the time of our lives.

7

How "Fast Response Organizations" Achieve Global Competitiveness

Martin K. Starr, Graduate School of Business, Columbia University

There is a lot of speculation about what makes one organization more competitive than another. Nobody knows the answer to the problem of how to become globally competitive next year or the year after that, because we are dealing with dynamic systems with changing rules and moving targets. Consequently, I can only tell you about the formula that successful companies seem to be following. Some rather interesting and unexpected elements emerge.

To begin, let me give you a feel for the situation. Many of us have a strong desire to have everything perfectly categorized. Then we sit back and write notes in our little books and say, "I think I understood that. Now if I could only do it." Winston Churchill once said that he thought Lady Astor was a wonderful person, and that her only flaw was that she suffered from hardening of the categories. Relating Churchill's point to our situation, we must be very careful in how we divide up the world and to what elements and dimensions we attribute success, because it's a "Rashomon"-type story. *Rashomon* is a Japanese film classic in which three different people give very different versions of the same occurrence as seen from their individual perspectives. The point is that one must be able to sort out error and discern authenticity.

In this regard, the following story is told about Picasso. An art collector in France bought a picture that he was absolutely sure was a Picasso. He went to a Parisian art dealer and asked him to authenticate the picture. The art dealer replied that he could do that, but it would take him a couple of months. The collector took the painting across the street to another dealer, where he got the same response. He became so impatient that he went to Cannes, where Picasso lived at the time. He went into Picasso's workshop and said, "Dear Picasso, I would appreciate it if you would sign this piece of work and authenticate that it is yours." Picasso looked at the painting and said, "It's a fake." The collector said, "That's impossible; I saw you paint this myself!" to which Picasso replied, "I often paint fakes."

World Class Systems. World class global systems — what categories can explain a subject like that? Our Center for Operations at Columbia University in New York City has been doing research on the behavior of foreign-affiliated firms in the United States. At first we concentrated on Japanese-owned and operated companies in the United States, of which there are currently over 1,000. We have been studying them since 1980. We have watched how they have altered the basic management model that is used in Japan and how they have adapted it to their U.S. operations depending upon where they are, what their industry is, and many other factors.

Our research team recently spent a week and a half in Tennessee. While there we interviewed representatives from five major Japanese companies to learn what was happening. One particularly significant finding was that cultural factors are superficial surrogates for the real forces that account for world class performance. Successful companies, no matter what part of the world they come from, are remarkably similar in management style.

In 1987 we added European companies operating in America to our study. We also began to visit European countries in an attempt to understand what is going to happen in Europe in 1992. By using meetings, conferences, surveys, and in-depth interviews, we began to capture the emerging characteristics of world class competition in Europe.

Computer-Integrated Manufacturing. The companies that are achieving and maintaining success are those which are using a comprehensive information system such as CIM, the acronym for Computer-Integrated Manufacturing. I am not just talking about off-the-shelf CIM software packages. Figure 7.1 illustrates the underlying concept of relational databased information architecture. At an even higher level of systems architecture, we encounter the Computer-Integrated Enterprise (CIE) — but CIM is the more common acronym.

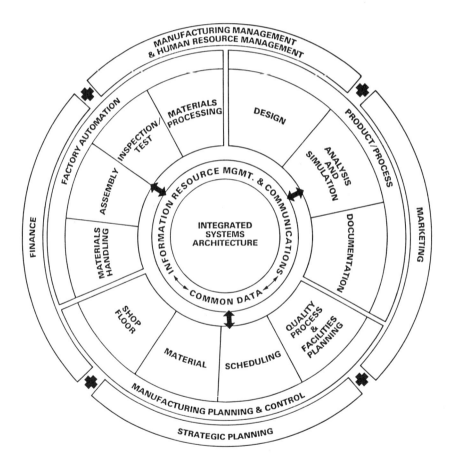

CIM "Wheel" Developed by the Technical Council of the Computer and Automated Systems Association of SME (CASA/SME) © 1985 CASA/SME, Second Ed., Revised 11/5/85.

Figure 7.1 Computer-Integrated Manufacturing Enterprise

The various concentric circles (or rings) of this diagram represent different levels of information in the firm. The outermost rings are the broad functions, which are all in communication with each other. Increasingly specific detail of the possible communications between the functional entities is represented as we move inward on the diagram. Each organizational function can be connected to every other one at all levels of detail. The information network and the rules for communicating are what is referred to as "integrated systems architecture." Each company has its own computer network and communication requirements, and so would have a unique ring diagram of its system's architecture.

Relational databases, which radiate their communication potential between all functions, are crucially important. They do not have to be formal databases. However, they must be designed to enhance communication between all the fundamental players who share data in the system. If two people don't talk to each other because one is on the eighth floor and the other is on the fourth floor, or they really don't like each other, or they are vying for the same positions in the same firm, or if they actually give each other misinformation, the ring is broken and the concept becomes nonoperational.

We have entered a new era in which companies are dealing with elements such as design information while simultaneously communicating about factory processes. Other interactive information elements in the ring include engineering design, costs, and quality. Successful companies view all of these things as interrelated by the flow of information within and outside of the firm. This helps managers reach decisions about what to do next, whether it is implementing quality improvement programs or designing new products. Good decisions depend upon a good information framework.

If the system is even halfway working on a relational basis, it makes you pretty close to world class. This simplifies the traditional dimensions of success. First of all, everybody in business talks about low cost. It is a *sine qua non*. Even if you argue that high quality is most important, most people will agree that, when push comes to shove, it boils down to a question of cost. We keep alternating between wanting the highest quality and the lowest cost. Successful firms strive for both, because multiple objectives and criteria are part of the notion of CIM and data-relational systems. Trade-offs are part of their architecture. You don't give one up and say, "I'm going for cost only," or whatever comes first on the list. Low cost, high quality, on-time delivery, and service: together these factors make up the interdependent package that the producer supplies and the customer buys. But there is something of great importance that is often left out of the package. What is it? It is the performance parameter, *time*, that increasingly has become a differentiating factor of successful companies. Our surveys show that companies that use *time-based management* principles are more likely to be successful in penetrating new markets and sustaining global competitiveness. They use domestic, local, regional, and international information databases to speed decisions and accomplishments. They are constantly extending their databases, which keeps them well-informed and minimizes their surprise at competitive moves. Their managers are conscious of the knowledge required for change: how long it will take to move from where they are to where they want to go. The crucial dimension is the time-response factor.

Fast Response Organizations. The title of this chapter is how fast response organizations (FROs) achieve global competitiveness. FROs are not the same as high-speed organizations, where a frenetic management is geared to "putting out fires." In fast response organizations, managers do not wait for something to happen before they take action. Part of time-based management involves *preplanned fast response* capability, which has also been called *anticipatory* or *corrective fast response* ability. Fast response managers are prepared to create new situations, to visualize and respond to likely scenarios, and to defer action until the time is right. Thus, they are acutely aware of *timing* as well as *time*.

Delays in lead time, lag time, think time, communication time, and so on, are continuously being cut down and compressed significantly. Within organizations all over the globe as diverse as Brunswick, Hewlett-Packard, and Honda, we have found that faster-response business units are more successful than their slower-response competitors. Often, some units are FROs while others within the same organization are not. CEOs of companies such as General Electric and Hewlett-Packard are using successful FRO-type business units to set the pace, and then are cloning or replicating them elsewhere in the company. This approach looks good; it works. In other words, you set up a pilot unit showing how the system can operate. Then you export the successful pattern to other business units.

A FRO pilot system is an artificial entity that creates interface problems for the organizational bureaucracy. While pieces and parts of it may be studied, it is not a functional reality until the normal organizational setup is totally altered. FROs will not operate in the traditional organizational framework. Why is that true? Traditional organizations emphasize *tactics* and tend to ignore the fast response aspects of *strategies*.

Strategies and Tactics. Most organizations have gone a certain distance with respect to tactics such as just-in-time, minimizing work-in-process, getting rid of waste, and improving quality (reducing defectives) in their processes. In other words, they are *doing things right* before *doing the right things* — those that are strategically correct. Global competitors believe that everyone should be *continuously* involved in doing strategically right things.

A lot of organizations are concentrating their efforts on the tactical aspects of operating without looking at the strategic aspects. That approach dooms them to failure. It just will not work in the long term, because FRO-type global competitors start with "strategizing" and move through "tacticalizing" (see Figure 7.2).

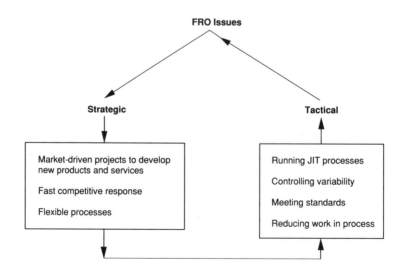

Figure 7.2 FRO Issues

The ability to have a reactive informational structure disseminated throughout the organization creates rapid decisional support capabilities. It adds the time parameter to the management information system (MIS) functions: it keeps track of things, but it also moves fast. If it is used only for tactical purposes, such as production scheduling and inventory, then the system cannot operate at the upper corporate level with respect to market-driven projects. Tactics alone do not address the key issues: What should we be doing, what are the products, and what are the services?

A variety of manufacturing companies are finding out that strategic-level service is a part of their business. They need to be able to respond to customer requests quickly. They must also be able to act flexibly if a competitor comes out with a new strategy for products or services.

Our studies indicate that most companies in the United States are well along the way tactically. Japanese companies in the United States consider these tactical problems — such as just-in-time (JIT), zero defects, and the way in which vendors are made part of the system — as solved or steadily solvable. A minimal number of vendors, strong trust relationships, keeping things moving, no waste, nothing on the loading platform, maintaining the highest quality — these are typical of tactical things that the Japanese take for granted. They may not have achieved perfection, but they keep trying.

It is interesting to note that American workers in Japanese-run plants in the United States seem to thrive under Japanese management, whereas American managers are more at odds with their Japanese colleagues. The American managers find it hard to deal with fast-moving, fundamental changes and continuously higher standards. Vendors in the United States find it difficult to work with Japanese companies for the same reasons. A lot of the Japanese companies are disappointed at their inability to develop highly reliable trust relationships for fast-changing product and service arrangements with American vendors.

American companies are doing fine with tactical issues such as getting rid of waste, making quality improvements, and bringing about continuous tactical change. They are learning to pay attention to detail and to leave nothing to chance. These priorities all come from survey statements by companies operating on the tactical side. Who is going to knock tactical FRO improvement which, it has been shown, can double your productivity, reduce costs by 20 percent, and allow growth three times faster than the rest of non-FRO industry? This is accomplished by getting rid of stuff just waiting around, thereby increasing the percent of total time dedicated to value-adding operations. But the underlying power of FRO will be missed if only tactical benefits are pursued. Although strategic benefits are harder to measure than tactical benefits, they are essential for survival in a fast response competitive environment.

Competitors and Suppliers in the Total Strategic-Tactical CIM Loop. Global competitors are bringing suppliers onto the strategy side of the CIM loop, making them a privileged part of their interactive information system. In some companies customers are also part of the strategy side of the CIM loop. There are now big companies with equally big customers hooked into their information systems by terminals directly connected to the producer's computer. They are sharing information about established and start-up products. Orders that used to arise suddenly (or so it seemed from the outside) have become schedulable, albeit with short lead times. For example, the sales managers of a large chemical company felt that they had to keep six carloads of a particular plastic outside their customer's plant on a railroad siding. By using a CIM-type information tie-in, the company has cut its rail-siding inventory down to one boxcar because it knows when the customer's orders are coming. What seemed sporadic has become logical as both parties jointly anticipate new product start-ups, special orders, last-minute orders, and even changes in longstanding orders. The key to success requires putting all of the players inside the same informational system.

Such success stories illustrate the savings that can be made using tactical CIM concepts. Strategic CIM capabilities, on the other hand, are not cost-oriented, but are strongly related to survival. Figure 7.3 depicts the total set of organizational activities that should be supported by the CIM system.

The major emphasis in Figure 7.3 is on the strategic components that operate through the "project management" box. The importance of the supplier's roles is very evident.

The cycle to note in Figure 7.3 is *find — design — build — ship.* To get this cycle working, you need to have an awareness of the FRO capability of project management (strategic) as well as process management (tactical). Our research indicates that the advantage today

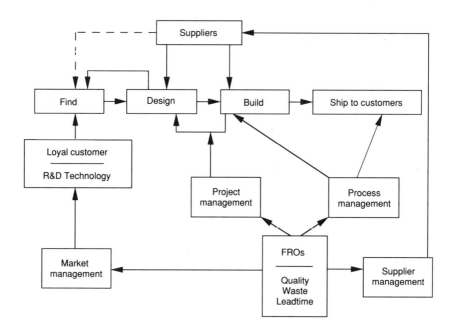

Figure 7.3 Profile for Excellence

goes to the company that is concentrating on *project* management rather than *process* management, except when the project is dealing with changes in process. Project management style is where global competitiveness seems to be emerging on a tremendous scale. Leverage is on the side of those who know what to design, build, and ship, and how to do this continuously. In this cycle, design, marketing, and production are joined in a new organizational form.

Organizational Change. Marketing, R&D, production, development — all of these functions, and others as well, are connected by the interactive information network. When these functions are forced to talk to each other on an ongoing basis, the organization changes. Organizational change is absolutely essential. To know what changes to make requires the collective intelligence of the entire organization. The flexibility of the production processes determines the ability of the organization to deliver the variety of outputs demanded by customers in the marketplace. R&D and production managers have to become aware of market research and market systems dynamics.

Designers of products, services, and processes in the fast response companies that we have interviewed sit down with market researchers and jointly endeavor to find out how people are using their products and what they might prefer. That is not a typical American approach.

Organizational Size and Learning. It is critical that the organization be small enough to ensure that the communication linkages between all of the functional entities are in place. Successful organizations can be part of giant companies, but they use *decentralization* to keep the information system of workable size.

The bureaucracy of large organizations is intended to constrain information flows. This is entirely counterproductive from the FRO point of view, which encourages individuals to take whatever actions are needed then and there. FROs require reasonable decision autonomy. Between 300 and 500 employees is the number that emerges over and over again as the optimal size for FRO-oriented companies. As soon as an entity within the business unit grows larger than that, the Japanese decentralize it. American companies such as GE and Ford Motor say they are doing this as well.

"Is the business unit too big?" You can't get these CIM systems working until you have a viable communication network. One of the basic principles I have already stated is that these organizations cease to be managed in the traditional way. They are *learning* organizations in which you are really managing *intelligence* rather than *information*. Managing intelligence — rather than data or materials or schedules — is the critical orientation for successful companies in this era of global competitiveness.

Continuous Project Management. Finally, let us turn to the ongoing project management that supports this system. What does the project plan (organization, system, team, unit) responsible for change look like? First, every employee in the business unit becomes part of a project management group. Not only are they responsible for the everyday affairs of production, marketing, and so forth, but they are now also part of one or more project teams. Although they have a variety of jobs to "keep things running," they must also get involved in project assignments to change products and processes. Second, there is no "start" or "stop" to these projects. The Program Evaluation and Review Technique, or PERT, model constrains creativity by requiring the total replacement of an old system with a new one. The major vested interests in the old system naturally resist disenfranchisement. Such "PERT" project management destroys the possibilities of working cooperatively to improve, rather than replace, an existing system. The new kind of incremental, ongoing project management seems to be working well for the companies that are using it. It takes a complete modification of traditional organizational arrangements to actually achieve continuous project management systems.

We have examples in the United States of FROs that are successful in both strategic and tactical modes (though many more of the latter). Some companies that have seriously addressed this issue are Allen-Bradley/Rockwell International, American Honda, Brunswick, General Electric, Hewlett-Packard, Northrop, Prime Computer, and Tandem. The same applies to European and Asian firms, and more companies are trying to enter the business Olympics all the time. The combination of knowledge and will is surfacing, and in companies where it is happening the project organizations are unique, cooperative teams. They are responsible for shaping the future, for determining emerging global leaders.

Time is the dimension that business leaders use for leverage. They minimize (not just reduce) time to innovate by continuously innovating. They use innovation to provoke general customer dissatisfaction with existing products. This destabilizes the marketplace and permits entry and reentry opportunities. These business leaders strive to upgrade quality standards to make obsolete the production investments of their competitors, and to supersede skill levels that formerly sufficed.

The message I wish to convey is that the traditional bureaucratic organization can no longer prosper — or even survive — in the present global business environment.

8

Organizing in the 1990s in the New Competitive Environment

Jay R. Galbraith, Professor, University of Southern California

I want to talk about organizing in the 1990s. Our Center for Effective Organizations at the University of Southern California has received a series of requests from our sponsors. They are asking what kinds of organizations are developing, what they should be preparing for, how they should be training people, what kinds of social structures will be created, and what kind of folks they are going to need to work in those social structures to be competitive in the 1990s. We have been looking at manufacturing firms to see what is going to be happening. This means looking at the kinds of strategies these organizations will be using, because social structures are ultimately determined by corporate strategy. The kinds of strategies people implement are going to depend on the business environment.

We have been assessing what the nature of the business environment is going to be in the future and what kind of strategies organizations will be using. From that we postulate the kinds of organizations that we are going to use to implement those strategies. Essentially, we see the globally competitive environment as being driven by technology.

Jerry Hage said that the new competitive environment began in about 1975. R&D spending among our competitors has increased every year since then, with the annual increase varying between 4.5 and 8 percent. Investment in R&D, in real terms, is doubling about every 10 to 12 years. The Japanese are increasing their R&D expenditures by about 17 percent per year. In real terms, they double the amount of money they are spending about every five years.

The implication is that the fixed cost of doing business is rising. You cannot rely upon domestic volume anymore to cover costs. If Hewlett-Packard introduces a spectrum series of computers that costs $400 million, they must rely on foreign demand to pay for that investment. That is true for everybody. Everybody is looking outside their own country for increased demand to be able to cover their fixed costs, and the demand is not there. You have more folks chasing less business — a much more competitive kind of environment.

The environment is essentially much more dynamic and turbulent. It is moving faster and is shifting power among the stakeholders. The customer is more powerful. It is becoming much more of a buyer's market. You have to be responsive to the customer.

Strategically, U.S. organizations started responding to these issues in about 1981. This is when the recession came about and the dollar was high. Organizations began to go to work to recover the competitiveness of their core business, cost quality competitiveness. Their initial remedial actions involved cuts: layoffs, early retirements, fewer middle managers, plant closings, open season on corporate staff. It didn't take a whole lot of brains to do this; it took a lot of stomach. The successful leaders were tough-minded individuals. Doug Danforth at Westinghouse shaped up the organization. He does not accept excuses.

Consolidation Versus Integrated Responsiveness. These initial cuts gave way to longer-term action. Now everybody has a quality program and a vice president of quality who reports to the CEO. We shop the world for cheaper money. We have to spend a lot of money on automation, consolidation, and trying to pull together a number of activities. In Europe everyone is consolidating across national borders. A lot of the mergers and acquisitions within industries are consolidations.

We are also setting up policies to enable us to move faster, and we get integrated responsiveness. In Detroit, this is called *simultaneous engineering*. Telescoping lead times down reduces the time needed to get to the market from five years to three years. It is crucial to design for manufacturability by bringing manufacturing engineers in to design the product from beginning. This is called *concurrent design* at TRW.

These two methods tend to work in opposite directions. Consolidation says size is good. Integrated responsiveness says size is bad. You want to be small in order to be quick on your feet. These are some of the pressures that lead us to the kinds of organizations that are evolving.

There is a lot of interest in vertical disaggregation, vertical disintegration. In the old days the winners used to do everything themselves. If you wanted it done right, you did it yourself. General Motors is vertically integrated. IBM makes its own polysilicon to make its own chips and boards. In the future, the winners are only going to do what they do well. You cannot do everything well. IBM does not run retail computer stores or sell consumer products very well. You only do what you can do well, and you cannot do everything well, so people are vertically disintegrating and disaggregating. They are subcontracting, buying much more, and doing less. Eventually these dramatic kinds of moves result in continuous improvement, and employee involvement tends to pick up.

Global Product Strategies. The other thing organizations do is take the core businesses that they have decided to keep and extend on them globally. They are run as a global business rather than as a group of regional businesses. When Ford spends $3 billion on Taurus and Sable and they need a new mid-range line of cars in Europe, they are not going to spend another $3 billion. They have to take Taurus and Sable to Europe. That means your products must be globally designed to begin with. You need a global products strategy, because you cannot duplicate everything in different sections of the world. This leads to globalization. Here again, you run into problems. There is always Newton's Law of Business: For every economic and technological force there is an equal and opposite political force that is not going to let you do what you want to do. You would like to have global products and sell from a single R&D site. Most countries agree with that as long as it is "my" country. You need, therefore, to be a good local citizen.

All of these things drive us to what is known as overlays, which is just a euphemism for "matrix." In most organizations I go into, if you even mention the term "matrix," people want to kill you. But don't look now: it is back. The pressures at HP to consolidate and be fast on your feet mean you have consolidated functions. To minimize the number of people you go functional. To be fast on your feet you need program managers to work a cross-function. So matrix is back in. Internationally, you need to have a global business manager to worry about Taurus and Sable for Ford. You'd better have someone worried about Europe and what is going to happen in 1992. Again, you have countries and businesses; you are into some kind of matrix organization. This time we have to learn how to get it right.

Companies are recovering their core businesses through a number of actions. They are globally extending those core businesses. When you get to a point where you are generating more cash flow from recovered businesses than you can usefully reinvest into the core businesses, the priority shifts to development. If you look at someone like Ford now, as they accumulate cash flow their priority shifts to development. If you go to General Electric, the expression is, "What are you doing for the top line? Where is top-line growth? Where are our new sources? How are we going to develop more?" In the 1990s I think the priorities for organizing will revolve around development and trying to develop new sources of revenue. This is one of the things that is driving us to investigate these new forms of organization.

The Network Organization. Particularly, the one I would like to spend the most time talking about is what Ray Miles calls the "network organization." If you look at successful organizations as they develop from scratch, they do not vertically integrate — the Nikes, the Reeboks, the Benettons, and the Sun Microsystems. They do only what they do well. They put together a network of joint ventures and alliances with other companies. There are a number of interesting design issues involved in putting those kinds of networks together, which I would like to look at.

Some new kinds of organizations come about in order to implement a shift to development. In general, these kinds of organizations are good at working across lines of authority. This is the old matrix kind of thing. Everybody is using teams and task forces of various ilks.

Cluster structures are occurring at the corporate level. We are clustering like kinds of businesses together and differentiating and decentralizing much more. A recent change at Hewlett-Packard created two clusters there. One cluster is composed of a group of instrument businesses that are stand- alone, high-performance, classic HP-way organizations. The other cluster is made up of all the divisions — those that are not classic HP — involved in the computer business. These are strategically centralized as they move into a systems business. Value-added goes to software, not hardware. The criteria for purchases are reliability and being able to integrate things; not gee-whiz technology. Two clusters, two different, independent kinds of businesses.

You can find similar things at Westinghouse and General Electric. Another word for these kinds of structures is "neoconglomerate." Conglomerates arc coming back in ways that allow us to incorporate financial services as well as business units. If you take a look at General Electric, you will find a collection of businesses, trading companies, and banks. What is the difference between GE and Mitsubishi? What is the difference between the Japanese *batsu*, Dinglerben and Dacha Bank, Volvo? More and more banking activities are going inside these companies. We also tend to use banking for developmental purposes. When Montgomery Ward does a leveraged buy-out from Mobil Oil, it gets financing through GE Capital. They do the leveraged buy-out, get the fees and so forth that go along with that, but they do business arrangements with the rest of GE. GE Credit does their financing and accounts receivable. GE also does private-label major appliance manufacturing for Montgomery Ward. GE takes 10 percent of that. As more banking activities move into corporations, we create these kinds of business clusters. The banking and financial services section also becomes part of the business-building activity.

Innovative organizations are still trying to learn to do something for the *first* time. Most of our organizations are set up for doing something for the *millionth* time. When you do something for the first time, you need to separate these things — put them off on a green-field site. The GM Saturn program is a typical example of actually forming a new company: starting with a clean sheet, little bureaucracy, full automation, and high employee involvement. When many organizations have the opportunity to start from scratch, they often create interesting nonhierarchical organizations. This trend is moving along fairly quickly.

Let's look at development. Organizations that are beginning to develop — General Electric or Westinghouse, for example — target software, service, technology, and financial services. These appear on everyone's growth lists. These are where new investments are being made. Why? Well, most of these things are already performing. People are taking software programs and are starting to sell them outside. It is the same with services. These tend to be the growth areas. They are less competitive. You do not have to fight for market share. Your margins are a little bit better in those businesses, particularly technology. These are the sunrise industries: get in early; get some market share. A lot of the service businesses tend to be local and fragmented. They are not subject to global competition. When GE buys RCA, they also get NBC. They can free themselves from Japanese competition and get a cash source to fund cash-flow battles in medical, electronic, and other, more globally run, businesses.

Many technological businesses are restructuring. When an industry restructures, the current participants tend to be at a disadvantage. The newcomer moves fast. He has the advantage of starting from scratch, with a clean slate.

Out of this shift to development comes pressure to use network organization. What do we mean by networks? Instead of monolithic, hierarchical organizations like IBM, most of the new organizations we see are really flexible networks of organizations. There is a hub firm or a firm that is a broker for the entire network and that looks out for the whole network. It establishes sets of relationships between these various kinds of companies and looks out for the good of the order. I would like to look at that particular hub company.

Networking. If you are going to go into these networks, what do you do inside the company and what do you do outside? How do you hold those activities that are outside of the company together? How do you coordinate it? The same pressures for vertical integration still exist. You still need vertical integration for guaranteed sources of supply. You need to be able to make money up and down the value-added chain. What we are finding, however, is that you do not have to own all of them to control all of them. We are moving from an era of vertical integration to an era of vertical control. How do you control these things? Let me work my way up to that.

Networks now are really seen as something in between markets and hierarchies by the people who study these things. For example,

Xerox used to have 3,000 suppliers. They used a market approach, purchasing all of their items. In order to become more competitive, they have been moving to sourcing. What does that mean? Well, they moved from 3,000 to 300 suppliers. They have tighter relationships, longer-term relationships, guaranteed high volume, and elimination of intermediate activities like incoming inspection. They share gains with the suppliers. There is a much tighter coupling between them. You can find the same thing with people moving from vertical integration to sourcing.

Proctor & Gamble used to run their business with a hierarchy. They did everything themselves. They crushed their own linseed to make linseed oil through a subsidiary called Buckide Crushing. But that is a commodity business. They looked at that business, and then they looked at Archer-Daniels-Midland, a company whose people know how to run a commodity business. The manufacturing skinflints dominate this. These folks run on razor-thin margins; they fly coach. That is a very different approach to the business than Proctor is used to. They say, "What are we doing running Buckide Crushing? Let's sell it to Archer-Daniels-Midland. We will keep a 10 percent equity investment, and then we will get a guaranteed 25-year contract. Let them run it. We do not know how to run that business." The idea of vertical disintegration is to get rid of the stuff that you do not know how to run. Moving to sourcing arrangements is one way to approach this.

You cannot afford to do everything yourself now, so you only do what you do well and find an alliance. Within aerospace these deals are called teaming arrangements. It is very tight coupling. There is teaming between McDonnell-Douglas and Northrop on the advanced technical fighter that is coming up. Then there are minority investments. When AT&T makes a 25 percent investment in Olivetti, it is sealing their relationship. Joint ventures are where there is an actual separate entity, and we argue over 49/51 percent ownership. These all represent different kinds of relationships between firms that are now getting together in networks.

Why do people do this? They cannot do everything well, so they give it to a pro. Why should aerospace companies at GE's aerospace division design their own test equipment? That is HP's business; Tektronix does that. Let them do it, and then buy it from them. They cannot afford the capital. The next semiconductor plant will cost $400 million. Not everyone can afford that; you have to share the risk.

Benetton: An Innovative Network Organization. Let's look at an example of the kind of organization I am talking about. Let me take the Italian company, Benetton. Anyone with young daughters would know they sell fashion merchandise to young women. They have been very successful with sweaters. The Benetton family runs the business. In one sense, it looks like any other business. The individual functions are all there. The only thing they do not have is stores. They work through agents, who do not work for them. Agents have territories there. They have something like 5,000 individual stores. They do not own any manufacturing. They used to, but they have sold it all off to various employees. There are about 12 subcontractors, each of whom does a lot of business with many very small weaving and textile firms. There are roughly 350 little textile operators. What is it that Benetton does? What do you put into this company? What do you leave out? What is the logic?

They control the brand. They do the marketing. This is a consumer business, a marketing-dominated business. They control the brand and the brand advertising activities. They put together the product line. They have a series of designers. Julianna, the sister in the business, drives this thing, and is very good at it. They control the products and the product line. They also control the design of the information system. They wire information from the stores all the way back to the individual contractors. GE Information Systems runs it for them, and they use their network. But Benetton designs that information system. They do the logistics for the entire network.

They also do the buying. Benetton is the largest buyer of wool thread in the world. When you are buying and selling, it is good to be big. They are big when it is good to be big and they are small when it is good to be small. You put activities where you want to be big inside the organization. They have a lot of engineers who design the processes to manufacture these sweaters. They buy equipment. Again, this gives them leverage by being big — buying it for everyone in the network.

They do 50 percent of the dyeing. Why do that? Well, because that is proprietary. Benetton has learned to dye sweaters after they are made. After the sweater is made in plain gray goods, they find out what the color demands are, dye it, and ship it. That allows them to cut their inventories roughly in half. That is hard to do. Not many other people know how to do that. So, they do it and keep the trade secret. They do what is proprietary. The rest of the manufacturing they put out to the little independently run places.

They do a lot of the cutting. If you want to control costs in a business, you want to do the buying. You need to get the buying cost down and then minimize waste. So, they design the CAD-CAM systems, do some of the cutting, and give it out to everybody in the network. They do these crucial activities themselves.

They also have stores in key markets. They own about six stores in places like Rome, Paris, and Fifth Avenue in New York City, which they use for market research. Nothing moves off the shelf that they do not know about. They analyze the transits when they try this stuff out. They try new designs, new architectures, and so forth. They also have 1 percent of the manufacturing. Why do they have that? Well, sometimes you have a new design and you want quick turnaround. You also must be a smart negotiator. So, you run the manufacturing shop and you understand the costs. You are not going to get smoke from the individual people. It is important to become educated about cost structures in the business in order to negotiate with everybody else concerning what margins should be.

Another interesting part of their system is the financial area. A lot of the financing activities are moving into Benetton. Benetton is predicting that in the 1990s, 50 percent of their profits will come from the sale of merchandise and 50 percent will come from financial services. They do not own the activities in the network, but they are the banker. They use that position to control the network.

If someone comes up with a new sweater, they want someone in their network to invest in a new machine to produce it. How are you going to convince an independent owner-manager to invest? How do you handle that? Well, you have a leasing subsidiary. You say, "Fine. You do not have to invest. We will invest in it and lease it to you."

What if someone does not mind the leasing, but they just don't like handling financial arrangements? "That's all right. We'll loan you the money." "Well, I don't want to borrow short to invest long." "That's okay. We have an investment bank, and we will do a private placement with an insurance company to help finance this thing." No matter what the arrangement is, they can arrange for the financing to hold all of these activities together.

Somebody says, "I have a couple of young folks in my department who would like to start their own business." Terrific; Benetton has a venture capital arm that will help people invest in new fashion businesses. Slowly but surely Benetton is becoming a merchant bank

— a *fashion* merchant bank. They don't invest in other types of financial services, but they will do initial public offerings and venture capital. They do all kinds of banking and lending in the fashion business.

They use this banking function to control the network and to hold a lot of the activities together. How does Benetton influence the network members that they do not own? First of all, they are the biggest one. They are the big fish in the small pond. They use size. Two, they perform the key activity in a consumer business — marketing. It is the same thing Nike does, the same thing Reebok does. All they are is marketing outfits. Everything else is subcontracted out to other people, but they control the brand and the advertising. They also control the financing for all of these things along the network. They look out for the good of the entire network. They do not see these people as competitors. They look at margins for the entire network.

In general, we are deciding what activities go in the companies, what activities go out, and what the basis of control is. Following the Benetton example, you put things *in* where it is good to be big. You put things *out* where it is good to be small. This allows you to be large and small at the same time and respond more effectively to competitive pressures. How do you control this? One way is with size. This is the kind of thing Sears has done for years. They use their buying size to influence and play the broker role as the hub firm. You also perform the dominant function. Benetton does the marketing. That is also what Reebok and Nike do. Nike does the marketing, and all manufacturing is done in the Far East. They do not own any distribution. They do not have any sales. All they do is the marketing. Seido does all the financing for them. Again, it is focusing only on what you do well.

Tapping the Value-Added Chain. The technology business is beginning to change as well. What do you do in a technology business? It depends on where the value-added function is. Sun Microsystems is an interesting example. They are pursuing something called open systems architecture, where you buy computers and run them on the UNIX operating system. You can buy anybody's equipment as long as it runs on UNIX. You do not get locked into proprietary software. If you go to open systems architecture, it changes where you make money in the business. For example, take personal computers. Who makes the big money in personal computers? It is no longer the people who make personal computers. The big profits go to the component manufacturers. Microsoft and Intel make the big money in personal computers, because you have to use their 8386 from Intel and MS-DOS software. Control over the components and the software is where the money is. Upstream and downstream in the value-added chain are changing. The battle is on for who can control the components. In the technology businesses, control over components is critical.

It is also a question of control over pricing. You do not have to be vertically integrated to get the advantages. Sedas Corporation, the biotech company, has invented a new biotech process which allows drug firms to manufacture and do research to create new drugs. Sedas has joined with Perkin Elmer. They make an instrument which they sell at a very low price to the pharmaceutical college at the University of Southern California, the medical college at Upjohn, to Eli Lilly, and to Merke. It is priced low, but for every pharmaceutical created with that machine, they get 10 percent of the royalties. They do not have to vertically integrate downstream to profit from the business. They have a different pricing scheme.

The control of intellectual property in the business, the control of the pricing, and where you make money determine how successful these technology businesses will be. This area is up for grabs. Right now there is an architect in Berkeley with an interesting way of doing business. If you have this person design a building for you, you pay him a fee. However, he *also* gets 1 percent of the sales price of the building every time it is resold. Again, different pricing schemes are being tailored to profit from intellectual property. In the technology area, intellectual property becomes quite critical. If you go into any technological firm today, legal counsel is included in the strategic planning group. Litigation strategy must be planned with product development strategy and R&D investment. Attorneys are a part of the top management team now, and the game is changing substantially.

What is the dominant function in the value-added chain? Where do you make money in the value-added chain, allowing you to vertically disintegrate, vary pricing arrangements, and so forth? In the technology area, it is in allowing these kinds of firms to stay small and yet profit. Financial services, again, is the tool with which organizations in a developmental mode are controlling the vertically integrated chain.

British Petroleum is in the food business. They have bought Purina Meals, the feed part of Ralston-Purina. They also have breeders. Through biotechnology they design the right male/female pairs for turkeys, chickens, hogs, or any other kind of meat animal. The result is designer cows that have the right cholesterol level, taste, and muscle texture. They will create a product the same way Proctor creates a product for us, and then brand it. Tyson has done this with chickens. Fresh meats are designed from the beginning to be what the consumer wants. The consumer is driving the business. There is an oversupply in farming. Professionally managed farms are replacing family farms. Government is presumably moving out, which makes restructuring more feasible. Biotechnology is reshaping the product as well. British Petroleum owns the feeds and the breeders. They do not want to get into the farming business. We have enough farmers. They will let someone else farm it. They will take a 10 percent investment in a packer so they can control distribution and branding, and then go into retailing.

They control this flow through financial services. They have a financial services joint venture with John Deere Credit and GE Credit. If you are a farmer who uses their male/female pair and their feed, they will give you loans. They will also guarantee you a spread through the hedging market. If you take their male/female pair, run the feedlot, and so forth, they will guarantee a margin through futures contracts. Farmers love this. They will hedge in the futures markets through their own financial services. By controlling the technology, controlling the brand, and doing financial services deals with other people, they get the same benefits you would get through vertical integration without owning it. This approach really conserves capital.

Network forms of organization are emerging. We see them primarily when organizations move into a developmental mode. It is folks like British Petroleum and Volvo in food. It is Sun Microsystems in high technology. It is the Nikes, Reeboks, Benettons, and The Limited in consumer products. They all are only doing what they do well. If you go into Sun Microsystems, the whole organization is geared to creating human resource development policies for high-technology talent. If you are a nerdy, workaholic engineer, this is heaven. Sun is designed for you, because they do not do anything else. If a project requires a body shop or a high capital-investment, they subcontract it. We do not know how to do that. They only do what they do well. They built an organization that only does what it does well. Benetton only has professional people. There are manufacturing process engineers, people who understand the textile business, people who design information systems. It is composed strictly of professional designers; there are no union relationships in there. They focus only on what they do well, and then set up a network of other people to do everything else. But they also have some scheme for control, some way to play the broker in that network. Financial services, performing the dominant function, technology, and control of intellectual property are all mechanisms that we are experimenting with.

Now, what kind of people do you want to run these things? They must be good negotiators. Authority is not a good power base to operate from. As a matter of fact, those organizations who did well in matrix have a leg up. When I am feeling like a smart aleck, I usually say that people who like matrix are going to love networks and joint ventures, because they are just matrix organizations with no tie-breakers. You have to do deals. You have to understand what power base you come from and how to negotiate with these people. So, in Benetton, they cannot tell any of these manufacturing people to buy a certain machine. They have to negotiate. Of course, they come in and make a deal that they cannot refuse and they understand what power base they are coming from. It is learning how to influence without authority, how to negotiate, how to put the deal together, and how to work interfaces with people of different nationalities. We need all of the skills that were necessary to man matrix organizations. We also need the ability to work effectively in an international environment. We need to be able to work with people who are willing to go through a cultural shock, to think in global terms, and to deal with governments and individuals who talk funny and do not share a lot of your values.

PART III

The Quality Equation

9

Quality: A Competitive Strategy

Paul A. Allaire, President, Xerox Corporation

At the outset, I would like to commend the College of Business at Utah State for sponsoring this series of seminars. Bringing representatives of business together with distinguished faculty members and students to focus on key business issues and concerns is a much-needed part of the process of keeping American business competitive in a global economy.

I don't believe I have to remind any of you that America is locked in a battle for global economic supremacy. Let me give you just a few facts to make this point:

- *Fact #1*: As recently as 1960, Japan accounted for only 2 percent of the world's economy. Today it accounts for 10 percent.
- *Fact #2*: When I graduated from high school, the United States controlled some 35 percent of the world economy. Our portion today is about 20 percent.
- *Fact #3*: Since 1984, we have gone from being the world's largest creditor nation to being the world's largest debtor nation.

These are fundamental issues for American society, with enormous impact on our way of life, our standard of living, and our ability to create meaningful employment.

The causes of America's economic decline are varied and complex. Each of us probably has our own favorite version of what went wrong. Almost all of us have pointed the finger of blame at someone else. We complain about the cost and interference of government regulation. Or the lack of management leadership. Or the high cost and the low productivity of the American worker. Or some mythical attribute of "Japan Incorporated."

There is some truth in each of these, I suppose. But in my judgment, the root cause of our trouble is that we became arrogant and complacent. Because America was on the top of the economic pile, we assumed it was our birthright.

Although I don't always like to admit it, in many ways Xerox is a microcosm of what happened to much of American industry. The students are too young to remember, but I'm sure many of the business people here today remember the Xerox 914, the first plain paper copier. We introduced it in 1959 and it quickly created an entire new industry. Some people have called the 914 the single most successful product ever made. It launched Xerox into an era of feverish growth and success.

But with two decades of success, we became complacent and took our eyes off both the customer and the competition. We saw the Japanese coming at the low end of the market, but we didn't take the threat seriously.

We went on continuing to believe we would always be successful, even as our market share began to shrink. After all, we told ourselves, this was our industry. We created it. We built it. And we owned it.

Fortunately, Xerox reacted in time. In the late 1970s we started to take a good, hard look at what we were doing at Xerox and how we run *our* business. And we started to take a good, hard look at the competition and how they run *their* businesses.

We were startled by what we found out. One of the first things we realized was that our costs were too high — and not just a little high. In fact, the Japanese were *selling* their small machines for what it cost us to *make* ours. We assumed that because they were low cost, they were poor quality — we were wrong! Then we tried to convince ourselves that they could not be making money. Wrong again! They were profitable.

That woke us up in a hurry and we went to work in earnest to begin closing the gaps.

We realized that to be a world-class competitor in the eighties and nineties, we had to challenge everything we had done in the past. We had to change dramatically — from the way we develop and manufacture our products to the way we market and service them.

We have been in the process of changing the corporation for about six years now, and although we still have a long way to go, the results are gratifying. Let's look at some examples:

- We have reduced our average manufacturing costs by over 20 percent despite inflation.
- We have reduced the time it takes to bring a new product to market by up to 60 percent.
- We have substantially improved the quality of our products. In fact, Dataquest rates our products as number one in five out of six market segments.
- We have decreased our defective parts from 8 percent to less than three-hundredths of 1 percent.
- We have improved our market share in the past few years — perhaps the first American company in an industry targeted by the Japanese to do this.

I am also proud to tell you that we did it without closing our factories or moving our manufacturing offshore. I tell you all this not to boast, but to illustrate that there is nothing inherently wrong with American business. We lost our way in the 1970s, but we have found it again.

People sometimes ask me how we are doing it at Xerox — how we have reversed our slide and begun the long, tough road back. Believe me, there is no magic formula. We are doing it by involving all of our people — union and non-union alike — in problem solving and quality improvement.

The entire management team has a deep and real commitment to employee involvement. Our incentive is a powerful one — survival as a successful business entity.

You've all heard a good deal about quality recently. We define it at Xerox as "conforming to customer requirements" — pure and simple. It is an axiom of business that is as old as business itself, yet many of us lost sight of it.

And when we speak of quality, we mean more than just product quality. We take the view that every person in the company has a customer for the work they do. For many people, the customer is someone inside the company — the person we type reports for or the person to whom we deliver parts.

It follows from this view of quality that it must work its way into the entire organization — into manufacturing, sales, service, billing, training, finance, and so on. Our quality policy sums it up well. It says simply:

Xerox is a quality company. Quality is the basic business principle for Xerox. Quality means providing our external and internal customers with innovative products and services that fully satisfy their requirements. Quality improvement is the job of every Xerox employee.

Xerox is hardly alone in this approach. Scores of corporations are finding that employee involvement in quality improvement is a powerful way to improve business results. And some of these companies are not in manufacturing. In fact, one of the leaders in quality is Florida Power & Light — the major electrical utility in the State of Florida.

The movement has spread to government as well. We recently hosted a meeting on quality specifically for representatives of the federal government. It was attended by senior executives of not only the Department of Defense, but also a wide variety of service organizations, including the Internal Revenue Service, the FBI, and the Social Security Administration.

This heightened interest in quality is not surprising. The Japanese have realized for years that you don't have to sacrifice quality for cost. In fact, quite the reverse is true.

A focus on quality — on satisfying the customer and meeting customer needs — actually drives cost down. That clearly has been our experience at Xerox!

The focus on quality that we initiated four years ago was built on some very fundamental assumptions about the American worker, which were that:

• Management does not have all the answers.
• All people have ideas about how their work can be done more effectively.
• People closest to the problems often have the best solutions.
• This almost unlimited source of knowledge and creativity can be tapped through employee involvement, and
• People are willing and eager to share their thoughts and participate in developing solutions to business problems.

Those beliefs have paid off handsomely. Today more than 80 percent of our workplace is involved in more than 4,000 problem-solving and quality improvement teams around the world. We still have a long, long way to go, but I am convinced we can do it. When I look back on where we've been and where we are going and ask myself what advice I would give to others, I come up with five specifics:

First, senior management has to be committed to change. Without genuine, hands-on commitment, all attempts at quality improvement and employee involvement are doomed to failure. And that commitment must take the form of action, not rhetoric.

Our expression for that at Xerox is that managers must "walk like they talk." In other words, their actions must demonstrate that they are willing to listen to the ideas of employees, they are sincere in their efforts to change the work environment, and they are serious about their drive toward quality improvement and customer satisfaction.

Second, the commitment of union leadership must be every bit as strong as that of management. That certainly has been and still is the case at Xerox. In fact, quality circles were a part of our manufacturing operations before we launched a companywide strategy of quality improvement and employee involvement.

Credit for that goes to the strong and enlightened leadership of the union that represents most of our hourly employees — the Amalgamated Clothing and Textile Workers Union. They understand that we must be competitive and that our union workers can provide significant help in that struggle.

M.I.T.'s Sloane School of Management has looked at the Xerox experience and summed up our success in one sentence: "The high level of trust built up over the years between labor and management in Xerox was clearly the instrumental factor in the company's success in employee involvement."

Third, it takes some initial investments. At Xerox, for example, we give every man and woman in the corporation six full days of training in problem solving, quality improvement, and team building.

For us, that meant training 100,000 people worldwide. That's an investment equivalent to 2,500 human years. It is a significant investment in both financial and human resources. But we are convinced it is one of the best investments we have ever made.

Fourth, it requires patience and discipline. Our experience has been that results don't come as quickly as we would like. There are some false starts. There are parts of the organization that lag behind others. There are teams that don't initially work on real business problems.

There are managers — particularly middle managers — who see employee involvement as a threat.

One of the Japanese experts on quality and employee involvement likens the need for patience and discipline to that of the bamboo farmer. Once the bamboo seed is planted, the farmer must water it every day. He does that for *four years* before the tree breaks ground! But when it finally does, it grows sixty feet in ninety days.

This is true also of employee involvement. It takes time. It takes nurturing. It takes patience. But when it finally takes off, its power is tremendous. We, like many other American companies, are proving this. It is a very powerful concept that can energize the total organization.

And fifth, the quality process is continuous. That is because as we improve, two highly dynamic forces are at work. First, as we get better, so does our competition. Second, as we meet the requirements of our customers, their expectations of Xerox also increase. What we see is an upward and never-ending spiral of increased competition and heightened customer expectations.

If you had told us that six years ago, we would probably have been discouraged by the thought of running a marathon race with no finish line. Today we find it invigorating. The pursuit of quality has taught us that as good as we are today, we must be better tomorrow.

That is a new concept for many of us in the West. I recently read a book called *Kaizen* by Masaaki Imai (Random House, 1986). Imai says that in the Western world we have an expression: "If it ain't broke, don't fix it." In Eastern culture, the philosophy is "If it isn't perfect, make it better." That's a powerful concept for all of us to emulate.

As you can probably tell, I have a great deal of confidence in the ability of American business to compete successfully in the global marketplace. I don't subscribe to the conventional wisdom that our foreign competitors are superior.

We still have the world's greatest financial resources, industrial capacity, and distribution system. And we have one other asset — the American people, with their immense resilience, strength, and creativity. Our people can win, as long as the competitive environment is fair to all. That means that government, labor, and industry must support one another.

10

The Johnson & Johnson Corporate Credo

James E. Burke, Chairman and CEO, Johnson & Johnson

I want to share a few thoughts with you today about the company I have been privileged to lead over the past 12 years and why I believe Johnson & Johnson has been so successful.

Let me start by saying that we do not have a strategic plan at Johnson & Johnson. We don't believe in it. I am sure some professors would disagree with that, but we don't. We think that business works best on a bottom-up basis. Our business runs through individually operating companies that do have strategic plans.

We believe in the enterprise system. If you can replicate that system within a corporation, you get the same kind of energy that we get out of it as a country. After becoming chairman of Johnson & Johnson in 1976, I spent a lot of time trying to put into writing the philosophies that I felt were responsible for the success of the company. Johnson & Johnson has a document entitled, "Statement of Strategic Direction." Basically, it verbalizes our fundamental philosophies. It states in part:

> We believe the consistency of our overall performance as a corporation is due to our unique and dynamic form of decentralized management, our adherence to the ethical principals embodied in our Credo and our emphasis on managing the business for the long term.

Those three phrases describe what Johnson & Johnson is all about. While we have had a dozen spectacular years since I have been chairman, they have not been any better than those of my predecessors.

Johnson & Johnson has been in existence for over 102 years. Our compound growth rate over that time span has been almost 11 percent. If you look at the business in ten- or five-year increments, you will find that the growth has been remarkably consistent. We went through a period of bad luck during the Tylenol tampering affairs, but basically I believe, and believe passionately, that the reason the business is so successful is wrapped up in the culture of the corporation. It is not wrapped up in Jim Burke or in my predecessors. The corporate culture simply attracts people like myself and others who preceded me.

Without a doubt, ethics and ethical conduct are critical to the success of any business, and Johnson & Johnson is no exception. But ethics is only part of the story. I think there are other, more fundamental factors that also play a major role.

One of these factors is the concept of public service. Public service is predicated on the perception that the interests of business and the interests of society are the same. I would like to advance the premise that public service is not a thing apart, but is implicit in the charter of every American corporation. It is, in truth, the corporation's very reason for being. That's what makes our enterprise system so special.

This philosophy is not unique to Johnson & Johnson, but is understood by most corporations. It is understood exceptionally well by quite a few. There is evidence suggesting that companies who organize their businesses around the broad concept of public service provide superior performance for their stockholders over the long run.

Let me offer you a quotation that crystallizes these thoughts:

> Institutions, both public and private, exist because the people want them, believe in them, or at least are willing to tolerate them. The day has passed when business was a private matter — if it ever really was. In a business society, every act of business has social consequences and may arouse public interest. Every time business hires, builds, sells, or buys, it is acting for the people as well as for itself, and it *must* accept full responsibility for its acts...

That was written right after World War II by a young brigadier general who had just served as head of the Small War Plants Board in Washington. His name: Robert W. Johnson.

This quotation is part of the preamble to a Johnson & Johnson document he entitled simply "Our Credo." Essentially, this document articulates our responsibilities to all of those in society who are dependent upon us:

First, to our consumers — doctors, nurses, patients, and mothers who buy our products and services.

Second, to our employees, whose creative energies are responsible for those same products and services.

Next, to our communities — not just where our plants and offices are, but all of the various communities we deal with, including the community of man.

And finally, to our stockholders, who invest their money in our enterprise.

We have often been asked why we put the stockholder last. Our answer has always been that, if we do the other jobs properly, the stockholder will always be well served. The record would suggest that is the case.

These guiding principles were disseminated among our employees in 1947, and to this day they continue to guide in the formulation of our everyday business and social responsibility decisions. I have to tell you that no matter what we did, or what I did, or what anyone else did, I do not believe we could have made it through the Tylenol crisis without the Credo.

Furthermore, I believe the reason we made so many good decisions was because we had the guidance of the Credo. We really had no alternative but to do what we did. In following the course we did we not only saved the brand, — which is now considerably bigger than it was before the poisonings — I think we saved the corporation and institutionalized a set of values.

It happened to us not only once, as you know. It happened twice. And in both cases we were successful. To be honest with you, I didn't think we would be successful the second time. I really thought the public gave us a hell of a break the first time because they trusted us. Part of that trust, by the way, is wrapped up in our history.

If you stop and think of it, virtually everyone in the country had been impacted by Johnson & Johnson at one time or another — whether by Johnson Baby Powder, Band-Aid or any one of a number of its products. Consequently, when the public became so frightened as a result of the Tylenol crisis and Johnson & Johnson came forward and said, "Trust us," the public believed us. So we cashed in the chips of all of the previous managements as well as living up to the values of the Credo.

The Credo reaffirms that serving the public is what any business is all about. That philosophy has been engendered by the founders and builders of some of the most successful American businesses in America.

I have long harbored the belief that the most successful corporations in this country — the ones that have delivered outstanding results over a long period of time — were driven by a simple moral imperative: serving the public in the broadest possible sense in a way superior to that of their competition.

In 1983, while preparing to receive a public service award from the Advertising Council, I attempted to find convincing evidence to support this contention. Since that year was the thirtieth anniversary of the award, I decided to look at companies who had been in existence for at least that long and who had, at the same time, fulfilled two very rigid criteria:

First, they had to have a written, codified set of principles stating the philosophy that serving the public was central to their being. Secondly, there had to be solid evidence that these ideas had been promulgated and practiced for at least a generation by their organizations.

My staff worked with the Business Roundtable's Task Force on Corporate Responsibility and the Ethics Resource Center in Washington, DC, in compiling the list. We found 26 companies that met these criteria. We then looked at the performance of these companies in terms of profits and rewards to the stockholders over the entire 30-year period.

We had to drop 11 companies from the 26 for lack of comparable data — Prudential because it is a mutual company with no stockholders; Levi Strauss, Johnson's Wax, and Hewlett-Packard because they were private corporations 30 years ago; McDonald's because it didn't even exist; and so on. But the 15 remaining companies still delivered an impressive record.

I think you will be interested in what happened to these companies. Keeping the base year of 1953, we've updated the data several times and we now have information over a period approaching 35 years. These findings were updated for me again recently and here's what we found:

First, profits: These companies show a 9.6 percent growth in profits compounded over this period. That happens to be more than 1.24 times the growth of the gross national product, which rose 7.8 percent during the same time.

To understand the effect of that difference in compound rate of growth over 37.75 years, the GNP is now about 13.4 times greater than it was in 1953; the net income of these companies is more than 24 times greater.

And how about the stockholder?

If any one of you had invested $30,000 in a composite of the Dow Jones 35 years ago, it would be worth $230,583 today.

If you had invested the same $30,000 — $2,000 in each of these 15 companies instead — your $30,000 would be worth over $1.5 million! $1,540,198, to be exact! If the Dow had grown at the same rate as these companies, it would stand at 13,998.

The results are, at the very least, provocative.

I know the people that run these companies and I know a lot about the companies. You would not be surprised at the names of anybody on the list. Included are such companies as IBM, J.C. Penney, Kodak, Procter & Gamble, Xerox, and other very well-known and successful companies.

The evidence suggests not only that ethical behavior is essential to you as individuals in living a life that is emotionally rewarding, but it is also very good business.

11

Business Ethics Is Not an Oxymoron

M. Anthony Burns, Chairman and CEO, Ryder System

I am delighted to talk about a subject that is very close to me personally and to the folks I work with, both at Ryder System and in various other corporations. That subject is business ethics.

It's kind of an interesting expression: business ethics. In fact, some people have said it's an oxymoron. They contend that the words business and ethics really don't go together, that they are inconsistent.

Listen to some of the statistics that are being quoted about business ethics in the United States. In *Ethics in American Business*, a report by the Big Eight accounting firm, Touche Ross & Company, 95 to 99 percent of those surveyed said they believe ethical problems exist in the business community.

The April 1989 *Journal of Business Ethics* reported that results of a 1988 Gallup Poll indicated that business lagged behind all other institutions, including churches, the military, the Supreme Court, public schools, and Congress — even Congress — in terms of ethics.

In a *New York Times*/CBS poll conducted last year, 55 percent of 5,000 Americans surveyed said they thought executives are dishonest. Only 33 percent of those surveyed thought that business executives were honest.

W. Michael Hoffman, director of the Center of Business Ethics, reports that "80 percent of managers say they feel pressure to compromise their integrity to achieve the corporate goals." He also estimates that white-collar crime costs business a shocking $200 billion annually. Fines and penalties run into the millions. Resulting governmental regulations cost more than $100 billion annually to implement. The damage to the public relations of firms probably has economic ramifications much more costly than that.

Yes, business ethics is a hot topic today. In fact, the Harvard Business School now requires its students to take a course in business ethics prior to graduation. A number of other schools, including Stanford, Columbia, Wharton, and Dartmouth, are making efforts to integrate ethics instruction into their curriculums.

What exactly is business ethics, and how does it really work within the business community? I'm impressed by a report that was put out by the Business Roundtable a month or two ago that said that there is not a contradiction between business and ethics in the best, most successful companies. Doing the right thing is not only proper in terms of morality; it is also very good business. The companies that are truly successful today are those that take their ethical responsibilities very seriously.

For the next few minutes, I'd like to share with you some examples not only of doing the right things, but also how these kinds of actions are good for business. I'd like to use Ryder System and some other companies that I am closely associated with as examples.

At Ryder System we currently have assets of over $6 billion, the highest of any Fortune 100 diversified services company. We had revenues last year of $5 billion, with net earnings of nearly $200 million after taxes. We have 45,000 employees worldwide and over 165,000 vehicles in our fleet. Not only are we the world's largest truck leasing and rental company, but we're also the world's largest contract carrier. Last year we delivered 6.3 million automobiles to dealers from railheads, ports, and manufacturing plants.

We are also the world's largest turbine aircraft engine overhaul and maintenance company. We overhaul and maintain more turbine engines for commercial airlines than several of the largest airlines combined through three large facilities in California, Texas, and Scotland. We're also the world's largest aviation parts distributor. We distribute aviation parts worldwide through about 80 locations.

We believe that our success comes from establishing a trust or a bond with all of our stakeholders: our customers, our employees, our suppliers, our shareholders, and the communities where we do our business. We believe doing that is not only the moral thing; it is also very good business.

The Customer Perspective. Now, let's take the customer perspective. Over 95 percent of the business that we do in our company is repeat business. Almost 95 percent of the business that we do at Ryder System is also business that the customer could do for himself, so we have to provide better quality for a lower price than the customers would pay by doing it themselves.

Let me give you a couple of examples. We lease about 1,500 vehicles — worth more than $50 million — to PepsiCo. PepsiCo could own those trucks and maintain them themselves, but they lease them from Ryder and we maintain them, wash them, provide fuel and tires for them — everything. Imagine what would happen if we were not honorable people.

We deliver more than 50 percent of all of the General Motors cars and trucks sold in North America to General Motors dealers. General Motors could buy trucks, hire drivers, and deliver those vehicles themselves if they wanted to. But we are partners with them because we provide better quality at a lower cost.

General Motors would not allow Ryder to deliver over half of their automobiles and trucks to dealers if we didn't have a high level of ethical standards. If we damaged the vehicles or if we cheated on the invoices, we would not be in business with General Motors. Not only is behaving ethically the right thing to do, it is also very good business.

The highest priority of our company is providing quality service to our customers through quality employees; that is critical to our survival.

Think about one of our largest customers for turbine aircraft engine maintenance, British Airways. We do wide-body engines for them in a shop at Prestwick, Scotland. It is the largest turbine engine overhaul shop in Europe. If we cheated on the vanes and the turbine blades in those engines — just a few times — would they come back to us for the service? The relationship and partnership that we have with them is very critical.

Another of our large customers is Thai Airways in Bangkok, Thailand. We have a very good relationship with them, but if we didn't treat them with dignity and respect as we carry out our multi-million-dollar contract, would they be back to do business with us?

For us, ethical behavior is not only a moral requirement; it is good bottom-line business. It helps us drive toward earnings that satisfy our shareholders in a market where they say, "I want it today, I don't want to wait until tomorrow. I want short-term rewards. I don't want to wait for the longer term." To be successful, your relationship with your customer must be based on a trusting, strong relationship.

The Employee Perspective. What is the key to all this? Our relationship with our people. The relationship that we have with our people, our employees, our associates, our colleagues will drive the resultant relationship that we have with our customers. The major issue is the human resource issue: finding, attracting, recruiting, training, developing, motivating, and retaining high-quality employees.

The Hudson Institute, located in Indianapolis, IN, is a very good social research organization that has studied changes occurring in the nation's work force. As a result of their studies, the Hudson Institute came up with a very interesting conclusion about the work force of the year 2000. I found that conclusion to be quite shocking. The report said that between now and the year 2000, 85 percent of the net new jobs will be filled by women, minorities, and immigrants. Only 15 percent of the net new jobs that will be created between now and the year 2000 will be filled by the traditional, U.S.-born, white male who has always represented the majority of the work force.

Now, with these changing demographics, companies that are good places to work, that treat people with dignity and respect, are going to be the true winners.

Let me tell you how we are responding to these challenges at Ryder System. I'm chairman of the National Urban League, which is the largest black organization in the United States. The Urban League was founded 75 years ago to integrate southern blacks into the industrialized Northeast. While the Urban League advocates affirmative action and equal opportunities for all people — blacks, whites, Asians, whatever — their primary mission is preparing people to take advantage of opportunities. That's the type of organization we like to work with in our company, because they offer us a new and excellent source of employees.

If you treat all people ethically — with dignity and respect — regardless of the color of their skin, regardless of the language they speak, regardless of the town or country they were born in, your company will be a success in the business community.

A second issue is education. Recent studies have indicated that by the year 2000, entry-level employees will need three years more education than is necessary today. Think about that for a minute.

I was told by the head of a big company headquartered in New York City that his company was seeking 1,000 new employees recently. They tested 23,000 people before they found 1,500 who could pass sixth-grade reading, writing, and arithmetic tests. Five hundred, or one-third, of the 1,500 failed a drug test. So they hired the remaining 1,000 people. But that's not the end of the story. One year later, 60 percent of the 1,000 had left the company for performance reasons. Education is critical.

I remember that back when we set up the Ryder System Charitable Foundation, we said our primary focus would be the cultural community. We wanted to help the Miami Opera, the Miami Ballet, the Miami Philharmonic, and so forth.

Today, however, only 20 percent of our foundation dollars go to the support of purely cultural programs. Eighty percent go into social services and education. I never dreamed ten years ago that we would be making direct-dollar contributions to public education, but we do. We are also very active in our relationships at the university and college level, where we recruit our employees.

A third important issue is the scourge of drug abuse. Drug abuse may be *the* issue of the 1990s. At Ryder System, we've dug in our heels and taken a tough stand on drug abuse. We say, "You take a drug test before you join the company. If you fail the drug test, you don't join the company."

We also have drug testing for two specific groups of employees with safety-related jobs: those in our highway transportation businesses and those in aviation.

We are the second-largest school bus operator in the United States. We transport 400,000 students to school and back each day. For our school bus drivers, our truck drivers, our turbine aircraft engine mechanics, and our aviation parts specialists, we have random drug testing. Why? How would you like to fly on a plane after a mechanic who had snorted coke had worked on the turbine engine?

You know, that is a very sobering thought. If you fail our random drug testing, you are fired. There are no exceptions. We make sure our people know the rules.

So, the employee is critical as we look to the future. You are not going to have the best employees if you don't have an ethical foundation upon which to build. If people aren't treated with dignity and respect where they work, they will go somewhere else to work where they *are* treated with dignity and respect.

Set the Example. Also — and this is very important — you have to walk like you talk. You have to set the example. A company's CEO and the senior officers have to be leaders in establishing the environment for an ethical relationship with employees. If the leadership doesn't have it, the company won't have it.

We also think that it is important for the company to have the right organization. As a wise old philosopher said, "Teach people proper principles and let them govern themselves." We have a very decentralized organization at Ryder System. Of our 45,000 employees, only about 300 are in the parent company. The rest are in our divisions. It is not only fundamentally right to allow people to make decisions. The fact is, they can make better decisions because they are in the marketplace. They are closer to the customer. Our organizational structure is based upon how we feel about people.

You can be centralized; you can be autocratic; you can make every single decision, if you are the CEO. But how does that work ultimately?

More and more companies are becoming increasingly decentralized, forcing the decisions closer to the customer, allowing more participation by employees.

We have made almost 100 acquisitions in the 1980s. One reason we have been successful in our acquisition program is that we will not make a hostile acquisition, and we want to retain management after we make the acquisition. Again, it's that relationship with employees.

A few years ago the *Wall Street Journal* surveyed a group of CEOs and asked them, "What are the key five ingredients you look for in the senior officers of your company?" It was interesting to me what the five were, and in what order they were listed.

Integrity was the highest priority. It is fundamental. You don't want someone to work for you, or you don't want to work for somebody, who is a liar. It really doesn't work.

The second priority was the ability to communicate. You have to be able to express yourself, both verbally and in writing. That is critical, especially for those at the senior levels of companies. You have to be able to communicate the mission statement, the goals, the objectives, the code of conduct, and what is expected.

The third priority was the ability to get along as a team. There are some isolated examples of real Titans who have personally turned around companies, but compare that to the tens of thousands of other very successful companies that are run by management teams.

I am really impressed with IBM. Paul Rizzo, retired vice-chairman of IBM, is on the Ryder System board. I also sit on the Pfizer board with John Opal, the recently retired CEO of IBM. They maintain that the key ingredient in the success of IBM is teamwork and the employees' ability to work together in accomplishing major objectives.

The fourth priority was job knowledge, and the fifth was pure intelligence. Integrity, ability to communicate, getting along as a team, job knowledge, and intelligence were judged to be critical, and most of these relate directly to ethics.

The Community Perspective. A key stakeholder for any organization is the community. At Ryder System, we believe that a corporation and its community are one and the same. A business entity creates pure economic opportunity. It creates jobs, it creates opportunities for vendors to sell to the business, it creates wealth, it creates an opportunity for a shareholder to enhance wealth.

A community, on the other hand, prepares people to take advantage of that opportunity. It gives them training, education, and social services to help them in times of need. A community and a company really work hand in hand, and a business that is truly successful over a period of time is a business that has a good, close relationship with its community.

Within our company we have a rather aggressive incentive program. Most of the total annual compensation for the top 50 or so officers of our company comes from a bonus. That bonus is based on two things. One is the achievement of the profit targets that were set for the business; the second is the achievement of certain other specific objectives.

We expect our officers to join and be active in social service organizations. For example, I am chairman of the National Urban

League and chairman of the United Way campaign. The president of our largest division, the fellow who runs our truck leasing and rental operations, is chairman of the local Salvation Army. We give our officers objectives to not only give of their monies, but of their time and energies in helping the community. We also give gifts in kind, such as trucks, to do certain things to support community activities.

Conducting your business in a socially responsible way means that you attract, again, the very best employees and the very best customers within the community. Customers like to do business with companies that are socially responsible.

Now, let me emphasize: sometimes that can be a lot of fun. As you may or may not know, we sponsor the Doral-Ryder Open golf tournament. The Doral-Ryder Open has the largest purse of any full-field tournament on the PGA Tour, $1.3 million. The winner receives a check for $234,000. But the key to that tournament is not just the public relations value and the visibility that the company gets. The tournament is a charity fundraiser, from which the American Cancer Society will receive $500,000 or more to help fight the scourge of cancer.

The Doral-Ryder Open helps South Florida because it is good public relations for South Florida. It is important to support the communities where we live.

The Wall Street Perspective. We also have other stakeholders that put tugs and pulls on us in a business ethics perspective. One that is very significant today is Wall Street.

I have been president of Ryder System for almost ten years. We are traded on the New York Stock Exchange; we have about 80 million shares outstanding and a market value of about $2.5 to $3 billion. We have never before seen the pressure for short-term results that is being applied today. It is really quite remarkable. The short-term pressure from Wall Street, the "I want it today rather than tomorrow" pressure, is the strongest that we've seen in terms of business ethics. You read about the problems of Boesky and Drexel, the problems on the Commodities Exchanges, the conflicts of insider trading. These are serious issues that have to be addressed directly.

Legislation isn't going to be the answer. There has to be a change in a lot of the attitudes on Wall Street. They have to learn to take a longer-term approach.

We have been pretty straight in our company. We have a good relationship with our shareholders. We've told them that we have invested for the future and that "if you want to invest with us, we want you to know that's what you buy." We think we have fulfilled our responsibility in communicating to our shareholders what we are going to do. But we have still had a lot of pressures on the short-term side.

Let me conclude with one final issue: business ethics as it relates to the senior management within a company. Senior management must set the example, wherein everyone can walk in cadence. If we see more of that throughout the business community, I think you'll see a much higher level of business ethics everywhere.

"Business ethics" is *not* an oxymoron. Those words really are consistent. Ethics is the foundation of good business. We have found that to be the case at Ryder System, as have many thousands of other companies in our country. You hear a lot about the bad guys, but don't give up hope. The good guys out-number them 1,000 to 1.

12

Work, Waste, and Quality

William E. Conway, President, Conway Quality, Inc.

I am going to talk about work. The world has seen a quality revolution in work. I happen to call the system behind all this "The Right Way to Manage." The Japanese call it "Total Quality Control." Here in the United States people call it "The Continuous Improvement Process." Call it what you may, we are talking about the continuous improvement of all the work and the work processes in our organization through quality. What does that mean? It means we find the trouble, errors, complexities, and waste and turn them into opportunities or track them down, get rid of them, and stay rid of them forever.

This is not just another project or program. We have all had plenty of those in our organizations: quality, cost reduction, productivity, participative management, SPC, and so on. The big boss makes a speech in January. Those of us who have been with the organization for ten or 15 years know that the program won't even stand the heat of July and August; we are going to do just enough to keep the big boss happy. Sure enough, in July it disappears from the company newspaper and the big boss's speeches. During the fall we watch the leaves change, knowing full well that in January the big boss will have another program for us. This kind of approach is no more going to get anyone to be competitive than the man in the moon. It is just a big joke. Think about that.

Continuous Improvement: A Workplace Revolution. A revolution in work took place 39 years ago. Some of us are already doing something about it; most of us are just doing a little here and there. Think about whether everyone in *your* organization does it. Does everyone think, talk, work, and act in the way that is necessary for continuous improvement?

My company was the first U.S. firm to decide to seriously work in continuous improvement. I called W. Edwards Deming on Tuesday, March 7, 1979. Of course, he wasn't used to hearing from people like me in the United States. When I called him, he had been working with CEOs and top-level executives in Japan.

After working together a few months, we came up with this definition: *Quality Management is the continuous improvement in all areas of the business to provide consistent, low-cost services and products to satisfy that external customer who pays the bills.*

One of the first things Dr. Deming talked about with those Japanese executives when he met with them in 1950 was the external customer. He said, "No customers, no orders, no jobs." He talked about the fact that variation is a technical tool we can use to find problems and turn them into opportunities, and to track down waste, get rid of it, and stay rid of it. He also talked about human relations: how to treat people so they will perceive that it is in their interest to work in this new way.

When Japanese companies started to work with Dr. Deming in 1950, they obviously didn't know how to do it. All they had was the theory — the principles of management — from four meetings with him. When they returned to their companies, they picked out one plant, one marketplace, or one product line, and started to make improvements in the quality and reliability of the product and the productivity of the people, as well as reductions in cost. All of those things resulted from working on *quality*. As time went by, they made huge improvements.

By the early 1960s they had come to the fundamental conclusion that created the basis for this entire management system: Only value-added work counts. Once we get rid of all the waste, what is left is value-added work, and there isn't very much of it. Most of us work on the waste rather than on what is real and value-added. What do we mean when we say something is "real and value-added"? If the external customer who buys your goods and services knew what you were doing, how much of that would they be willing to pay for? If you think about that, you will begin to get an idea of the amount of waste that we have in Western society.

When Dr. Deming initially visited us on March 10, 1979, I began to see what the new system was like. Dr. Deming, my six vice presidents, and I had been meeting in my office for about five or six hours. At about 3:30 in the afternoon, he said, "Well, I have to go to the men's room." While he was gone I said to those six vice presidents, "This guy really knows and understands what this is all about. He has told us what he has done to help companies like Toyota. He has told us about the principles under which he worked. It all makes sense. I think we ought to hire him." They all looked at me like I was crazy, and one of them said, "Bill, the guy is a nut!" I said that I was going to hire him anyway.

When Dr. Deming came back to the office, I asked him to work with us. He said, "Bill, I will work with you under one condition: that you will be the personal leader of the change, and will see to it that these six vice presidents are the leaders of the change in their areas. Furthermore, you must see to it that throughout every level of the organization every single manager, supervisor, administrator, and engineering lead person is the leader of the change in their area. Otherwise, I won't work with you."

You Have to Want It. What is the system? First, you have to *want* continuous improvement of the work and its processes. Work is not just the work of people. It is also the work of machines, chemical processes, air, steam, and water. It is the front-edge design engineer, the salesperson in the field, the chemist in the laboratories. It has two sides to it: what we work on and the way we work. Continuous improvement is *not* just improving the way we work. If we aren't working on the right thing, what is the sense in improving the way we work?

Believe It by Doing It. Next, we have to believe it can be done. You can only get the belief by doing it! You really believe only when you understand the new management system and the tremendous power it has to make huge improvements in quality, productivity, cost, and flexibility in delivering products and services to customers.

There is no other way. You don't get it by reading a book. You get it by being actively involved in doing it, acting as the leader, seeing what is going on, and participating.

The Wherewithal. The third part is the wherewithal, or the means by which we do it. It is made up of six things:

1. *Human relations.* Help people understand that it is in their interest to work in this new way. Treat all people with *respect*, the way that you would like to be treated yourself.
2. *Surveys.* Find out what to work on. If this isn't done properly, nothing else will make much difference.
3. *Simple charting techniques.*
4. *More sophisticated statistical tools.*
5. *Imagineering.*
6. *Principles of work.*

The last two ideas, "imagineering" and principles of work, are the most crucial. They enable us to reach *all kinds* of work. Unfortunately, most companies don't teach them.

If we understand imagineering we will be on the road to making improvements. It is the most powerful and least-used variation tool. Imagineering is visualizing the difference between the way things are now and the way things could or should be. That difference is *waste*. Imagineering takes into account not only the troubles and problems that need to be addressed in our current processes, but also new technology, the marketplace, and the competition. This is where innovation comes in — how to change and improve all those systems.

Principles of work are basically industrial engineering concepts. First, we must find out about *all* of the work: its troubles, problems, errors, and complexities. Only then will we know what to automate. If we don't *find* the problems and waste, how are we going to get rid of them?

The "Right Way to Manage" is using these six tools — starting with the CEO and going right down to the technician or janitor or clerk — to identify and solve all the problems and identify and exploit every opportunity available to the organization. This is the heart of the revolution. World competition is demanding that we practice the "Right Way to Manage."

The last and easiest part is *doing* it. The *hard* part is to create the system so that *everyone* in the organization changes the way they work 24 hours a day, 365 days a year, forever. That's what makes the miracle happen.

What do we expect out of this?

First, I am talking about a huge change, not a little change. I am talking about a revolution in work. I am talking about fabulous improvement in the reliability of the product or the service; tremendous cost savings; doubling, tripling, quadrupling the productivity of our people; reducing in half the time it takes to develop a new product; improved planning; and flexibility to make rapid changes in the product according to customer demand. The emphasis is always on satisfying that external customer who is paying the bills. That is the revolution.

The next part of the definition says that it is not methodical, not just a little change. It is theory shattering, a quantum jump, a huge change.

The last part of the definition says that the new paradigm always discredits the old. If you are still working in the old way, you are becoming more obsolete with every passing day.

Getting Rid of Waste. We have to find the waste, get rid of it, and stay rid of it. The level of waste in American industry runs between 20 percent and 50 percent of net sales, averaging around 35 percent. When I say waste, I don't just mean the scrap out in the plant. I mean all the material over and under specifications; dealing with suppliers who are not working in the new way; wasted capital, inventories, and receivables. I mean all the wasted time of all of the people, all of the things we didn't sell, all of the gross margin contribution to fixed expenses from all of the things that we should have sold but didn't. *That* is what waste is.

Imagine running a $100 million business. You will probably have a least $35 million in waste. Does anyone have employment security in this kind of organization? No! You are just hoping and praying that you won't have to compete against someone that has been working the new way for 10 or 15 years. You have been lucky so far; very few U.S. industries have had to compete against companies that work the new way.

What is that waste? It's the difference between the way things are now and the way they could be or should be. I like the phrase, "Not failure, but low aim is the crime." In December 1987, *Quality Progress* magazine ran a survey of all the CEOs of the U.S. Fortune 1000 companies. They asked them what was the size of the waste in their organizations. "A little over 5 percent," said the CEOs. Then the people who conducted the study went out and got two CEOs who they were sure would *really* know something about waste. They went to Jack Curran, CEO of Xerox, and John Young, CEO of Hewlett-Packard. In 1980, Xerox became the first non-Japanese company to win the Deming prize for quality; a Hewlett-Packard subsidiary was the second, in 1982. *They* said that the waste in their organizations was 30 to 40 percent of net sales. Not failure, but low aim is the crime.

There are five ways to find waste:

1. *Macro.* Follow the market, the technology, and the competition. Find out what big technological changes are needed.
2. *Imagineering and Innovation.*
3. *Follow the money with P&L/Balance sheet.*
4. *Follow all the systems in the processes.*
5. *Cost of quality.*

Work and Work Concepts. Work is a set of tasks performed by people or machines to meet an objective. We measure it in terms of the quality of the resulting products and services and the time it takes to produce them. The principles of work are:

1. All waste comes from work — what we work on and the way we work;
2. A small amount of time is spent on the things that really count;
3. There is little work in anything once we get rid of that waste;
4. Almost all the troubles and problems come from the system, and only management can fix them.

Work, pace, and time are the *concepts*. The *tools* are: (1) work sampling, (2) process flow charting, (3) work simplification, and (4) methods analysis.

All of our employees — who utilize those tools five days a week, 24 hours a day — must be trained. Human relations must be set up in such a way that people perceive it is in their interest to tell you what they are doing. Since 80 percent of all work is knowledge work, you won't find out about the work unless they want to tell you, because it is in their heads.

A study has been published about the time people get paid for. It says that 25 percent of the time we don't work (vacations, holidays, breaks); 35 percent of the time we do necessary, value-added work; and 40 percent of the time we work on unnecessary work. Do you know all about the work in your company? Have you got all of the information from work sampling? As soon as you do, you will see how you can double and triple the productivity of the people. Is everyone educated to understand that it's true? Until we are educated and believe that, we will never work the new way.

Managers are needed on each level who are curious about work and waste. They must be suspicious. Once we find out about work, we have to collect data about the work and the waste to see what level it is operating at. When we can see how the range is moving up and down, we must be dissatisfied with the level or the amount of variation in it. If we are not dissatisfied with it we won't take any action, and nothing will happen. I am talking about the continuous improvement of all the work and work processes forever, through quality.

Doing It. Once we understood the new system for working on continuous improvement, we applied it to a whole business. We started out with one that had about $45 million in sales. There were 225 hourly people and 225 salaried people. It was a high-tech business, hard disks, competing directly with IBM, 3M, Xerox, Control Data, Memorex, BASF, Hitachi, and Fujitsu. We trained the people in the six parts of the system and all the principles of work. The vice president and general manager were 100 percent behind it, acting as the leaders. There were two management-directed programs:

- Improve the yield on the main line of disks. We had to get the people from marketing, sales, R&D, maintenance, purchasing, and planning involved along with the manufacturing people to make it happen.
- Improve the productivity of all the people. We did work sampling. Everyone sampled their own work: salespeople in the field, R&D chemists, physicists, accountants. Everyone sampled their work, and found the work was full of waste.

Everyone agreed to try to improve the productivity by at least 3 percent per month. That meant *doubling* productivity in 24 months. They all went to work, and they did it. We started with a yield of 65 percent in November. By February we were at 75 percent; April, 80 percent; May, 85 percent; June, 90 percent; and by the middle of August,

95 percent. Imagine the cost, consistency, and quality. Absolutely incredible!

As a result of these phenomenal improvements, the products and services were all different, and we had to retrain general management, sales, and marketing. Our first big new account was Hewlett-Packard. They sent their top people out to see what we were doing, and started to buy immediately. Within six months we were their main supplier. From there we went to Digital Equipment in Colorado Springs, Nixdorf in Germany, and then all around the world. Business just took off.

Then we instituted a new rule: Nobody could have any more people. At first everyone resisted. During the first couple of months, a few people quit. After a few months, people were working nine- and ten-hour days and on weekends. Finally everyone decided to find the waste in the work and get rid of it. In the next two and a half years productivity increased 2.5 times. Inventory went from three months to one month. Receivables went from 73 days to 35 days. Everything showed that same pattern. We were using the same people. It wasn't the people — it was the system.

In 1981 the company had operations in Mexico and Brazil. People said it would never work down there. They said it wouldn't work in Australia. Well, it didn't make any difference at all. Local managers of every nationality, once they understood what the system did, were ready to act as leaders level by level. It didn't make the slightest difference *where* we were talking about.

What happened in that hard disk business? Xerox, 3M, Memorex, Control Data, and BASF went out of the business. A few of the Japanese leaders and my old company are the only ones left in the world. Why? The other people couldn't compete.

The Role of the New Leader: Lifting People Up. The job of the new leader in the new management system is to lift everyone who works for them up and make them all better people. How do you do that? The first thing you do is create the system and educate the people. Once they understand the "Right Way to Manage," they understand total quality control. The people at the very top need this education the most. Only by being educated in the system can we get the mindset. This whole system is based in our mindset — what is going on in our heads. If we don't believe that the work is full of waste and that people can eliminate it if they are in the right frame of mind, then we will never make it. The process of education never ends.

I wish we had all been working this new way for the last 20 years and the country was now competitive. The question is, when are we all going to change and work the new way?

13

Quality: America's Path to Excellence

Joe C. Collier,Jr., Senior Vice President, Florida Power & Light

Several years ago when our company was contemplating whether we dared even think about applying for the Deming Challenge, the chairman of our holding company, Marshall McDonald, said, "Tell me this. Can you tell me who was the first man to run the four-minute mile?" Immediately everybody said, "Sure. Dr. Roger Banister. We know that." He said, "Tell me who was the second man to run the four-minute mile." How many of you know that? Of course, the point is that if we are going to do something, let's be the first. He challenged us with that, and we have been pursuing that philosophy ever since.

We did a little bit of research and discovered that, prior to Roger Banister's feat, no one had ever run a four-minute mile in all the history of mankind. It was a barrier; conventional wisdom said, "It can't be done." Ever since that landmark day in the 1950s, someone has run a faster mile every year. I believe the record is now down to around 3.47 minutes. In 1910, the first Kentucky Derby was run by a horse in two minutes and ten seconds. Last year the Kentucky Derby was won in two minutes and eleven seconds. Statistically, it looks like in another 47 years a man will be able to win the Kentucky Derby!

We have some great fun with statistical quality control. We have a group in the company we call "Applications Experts." We have identified people who want to volunteer to teach graduate-level statistics courses to the rest of our company. They are sort of our gurus of statistical quality control. If a complex question arises, we just turn to them. I challenged them with a study that indicated that a good way to decide what to study in college is to look at the starting salaries of college graduates in various fields. I found a statistic that said the graduating class in geography at the University of North Carolina in 1986 made an average starting salary of $280,000. Before everybody rushed to sign up for geography class, we told them that Michael Jordan was one of the graduates. Statistics can do some funny things.

It is good to see companies talking about quality in America. It is like when a politician changes his mind. You don't know whether he has seen the light or whether he has felt the heat. I think maybe in America our companies have felt the heat regarding quality for the past 20 years.

Twenty years ago about three out of every four cars in the world were built in America. Today that figure is less than one out of four. In 1988, only 60 percent of the automobiles built in America were manufactured by American companies. Twenty years ago, three-quarters of all of the television sets and 90 percent of the radios in the world were built in America. Today, America accounts for only 6 percent of the world production of radios and televisions combined. It doesn't stop with electronics. Last year the three leading companies that were awarded patents in the United States were Canon, Hitachi, and Toshiba. The Japanese percentage of patents in the United States has grown from 4 percent to 19 percent in just 15 short years.

This raises two questions. What happened? What can we do about it? I think that you all know what happened. We suddenly found ourselves in a global marketplace with competitors who had a desperate economic imperative to succeed. We discovered something strange — customers didn't have an emotional attachment to our products. We are learning that at Florida Power & Light (FPL). We are finding that our customers can put in their own generators and generate their own kilowatt hours. It shocked our older managers to learn that our customers don't have an emotional attachment to FPL's kilowatt hours. They buy warm water and cold beer. They don't really care where it comes from if it does the job more cheaply.

Well, I think we know what has happened. Now, what are we going to do about it? I think that the answer is to adopt an entirely new philosophy toward quality and productivity based on a new understanding and a new economic imperative for America. Are we going to be a first-class economy, or are we going to be a second-class service country? The good news, though, is that business has awaked and is catching on. You can see it on your television, in the news and in the commercials. I sort of study commercials, and I have noticed that more and more the idea of quality is creeping into the marketing messages of American companies. Some that you are familiar with are very direct — "Quality is job one;" "Quality goes in before the name goes on." Some are a little more subtle. MCI "wants you to hear a pin drop" long-distance. "The tightest ship in the shipping business," "Fly the friendly skies." "Clarity you can see, purity you can taste." Budweiser has one that says "Beechwood aged." I wonder if those steelworkers in Pittsburgh really care if it is beechwood aged or not.

Everybody has slogans, and that is okay. We had a slogan when we first started. It was "Do it right the first time." Dr. J.M. Juran came for a visit and said, "Do *what* right the first time?" We thought about that and said, "Do the right thing right the first time." He said, "What is the right thing?" We said, "We don't know, but we will know it when we see it." That sounds like the Supreme Court's definition of pornography: they can't define it, but they know it when they see it. That is the case with quality. We all think we know what quality is. But without a road map, without a plan, without a process, you won't know how to get to a state of excellence in your company. What is more, you won't know how to maintain it when you get there.

The ten top companies that Tom Peters and Robert Waterman listed in their book, *In Search of Excellence*, are no longer the ten top companies today. If, however, you look at the Deming Prize winners in Japan, the ten top companies stay on top the next year and the year after that. Companies who have invested 30 years in becoming excellent stay excellent throughout time.

Quality: A Management Process. That is why at FPL we think that quality is first and foremost a management process, a process that has to be believed in by everyone from the CEO to the first-line supervisor. Each member of the team must demonstrate that sense of commitment by their involvement and constant participation in management. It has been said that 80 percent of all business problems lie in the hands of managers. If they will just get out of the way and let their people perform, they can solve a lot of those problems. We know that employees want to do the right thing. It is human nature to want to do a good job. The role of management, then, is to provide the environment, training, tools, and leadership, and then get out of the way. Let your people do a good job.

Tom Peters has a wonderful story about a gentleman who had made a very successful career out of turning failing businesses around. Someone asked him, "What is the secret of your success?" He said, "Well, I go to a business and I take off my coat. I go down on the shop floor or down to the front line and I ask the people, 'What is wrong with this company?' Then they tell me and I say, 'Well, can you fix it?' They say, 'Yeah.' I say, 'Then go fix it.' They go fix it, and I make a lot of money." The people closest to the problem, the people closest to the customer, are the ones with the solutions. We have to learn to give them the tools, techniques, motivation, and leadership to do their job.

I know that all of your companies have objectives. All of you have mission statements, all of you have quality directives, and all of you want to do the right thing. We don't take credit for inventing anything. We have discovered a magic formula. Thomas Edison was credited with inventing the talking machine. He said, "I didn't invent the talking machine; God did. I just invented the first one that could be turned off." We have not invented quality. I give all the credit for what we have come up with to our friends at Kansi Electric in Osaka, Japan, who have been very generous. They have shared with us and have allowed us to go over there year after year after year. They are very gracious and have shared with us not only their knowledge, but their people. Their employees come to Florida and spend two years working with us in our shop. They have been tremendously helpful. There are many different definitions of quality. If we spoke a common language, maybe we could share. What I hope to do today is to share some of our program with you and try to bridge that understanding gap in explaining what total quality control (TQC) means.

I want to share a personal story with you about filling in for your boss. About ten years ago, there was a national conference on quality and productivity in Washington. Our president at the time was Marshall McDonald. He was invited to be a speaker. He couldn't go, and sent me. Dr. Juran, Philip Crosby, C. Jackson Grayson, and all of the great names in quality that I had come to know were there. I was so enthusiastic and excited about quality when I came home that I wrote a long, thoughtful memorandum to the president of our company about what we should do. He tracked me down and said, "Well, what should we do?" I said, "Boss, we need a quality council." "Well," he said, "who should be in charge?" I replied, "You should be the spiritual leader, Boss." He said, "Okay then, we'll start one, and I'm putting you in charge." Therein lies an important lesson for junior managers: When you invite a gorilla to dance, you don't sit down until the gorilla gets tired. We have had two successive gorillas since then. They have shown no signs of tiring, and I don't think they ever will. Our employees have accepted the fact that this program is not one that is here today and gone tomorrow.

We have tried everything anybody ever published — management by objectives, managing managers' time, extended MBO, and so on. Winston Churchill said, "You can always count on Americans to do the right thing after they have tried everything else." We think we have tried everything. Now, we have found the right thing, and that's this management process we call Quality Improvement, or TQC.

Designing In Quality. Most of you are familiar with the continuum of quality. It was the purview of the manufacturers. People who made widgets could weed out the bad ones. Only good quality widgets would be left. The problem was, 40 percent of the widgets were being rejected. This was very costly. Eventually the emphasis has shifted to designing in quality. The trunks of the early Toyotas all leaked, mostly because of weld points. Those early trunks had 57 welding points. Toyota redesigned it down to seven welds, thinking that if they could eliminate the trouble points they could eliminate the problem. The history of Toyota is, of course, well known. Designing in quality became the new continuum. As we moved into a service-sector economy, managing in quality became a strong part of the continuum. We think that managing in quality is what we are doing, what we are attempting with our program.

What is quality? We have more and more philosopical arguments about that question. Is it Rolls Royce quality, or is it K-Mart quality? It is both. We have adopted Dr. Deming's statement, "Quality is conformance to valid requirements." In order to be valid, requirements must meet user needs. They have to be current, realistic, and somewhat measurable. A man came into a coffee shop and told the waitress,

"I'll have cold coffee, burnt toast, half-cooked eggs, and greasy bacon." She brought the order just as he requested and said, "Will there be anything else, sir?" He said, "Yes, sit down and nag me. I feel homesick." If you satisfy the customer's needs and wants, then we would argue that the requirements are valid.

This conformance applies to specifications, procedures, materials, workmanship, everything that it takes to produce quality. An important part of our program is taking quality upstream, if you will. We buy 60 percent of the materials we use in our business from outside vendors. If their products don't meet our standards and our customers' specifications, we can't produce quality. We spend $2.6 billion every year with our outside vendors in an effort to produce quality for our customers. Some of you are here today. We seek out, recognize, and reward vendors who work well with us through our vendor quality program. One of the toughest decisions that businesses in America must make — we are no different — is to weed out those vendors who don't want to play according to the quality rules. We are now at the point where we are weeding down our suppliers to those few who meet our standards and help us meet our specifications.

Focusing on the Customer. This leads me to the first of four principles upon which our program is based: Focusing On the Customer. We do an enormous amount of research every year to find out who our customers are, what they want, how much they are willing to pay, what they need it for, and how we can better serve them. We were one of the first utilities to spend literally millions of dollars on market research to determine what it is our customers want and how we can supply it better. We measure our performance every quarter on 22 quality elements that our customers tell us about. Focus on customers should not be only on the external customer; focusing on your internal customer is also important. Every department must identify their product, service, or output and then identify the customer for that product, service, or output. They have to negotiate valid requirements between themselves and that customer for that service, product, or output. An interesting thing happens when you do that. You find that you have a list of products for which there are no customers. The accounting department found they didn't need to produce all those monthly reports and stacks of computer printouts. They found that nobody was reading them, nobody wanted them, and once a month would have been better than once a week. We have saved a lot of paperwork just through the customer-identification process.

I could give you several examples, but I will just stick to one. Our customers have told us that accurate bills are one of their high priorities. They want to be confident that their electric bill is accurate and correct. The truth is, 99.99 percent of our bills are exactly correct. There is a perception, however, that they are not. To get an accurate bill requires that we buy a good meter, test it properly, install it properly, put the paperwork in the computer, read the meter accurately every month, and so forth, right down the line to the point where the customer gets his bill in the mail. It is like one big assembly line, with people in varying locations 500 miles apart each playing their role to deliver that customer's accurate bill. We teach our people that everything they do has an impact on that chain reaction which creates accurate bills for our customers. Each one of them can contribute by keeping their share of the assembly line working properly. By using the quality tools, they can do that, and actually calculate their contribution to the chain effect. We can show that in case after case after case. It is a very powerful part of the business.

Continuous Improvement. The second part of our fundamental program is Continuous Improvement. We do it through Dr. Deming's wheel, the Plan-Do-Check-Act (PDCA) Cycle. At the end of the day, each meter reader can check his or her daily work to see if they have done it correctly. If they didn't get it right, they correct something and get it right the next time. Every supervisor has a process flow chart that helps him keep his process under control. We have moved from measuring things in parts per million to parts per billion through PDCA. We have reduced errors through good process control. The beauty of this is that everyone can use it — the first-line employee right on up to management. We are constantly looking for ways to turn the wheel and practice PDCA.

Management by Fact. The third fundamental aspect of our program is Management by Fact. Believe it or not, this is one of the toughest cultural changes an organization can make, especially one like ours. We have a 60-year history of tough, individualistic people who built a system out of the swamps and the Everglades. We created these supervisors. We put them where they are because they are tough and can make decisions. They operate on what we now know as their calibrated intestines; in other words, gut feel. When these senior managers are confronted by some young engineer with a better set of facts, better data, or better information that calls for a different decision, it is often very difficult for them to swallow and say, "Well, looks like you may be right."

Management by Fact, though, has become a part of our business. Our people no longer say, "Well, it seems to me..." They have been trained to immediately question what the evidence is, what the facts are, what the data shows, and why you came to that decision. This has been a cultural revolution in our business. We have a saying that "Sometimes it is easier to change *people* than it is to *change* people." When you think about that, it *is* tough to *change* people. Last year we had an early retirement program, and 900 people chose to leave. Not all of them did so because of quality programs. It was just a great opportunity for a lot of them. However, a large number said, "I am too old to learn statistical quality control," and when they found a window they took it. That is what is going to have to happen if we are going to have a new attitude toward total quality control.

Respect for People. The fourth fundamental is Respect for People. We demonstrate respect for people through our quality teams program. As I said, no one knows the customer better than the person who deals with him every day. No one knows the process better than the employee who does the process every day. By allowing these teams an audience, an opportunity to put their ideas forward, we are demonstrating respect for people.

Last year we conducted our very first total employee attitude survey. Believe me, it was not easy to talk our management into letting us do it. We hired an outside behavioral firm and conducted a scientifically based survey. Ninety percent of our employees said the thing that would motivate them more than dollars, more than recognition dinners, more than tie tacks and lapel pins, more than anything else, would be having management pay attention to their ideas, and put them into practice throughout the company.

Replication of good ideas is a basic part of our program. We do just about the same thing in Daytona that we do in Miami. If we can find a good solution to a problem in Miami, there is no reason it shouldn't be replicated somewhere else. We even tried to come up with an incentive to get one team to steal another team's idea. We were going to call it the "Buccaneer Award." Respect for people is a strong, strong program.

Components of Total Quality Control. I have given you the four basic principles. Now I would like tell you about the three component parts of our program. First of all, there are different types of teams. We have what we call lead teams. I am on a lead team. Every member of management is on several teams. I think I am on five. There is a lead team of all department heads in a cross-functional area.

Functional teams are those people who have similar work assignments. All of the linemen would be a functional team. All the cable splicers get together and talk about cable-splicing techniques.

Then we have cross-functional teams. People from marketing, sales, engineering, regulatory, and accounting would be a cross-functional team. We practice cross-functional management all the way to the very top of the company. We are knocking down all those barriers that it took us 60 years to build between accounting, marketing, engineering, and so on.

Task teams are those teams that we assign to a specific, known problem. When we find a problem, we pick people to work on it. They solve the problem, dissolve the team, and go on. The others are ongoing, continuous team activities.

We initially started with quality improvement teams. We started with two pilot teams back in 1979 or 1980. In 1981 we developed some formalized teams. We probably had eight or nine the first year. We are up to about 2,000 teams now. Typically, eight or nine people make up a team. The supervisor is the team leader. We have someone called a facilitator who helps keep the teams on track. Facilitators also help with training, teaching them about the tools, and recording minutes.

Policy Deployment. The next part of the program is Policy Deployment or Goal Setting. While teamwork is a bottom-up approach, policy deployment is a top-down approach. Management decides what we want to be, when we want to get there, and how we can set the goals, and then asks people to follow. A good example I have used in teaching our people is that each one of us could go up to a freight train and push on it, and nothing would happen. If all of us pushed on the freight train in exactly the same direction at the same time, we could move the train. You get that kind of synergism from policy deployment. We can't fix everything all at once, so management chooses four or five high-priority areas on which to concentrate. Those are typically drawn from what our customers tell us.

Our customers have told us in quarterly surveys that they are interested in (1) reliability, (2) safety, (3) price, (4) courteous, kind treatment, and, (5) accurate answers and accurate bills. We have tried to establish our corporate priorities according to what our customers constantly tell us. As our Japanese friends say, "The hunter who chases too many rabbits goes hungry." We try not to chase too many rabbits at the same time. By focusing the attention of all of our people on those four or five crucial issues at any one point in time, we make some serious breakthroughs.

A good example of setting goals occurred at NASA. When President Kennedy challenged NASA, we had one goal. You all know what it was: Put a man on the moon and bring him home safely within the decade. You could walk up to anyone at NASA — from the engineers in Houston to the operations people at Cape Canaveral to the janitor in Huntsville — and say, "What is the mission of NASA?" and they could tell you. They knew what their mission was. Unfortunately, when they accomplished it, they didn't have another mission. NASA fell into some deep problems and took awhile to get out. I know there is much more to it than that, but that is a classic example of how having everyone focus helps you meet your goal. Policy deployment, then, is the process by which we achieve breakthroughs by concentrating and focusing all our efforts on a few selected issues. We publish those issues in a book every January. They all have indicators. Every department makes a contribution to the improvement of those indicators.

Quality in Daily Work. The last component of our program is Quality in Daily Work. The Marriott people call it "staying close to your business," because you do it on a daily basis. The supervisor who has process control charts and monitors his daily, weekly, and monthly operations is using this approach. This constant monitoring helps to maintain the gains that we achieve. It promotes consistency and clarifies everyone's contribution. If power plant employee A knows that he has to improve his first outage rate by three percentage points and monitors that on a daily basis, he knows how his contribution is going to impact the overall effort. We operate some 13 different power plants. Each plant has process control charts for 80 or 90 processes, which they follow every day.

Those are the three parts of our Quality Improvement Program. We should have called it something other than a program, because it is not bounded by any completion date. It is an ongoing, continuous journey. It won't work without committed managers. Our program may be a little different, because we are a service industry with 3 million customers. We deal with an enormous number of things that we have to do on a repeated basis. We believe it is the role of management to bring all of this together by demonstrating commitment, managing throughout the process, staying informed, encouraging employees, and recognizing and rewarding those employees. Without the enthusiasm of management, employees won't know that we are really serious about it.

Zig Zigler, who is a very humorous and warm public speaker, has a wonderful story about enthusiasm. It seems this family of Scots from Tennessee were taking a winter vacation. They were going to Florida for the winter. They passed by a paper mill in southern Georgia. One of the children lifted up his nose, sniffed the air and said, "My, what is that?" And the father says, "I don't know, but we have got to get some of it." We think managers have to get enthusiasm if the quality process is to be successful.

Quality and the Bottom Line. What about the bottom line? We teach our people that if you achieve quality, productivity will follow. We now have about 12,000 people who have gone through basic and advanced quality training and who are on some sort of team. We don't have to sell quality to our customers, we just have to create it. The customers will buy into it. Everybody wants to know about the bottom line. I certainly understand that. As a regulated business, we have to explain to our regulators in Tallahassee how these benefits are flowing to our customers.

1977 was one of our worst years. Our sales started to slide. Total annual energy per customer was sliding, and at the same time our costs were increasing greatly. The conventional wisdom was that electricity was not price-elastic; customers were going to use what they were going to use regardless of the price, and we shouldn't worry about it. We learned the hard way that this is not the case. As our prices went up, our customers began to leave. They went elsewhere, built their own power plants, or just quit using so much. We were in what economists call a "death spiral." That is when you raise prices to maintain earnings. That depresses sales, so you have to raise prices again to maintain the earnings. You can keep that up only so long before you reach your resistance level. We were dangerously close to that kind of situation. We got hold of our prices and did some drastic things. We started applying TQC at every level; cut our overhead and maintenance (O&M) cost growth significantly; and had some good luck with oil prices, because we had gotten off of foreign oil. As a result of our efforts, prices are now very stable and sales have rebounded. They still aren't back to where they were in 1977, but they are returning. The situation is much more stable. We have not had a major rate increase since 1985, and don't anticipate one in the near future.

We measure service availability because our customers say reliability is their first priority. We are very proud that our service is available 99.9 percent of the time. But being proud of yourself doesn't help you solve problems. In 1986 we decided to turn the equation around and look at *non*-availability of service. Now we look at how many hours or minutes per customer our service is *not* available each year. We started out at 110, I believe, and it is now down to 60. Since 1986 we have had steady improvement in our customer reliability. We have set a 1992 target of 32 minutes per customer per year for service unavailability. According to the data available to us, if we achieve that goal our service availability rate will be the best in the United States.

We are in a dangerous and sometimes complicated business, so safety is a major concern to us. We have 3,500 construction workers out on lines every day, all day long. Our lost-time injuries have been cut in half, and we propose to cut them even further by 1992. This will be difficult. We cannot always explain the source of the improvements that have been made. We know that making safety a visible issue has produced a Hawthorne effect, in that everyone is now conscious of it, thinking about it, and ultimately practicing safety procedures. It is very difficult to measure how much of this improvement came from specific programs. Everyone recognizes customer complaints. Ours go to the Public Service Commission. Ever since we started measuring the number of complaints per 1,000 customers, they have shown marked improvement. We know that for every complaint we get, there are another 25 that we don't know about. This is a serious component of our indicators.

During our formative days, we established a corporate vision. We have been working to explain what that vision means to our employees for the past eight years. We do think that we know how to manage effectively. We have 25 other major utilities in other parts of the United States. The data that is available to us shows us where we have to be in 1992, assuming that they are going to continue to improve as well. Recognition is nice, but it is only good insofar as it motivates us and others to move forward and do our best.

As our present chairman, John Hudiburg, testified before Congress, we were instrumental in the establishment of the Malcolm Baldridge Award. We are very proud of our role and the fact that Mr. Hudiburg serves as a trustee. We hope that in time this award will come to symbolize American excellence in quality, as the Deming Prize has come to symbolize this excellence in Japan. We would urge all of you to consider grooming your companies to challenge for this award, to be aware of it, and to recognize those companies who achieve it. Last year there were three companies who won it for the first time. This year I understand the number of applications is up nine-fold from last year's level.

Coach Vince Lombardi once said, "The quality of a man's life is in direct proportion to his pursuit of excellence." I would like to paraphrase that, and suggest to you that the quality of life in America in the next decade or so will be directly proportional to our efforts in the pursuit of excellence. We encourage you to join with us in this pursuit.

PART IV

The Productivity Equation

14

The Productivity Paradox Explained

Wickham Skinner, Professor, Harvard University

The theme of this conference is "Productivity Strategies for the 1990s." My approach may strike you as somewhat unconventional and contrary. I hope it doesn't strike anybody as disrespectful, because it isn't intended that way. In fact, my respect for an audience of this sort goes back to when I was at the Harvard Business School and was struggling to get people interested in production operations management. I tried to convince them to work in factories and operations instead of going to Wall Street and dealing with second-order abstractions and pushing pieces of paper around. In the *New York Times* Russell Baker said, "It's only the Japanese and the Asians that manufacture. Americans merge, acquire, divest, and declare bankruptcy." This is an audience, I think, that is dealing with some of the most fundamental, difficult, and important problems in our society.

I want to propose an approach to productivity strategies for the 1990s that is quite different from what we have been doing in the 1980s.

For the last 10 or 11 years, all of us practitioners and teachers in the field have been dealing with a very sick institution, which we all know and love, called manufacturing. We have prescribed very strong medicine for it. Has that medicine cured the patient, or do we need to not only build on what we've been doing, but also prescribe some different medicine? I think we need to change the prescription.

The title of this chapter, "The Productivity Paradox," is kind of cute. My greatest detractors say, "Well, Wick, we seldom agree with your articles, and you don't say very much, but you sure are great at titles." I want to tell you what the title of this little talk really ought to be. It ought to be called "Wallflowers at the Global Competition Ball" or "Why Elephants Can't Dance."

I used to argue with my colleague, the great Bill Abernathy. He wrote a book called *The Industrial Renaissance* in the very early 1980s. I said to him, "Bill, I don't see the renaissance." Ladies and gentleman, I was wrong. My great colleague, who died at a very early, unfortunate age, is probably sitting up there saying, "Wickham, I told you so."

In the last 10 years we have seen a remarkable reindustrialization effort. There has been the greatest outpouring of energy, rededication, enthusiasm, and determination to turn this great institution around that I have ever seen in my long career. I'll bet that history will show that we have learned, relearned, and tried more in this 10- or 15-year period and that more people have become seriously, thoroughly, and enthusiastically involved in greater change than has taken place in almost any period in industrial history. It has been an extraordinary period. Its purpose was to try to regain our competitive ability. That's what got us all going. It was absolutely essential to the American economy. We learned that manufacturing does matter, that we can't survive and prosper on a service economy alone.

After this fantastic Rip Van Winkle-reawakening of our whole field, the results are a bit of a paradox and a mystery. Productivity got off the 75-year curve of roughly 2 to 5 percent a year in 1973, and stayed off that curve for about 11 years. We are now back on that curve. This is part of this extraordinary turnaround that we have had. Look at what has happened in quality. Sure, it isn't what it ought to be, but on a scale of 10 I would say we went from about a 4 or 5 to a 7 — just tremendous improvement. We all know it. Look at the products you are buying. Look at what has happened to the American automobile in this ten-year period.

Wallflowers at the Ball. The data that comes out of our factory operations says that this effort has really succeeded. The question is, however, have we really regained competitive ability? You can pick certain industries and certain terrific companies and the answer is "Yes," but I'm going to tell you that the overall answer is pretty clearly "No." We are still struggling, we are still chasing. Have we stopped imports? Of course not. Have we stopped the constant, steady rise in imports? No way. Those imports are still coming in, and they are still rising. If you look at the curve, it has started to drop off a little bit. Imports are now roughly 13 percent of our domestic market.

How about exports? We have finally started to export a little, particularly in some commodity products, but our export picture is dismal compared to our Asian and Western European competitors. Our share of foreign trade, in total, has dropped over a 10- or 12-year period from about 21 percent to 14 percent. Our share of the world's manufactured goods is now down to 11 percent, while Japan's has risen 50 percent over the last 10 years. Global international trade is expanding and shooting up, the tempo is rising, and — to carry out my new title — it really is a ball. But sadly, we are like wallflowers at the ball. We are watching, we are trying to learn, we are trying to get back in the party.

We certainly are not there yet. But with the tremendous improvements we have made in productivity and in quality, even though we are not there, it is kind of surprising that we haven't done better. You also have to add to those terrific improvements what has happened to the value of the dollar. Look at different currencies: there has been a 20 percent to 60 percent change. Why hasn't that done it for us, practically by itself? Look at declining unit labor costs. With the increases in productivity, our labor costs have actually declined on a per-unit basis. They have gone up in Japan. Look at the decline in union membership. We have had all these things going for us outside of the factory. Yet, it still hasn't come off.

My conclusion is that the productivity and quality strategies that we pursued in the 1980s will not be enough in the 1990s. We have improved, but our competitors have improved even more. Look at the statistics in the auto industry. Ford has shown about a 40 percent improvement in the last six years, based on returns to the dealer for any reason. Toyota has done even better; about 45 percent. General Motors is about 15 percent; Chrysler is about 12 percent. In other words, while basic quality in the U.S. auto industry has improved, the Japanese have done even better.

When I was in Japan a couple of years ago I visited NDK Tapes, the giant manufacturer of video and cassette tapes. We went through the most highly automated, unwasteful, absolutely gorgeous plant you have ever seen. I was taking a group of Eastman-Kodak people through it. There were about 30 of us. After we went through the plant we sat down in a conference room. Our Japanese hosts said, "What did you think of our facility?" It was a very bland and open-ended question. We all said, "This is the most extraordinary, fantastic, productive, high-quality plant we have ever seen." Our guide honestly looked really surprised. He said, "You really liked it?" We said, "Why are you so surprised?" He said, "We have seen the value of the dollar starting to change, and we predict that it is going to go that way for at least three years. We think the change against the yen is going to be large. We have decided that our plant performance is about 45 percent of where we ought to be. We will not survive in this business if we don't get that 45 percent up to 90 or 95 percent, and we think we have about a year and a half or two years to do it." We said, "Well, what sort of things are you going to do?" They said, "Well, if you are really interested, let's change the schedule and talk about this some more."

They brought in a lot of other people and got up the vue-graphs. They had 21 projects — all the way from cutting waste to improving quality even further; things with vendors, scheduling, inventories, movement between machines, information systems. We asked, "They all look very good and potentially effective, but how are you going to do them?" Then they showed us more graphs. There were Program Evaluation and Review Technique (PERT) charts on every single one of these projects with mile posts, due dates, specific achievement targets, who had to do what, and who was responsible. It absolutely blew your mind. With an already superlative operation, they were planning difficult and demanding improvements. I have heard that they were successful.

In the meantime, we are struggling to get ourselves back up on this productivity curve. The Japanese knew the currency was changing. They hitched up their belts and went to work. Don't mistake me. I am not saying that we have wasted effort or that we have done the wrong things. We absolutely had to do what we did. Have we been barking up the wrong tree? Absolutely not. We have to *keep* barking up it, but that is not enough.

Are these kinds of things, necessary as they are, going to lead to competitive advantage? Those of you who have studied Herzberg in organizational behavior know about what are known as "hygiene factors," such as working conditions. If the working conditions are bad, it hurts motivation and productivity. But if the working conditions are good it doesn't motivate anybody. I think productivity and quality are those kind of phenomena. They are absolutely essential and critical, but is that the way we are going to beat the Koreans, the Asians, and the Western Europeans? Everybody these days can copy and learn from everybody else. We are copying and learning from the great teachers of Japan, and we are relearning from the great teachers of America like Mr. Deming. He began writing his first papers in the 1930s or 1940s, but he had to go to Japan to get people to listen to him.

We are learning fast. We go to conferences like this. We go to Japanese conferences and they come to ours. We exchange literature. Everybody says, "Hey, this is what I just learned. Let me tell you about it." Competitors are even visiting competitors. We are in a totally competitive world. My sense is, we are chasing and chasing. Thank heavens, we can still see the leaders going over the next hill each time we come to the top of one. We don't lose sight of them for long. We are with them, and we are in the race. But I am not so sure we are going to win the race in the 1990s the way we have been doing it in the 1980s.

Facts of Global Competition. What do we need to do? I think first we need to look at twelve or so facts of global competition. You know them all. What do we have to do in the 1990s? We must deal with these facts of global competition. Decreasing trade barriers is one. More big international companies are producing everywhere. They are moving, buying, shifting, and trading across international boundaries. There are more alliances, consortia, trading of information, partners, and technical exchanges. Everybody is going everywhere. Look at the Japanese coming in here; look at us finally getting into Russia and China. A very interesting thing is that low labor rates rise. We were worried about Japanese labor rates ten years ago. I am a director of a medium-size company that has a factory in Japan and a factory in Waltham, Massachusetts. Our labor rates are lower in Waltham than they are in Japan.

Everywhere more small, aggressive, high-tech companies are coming on fast, penetrating the market, and increasing employment and growth. Employment in Fortune 500 companies is actually declining. This is happening everywhere. This kind of competition is not just global; it is big company/small company. It is competition coming from outside of your industry and blindsiding you. Increasing management expertise is everywhere — much more sophisticated management, and people who know and understand management. Over 60,000 MBA's are graduating every year now, (heaven help us all!). We are getting swarmed over with management expertise. Some of it is pretty bad, some of it is pretty superficial, and some of it is very academic. But it does improve the rate of communication, exchange, and learning.

There is a more rapid flow and exchange of technology products and techniques — Just-In-Time, TQC, MRP, and CAD/CAM. Everybody is learning very fast. There is no monopoly on concepts and techniques. There is a great deal more communication. There are fewer secrets. The response time to competitive change is being cut down.

It is rough, but I think this is all going to get worse. We know about Korea, Taiwan, Singapore, and Hong Kong — the dragons of Asia. Mexico is just getting good; Brazil is very good in many, many fields. What is going to happen in Indonesia, India, China, and, of course, Russia? It is a very clear change. We didn't have to worry much in the past about competing with the Communist bloc. Very clearly, they are giving up much of their economic philosophy. Those people are going to be competing with us, as well as offering us more markets, very soon.

What does all of this demand of manufacturing, competitively, in the 1990s? I think the name of the game is changing from cost and quality — where everybody is getting so much better — to product development. It is changing to developing products that are targeted for specific customers, markets, and locations. The competitive game is changing to managing your new product development cycle much, much better. This change is going to require a lot more speed and flexibility, and the focus must be on time, time, time.

Seven Prescriptions for Productivity. Let me step back once more to ten years ago. What were the formulas, the recipes, the medicine, if you will, that were being prescribed for us at that time? There were seven things. One was that we had to get back on that productivity curve. Two, we had a tremendous amount of work to do on quality. Three, we needed more automation, more robots, more lasers, more flexible automation, and more computer-integrated manufacturing. Four, we needed to do a much better job with our people. There needed to be more involvement, more participation, and more teams. Five, we had to do a better and quicker job on new product development. Six, do a better job on scheduling and inventories, including the whole field of procurement. Seven — Skinner Snake Oil — is manufacturing strategy in which you stand back from operations and learn to focus your plants on limited tasks, and do those very well.

Just think for a second about those seven areas. How have we done? Fairly well in productivity and fairly well on quality. Miserably, in my opinion, on buying, introducing, testing, working out the bugs, and moving ahead with more automation and mechanization. We are doing better in human resource management, but how many of you can really say you have tapped the spirit, energy, and creativity of your people?

There is fascinating literature on new experiments in human resource management. The data shows pretty clearly that two out of three companies succeed for the first few years, but three out of four of them fail after that. There is a rubber band effect; we tend to snap back to the old ways of treating and handling people.

In new product development we are only a little past the old engineering attitude of "Do it, then throw it over the wall." Now manufacturing and engineering do it and throw it over wall of production. All those walls add up. Any new product takes six or eight years to hit the market. A fascinating study was done by Kim Clark of our faculty, who visited every major auto company in the world. He collected data on new product development, showing that Americans take roughly one-and-a-half to three years longer than our Japanese and other competitors to develop a new model. In many companies I have visited, that is a major competitive weakness. We haven't made very much progress.

Production control and inventory control: Who hasn't been through an MRP disaster? It has been tough and slow. I am not saying that we shouldn't do it. Just-In-Time has made some inroads. There has been some fairly good progress there. Skinner Snake Oil is still on the shelf, the prices are going down all the time, and there is a surplus. Companies talk about manufacturing strategy, but few have penetrated very far.

My conclusion from this data is simply this: We have made only mediocre progress during the last ten years on the major ingredients required for improving competitive success. But why has progress been so slow? We knew what we had to do, but it takes too much time and talk and persuasion to get our corporate organizations to focus every element of the system on competitive performance in manufacturing. Many of you say, "I need a better accounting system. I am always arguing with those people in accounting. We still have old-fashioned accounting with everything based on direct labor, and I don't have much direct labor anymore. I have to get out of overhead costs, and the accountants really don't help much." You can also blame a lot of things on the finance people. The hurdle rates are so high, you can't get needed investments approved. I have seen company after company turn down investments with the low predicted return rates only to find themselves virtually out of business after six or eight years. We don't look at investments in a strategic way, so we have manufacturing companies that are not focused on manufacturing. Instead, each function has its own separate objectives and performance measures.

Basic Issues for Quality Productivity. I want to leave you with three suggestions for achieving productivity quality at a basic level in the 1990s. First, there is a productivity paradox. It goes sort of like this: "If you go for quality you often get lower cost." If you go for efficiency, productivity, and lower cost per se, you often don't get it. You also often get worse quality rather than better quality. I see kind of an obsession with "productivity." There is a backlash to this obsession. It can easily cause reversion to the old-fashioned industrial engineering attitude of, "Scrimp and save, hire efficiency experts, cut and slice, and get out your stopwatch on everybody." A book entitled, *The Uneasy Alliance* looks at the conflicts between achieving productivity and achieving innovation. It is interesting that technology and productivity aims often run headlong into each other. Furthermore, managers are often so preoccupied with working at the operating level or focusing on the short-term horizon that they fail to look at fundamental structural problems. There is no way to succeed with the wrong structure.

I am talking about a manufacturing structure that starts with a make-or-buy decision, then goes to a capacity decision, then to the main choices of equipment and process technology, and then to the main infrastructure of operating systems. If those things aren't right, heaven help you. If you have the wrong plant, the wrong size, the wrong location, the wrong equipment, or the wrong production control system, the best group of managers in the world can't succeed. I don't think that we think enough about those structural decisions.

Are our best management people going into production manufacturing and operations management? It used to be a struggle with our MBA's at Harvard, but last year the production operations management course at Harvard got the highest educational value ratings of any course in the first-year MBA curriculum. Even more interesting and encouraging was the fact that more students chose operations management/production manufacturing courses as second-year electives than any other area of the school. That includes finance, investment banking, and all the great, jazzy things of the day. Now, that is not because we are so smart and such good teachers. I am not there anymore, so I can't take any credit, but our students read the newspapers and have learned the importance of manufacturing excellence for survival. But the best of our management people are still not going into manufacturing.

I did a survey of 12 companies about four years ago. We said, "You pick out your comers. They should be five, six, or seven years at the most away from senior manufacturing and operations management positions." We then interviewed their "comers." The question was, are these young men and women really going to help turn around American industry and take us where we need to go? They were bright, energetic, marvelous people, and very impressive, but they worried me on three counts. First, they all had very short-term operating points of view. Second, the engineering people generally had very little sense of the business. They could hardly talk about what was happening in competition, their division, their product group, or the company. Third, there was a surprising lack of interest in the technology of their company, plant, department, and industry. Four out of five of them said flat out, "Technology is not important." I worry about whether we are getting the right people.

Let me close now with my third and final major concern, which I would urge we think about and do something about in the 1990s.

This is the biggest problem of all. American industry is organized on a traditional corporate basis much more than are our competitors in Asia and elsewhere. By that I mean functional department structure — manufacturing, marketing, sales, accounting, finance, and personnel. The theory is that the job of top management is to recognize that all of those departments and functions have legitimate and professional objectives. The job of top management is to balance among eight functions. I think that we have hung that functional/departmental kind of organization on ourselves for too many years, and it has become a very serious impediment to our growth, our learning, our adapting, and our moving fast in the globally competitive world.

What can we do about that? In one sense, the biggest problem for the 1990s is *outside* the factory. We have done pretty well on improving the factory. We really have gone to work on it with tremendous enthusiasm and vitality. Now it is up to top management to get off our backs and help us get things done with these other departments so we aren't always fighting with engineering on manufacturability, with accounting on getting a good accounting system, with personnel to let us experiment and rock the boat a little bit. We could easily say our hands are tied. In some respects, American production managers have been fighting with one hand tied behind their back. But the tempo in this global dance has increased.

Many of us in manufacturing are lions in the plant. We are pussy cats when we get to top executive levels and try to get some money and convince other departments to see things our way. We need to stop that. We have to insist, take charge, set up teams. We need to tell accountants and finance and personnel people what we need. We have to experiment with new types of organizational systems. There is no reason why manufacturing — with 80 percent of the employees and typically 90 percent of the assets and an absolutely enormous stake and role in corporate survival and manufacturing excellence in this decade — should have to be just another one of those eight departments. Those checks and balances are checking and balancing us into oblivion.

What did we learn in the 1980s? We learned that manufacturing excellence is absolutely critical to global survival. We also learned something else: if you have second-rate manufacturing, your strategic position becomes virtually impossible. We have got to continue what we are doing in productivity and quality and do it even

better. But we have to do more. We have to get better people in manufacturing, the best in the company. One CEO, whom I admire tremendously (and who didn't come out of manufacturing) said, as he
thought about his manpower planning problems, "I need the
brightest people in the whole company in operations." I said,
"Why?" He said, "Because it is so complicated, it requires the best
minds." We need to think more about our structures and less about
the short term. Finally, we need to get at these organizational barriers, take hold of them, take charge of them, and break them down.

To rebuild, manufacturing companies need to be truly focused
on competitive superiority in *manufacturing*, rather than the collection of "professional" functional specialties we have now. We can't
compete with the conventional "line and staff" form of organization
described in management literature. This is the fundamental task before us if we are to answer the dilemma of the productivity paradox.

15

Productivity: Who Cares?

John A. White, Assistant Director for Engineering,
National Science Foundation

I recall an incident that occurred several years ago as I was delivering an after-dinner speech in the Pocono Mountains. I had to deal with my first heckler. The individual was quite persistent and very obnoxious. Despite his attempt to replace me as the after-dinner speaker, I persevered and completed my address. Following the address, a member of the audience approached me and apologized for the behavior of the heckler. To console me, he told me that during the cocktail hour he had asked the heckler, "Which do you think is worse, ignorance or indifference?" The heckler responded, "I don't know and I don't care."

I am also reminded of the story of a young, male engineering graduate who had purchased a new sports car. He was driving along a mountain road, putting the car through its paces. As he approached a curve he saw a car coming at him, out of control. It was swerving all over the road, fishtailing right and left. It seemed impossible to avoid a head-on collision. But, as though by a miracle, at the last minute the car was brought under control and missed him by less than an inch. As the two cars passed, the driver of the other vehicle, a woman, looked at the young man and screamed, "Pig!" "How dare she!" he thought. He turned around and shouted after her, "Sow!" He then drove around the curve, hit the pig in the middle of the road, and was killed. The moral of this story is that there are people sending us messages that will lead to our destruction if interpreted in traditional ways, but which, if interpreted in new, creative ways, will ensure our survival.

What do these stories have to do with the state of productivity in the United States? Despite considerable coverage by the business press, few seem to care about productivity; the American public, as well as industrial and governmental leaders, appear to be quite indifferent to the productivity situation that exists. In a sense, many voices are screaming "Pig!" at American management. Unfortunately, for too long their response has been, "Sow!" New, creative responses are needed to deal with a broad range of issues. And too many managers and governmental leaders are like the heckler — they don't know that anything is wrong and, furthermore, they don't care! Clearly, indifference is worse than ignorance. Hopefully, the ignorant will be converted once they become informed. Awakening the indifferent is a different matter.

A third story that comes to mind concerns the proper technique for boiling a frog. I don't know if you have ever tried to boil a frog, but if so, then you know that if you try to drop, toss, throw, or otherwise force a live frog into boiling water the frog will simply hop right out. To boil a frog, you place it in a nice pan of cool water. While the frog is enjoying itself and swimming around, you gradually begin to turn up the heat. As it gets a little warmer the frog thinks, "This isn't so bad; it's kind of like a whirlpool or a sauna." As you continue slowly turning up the heat, the frog is gradually cooked.

The temperature of the "competitive water" is slowly being increased by foreign competition. It is also being increased by an attitude in this country that is most alarming. Most of us have our hands on the controls; we are "boiling" ourselves. The great philosopher, Pogo, was correct in identifying the enemy as ourselves. Too many of us are ignorant, and too many of us are indifferent about the effects productivity declines are having and will have on the future of the nation.

The spotlight has been on the need for productivity improvement for many years; the first alarm was sounded in the early 1960s. In an attempt to awaken corporate management to the impending crisis, Utah State University (like Paul Revere) rode from company to company (through its Annual Productivity Seminar) crying, "The Japanese are coming! The Japanese are coming!" The national response was, "Let's go back to sleep. It will take them a long time to get here." It didn't take long, did it? Yet we are still talking about productivity at the Fourteenth Annual Productivity Seminar, attempting to awaken new generations of managers to the continuing need for productivity improvement.

What is Productivity? Despite the focus that has been given to productivity for the past two decades, many continue to define it in very narrow terms. Productivity is often defined as "the output of goods and services per unit of input by direct labor." The focus is often on the output of the *hourly* worker, rather than the *knowledge* worker. I prefer a very simple definition of productivity: "getting more for less." By this I mean getting more goods and services from less input of human effort, capital, material, space, energy, and technology. Of these, the factors that appear to have the greatest impact on productivity are technology and capital.

How Does America Compare? For almost two decades, America's productivity has lagged in comparison with that of Japan, West Germany, and several other countries. The impact of this decline has been felt in many quarters. For example, the U.S. trade position in high technology has suffered; in 1986, the first negative trade balance occurred in high technology products. The erosion of the U.S. share of domestic technology markets for products pioneered in the United States includes phonographs, televisions, video recorders, tape recorders, telephones, cellular telephones, machine tools, facsimile machines, and semiconductors, among others. Few signs of improvement exist on the horizon.

What Caused America's Productivity Problems? A number of explanations as to the source of America's productivity problems is given by a number of people attempting to explain it. For example, tax policy, the cost of capital, labor costs, stockholders' short-term goals, and the low priority placed on manufacturing are often cited.

The lack of a "level playing field" is not entirely due to action by state and federal governments. Rather than focusing on the use of trade barriers, why not "level those parts of the playing field that can be leveled" by a firm's top management? For example, Japanese firms have at least a three-fold capital investment advantage over American firms because of the differences in the planning horizons and investment return requirements. U.S. firms typically require double-digit "hurdle rates" and payback periods of less than five years, whereas Japanese firms are satisfied with single-digit returns and payback periods of fifteen years or more. As a result, a Japanese firm can invest at least three times as much in technology as an American firm with the same annual savings; likewise, for the same level of investment the Japanese firm will accept one-third the annual earnings as its American competitor.

In addition to the cost of capital differences, many agree that a major contributor to the relative decline in productivity improvement has been a decline in technological development. Several studies have shown that growth in technology is highly correlated with investment in research and development (R&D). We know the R&D investment in the United States has lagged behind the GNP. The cumulative effect of under-investing in R&D is manifest in the nation's productivity level. When R&D investment as a percentage of the GNP is compared with national productivity rankings, their relative positions are very similar. In both comparisons, the United States ranks behind Japan and West Germany. (When you compare non-defense R&D investments, the U.S. position is weakened considerably.)

Recently, defense research has dominated. The percentage of available funds that are directed to basic research has shrunk during the same period. In 1987, approximately $9 billion was delegated to basic research by the federal government; of that, $8.1 billion was for non-defense purposes. The NSF share of federal support for R&D is almost 3 percent of the total, but is 16 percent of total basic research support and 25 percent of basic research in colleges and universities.

The Council on Competitiveness, in its report, "Picking up the Pace," noted that it would be incorrect to conclude that preeminence in science guarantees technological and commercial success to a nation. By any measure (patents, Nobel Prizes, doctorates granted, R&D investments) the United States maintained a leading position in science during a period of productivity erosion. American higher education is still the envy of the world. Yet American industry has been unable to derive direct benefits from the nation's preeminence in science and engineering education.

After World War II, American industry benefited from a "research-driven" model of the innovation process in which generic research led to new products and processes in a linear fashion. However, other countries (particularly Japan) demonstrated an ability to be competitive by using a different model, a "market-driven" model, which depended on market-specific research. Furthermore, the Japanese companies showed they were adept at translating research results developed in other countries into marketable products much faster than their U.S. counterparts. Speed, quality, cost, innovation, and service proved to be the real dimensions of competitiveness, not simply R&D investments. It has become quite clear that U.S. firms must become more adept at "hunting and gathering" technology developed elsewhere; depending solely on internally generated technology is no longer a winning strategy. Not only have the *rules* of the game changed; the game itself has changed. The United States must learn a new game, not just new rules.

What Can Be Done to Improve Productivity? There are many answers to what the United States should do to improve its productivity. Among them are government regulations, capital and energy costs, labor skills and availability, and R&D investments. Because of the correlation in productivity increases and investments in capital equipment, incentives must be provided for U.S. firms to invest in modernization programs. (An extension of the R&D tax credit has been proposed by the Administration.) However, as other nations become more capital-intensive, their technology also improves. Productivity is a worldwide consideration. All nations are striving to improve their productivity; the target is not stationary.

How Does Productivity Lead to Economic Health? Productivity increases lead to improved standards of living; similarly, declines in productivity lead to declines in the standard of living. For this reason, today's generation of adults may be the first Americans whose children will experience a lower standard of living than their parents.

For years, America depended on the technology-employment spiral: the development of new technologies provided new jobs, which provided capital to produce new technology, which provided new jobs, and so on. Examples of the beneficial effects of technology abound and include automobiles, televisions, computers, and machine tools, among others.

The relationship between jobs and technology is well understood by those in state governments. The competition among the states for a new Toyota assembly plant was as fierce as the competition for GM's Saturn plant; the parentage of the firm was not of concern. What *was* of concern was the number of new jobs that would be created.

Increasingly, less attention is being paid to national parentage of industrial firms. Furthermore, it is difficult to distinguish the American firm from the international firm. While it might have been true in the past that "whatever is good for General Motors is good for America," today corporate decisions are not necessarily being made on the basis of national interests. The globalization of the economy is such that a global perspective is needed for states, corporations, and universities, among others. General Electric's global partnerships are typical of new alliances being formed by a diverse set of institutions and organizations.

Clearly, for American companies to be more competitive, they must become more productive and more innovative. Those seeking a competitive advantage are likely to find it through improved design and manufacturing. Since technological improvements were the source of much of America's past increases in standards of living, it is important for incentives to be provided for U.S. firms to place a greater emphasis on improving technology.

Cohen and Zysman, in *Manufacturing Matters*, argue for increased attention to manufacturing by corporate management. There is little doubt that America's decline in world trade is directly traceable to a decline in manufacturing prominence. Yet the nation's best and brightest people do not pursue jobs in manufacturing. Corporate management has yet to see the benefits of encouraging their best people to include manufacturing in their career paths.

Does American industry need to use better processes or does it need to use processes better? Both. The Council on Competitiveness found that foreign companies often beat their U.S. counterparts by using more efficient manufacturing processes, rather than by relying on lower wages. Japanese manufacturers spend two-thirds of their R&D budgets on process innovation, while their U.S. competitors spend only one-third on process-related R&D. In 1988, Japan passed the United States in per capita GNP for the first time. The success enjoyed by Japan is undoubtedly due in part to their long-term manufacturing perspective.

We have said that competitiveness depends on productivity and innovation. We have also said that productivity depends on capital, technology, and human skills. What does innovation depend on? The Council on Competitiveness found that innovation depends on knowledge, people, and infrastructure. For this reason, new knowledge must continue to be generated. But who will generate the new knowledge?

When confronted with the question, "Will science and engineering be more important or less important to America's future in the year 2010?", practically everyone would answer that they will be *more* important. If that is true, who will be America's scientists and engineers in the year 2010? Those who will enter the work force as scientists and engineers in 2010 are alive today; in fact, they are enrolled in preschool programs throughout the country. Unless dramatic improvements are made, the people needed to generate the new ideas that will lead to new technology will not be available.

The Pipeline Issue. Considerable attention has been given to the pipeline issue. Why is it receiving so much attention? By the turn of the century, more than 80 percent of those entering the workforce will be women, minorities, and immigrants. In 1982, 74 percent of five- to seven-year-old students were white; in the year 2020, 53 percent will be white, and half of those will be female. Why are these statistics of concern?

A recent NSF study found that only 1,800 high school sophomores out of 10,000 expressed an interest in science and engineering. By the time they were seniors, the number had decreased to 1,500, and by the time they entered college the number had declined to 850. Only 500 of these students received a bachelor's degree in either science or engineering, and 150 of them enrolled in graduate school. Of those 150, 110 received a masters degree and 23 received a doctorate in engineering or science.

As poor as the statistics are for *all* students, when the study focused only on the career paths of under-represented minorities, the results were much more disturbing. It required 856,000 minority high school sophomores to produce 23 doctorates; whereas 23 doctorates were produced from a general sample of 10,000 students. The evidence is overwhelming. America must take strong, positive steps to prepare, develop, and retain women and under-represented minorities as scientists and engineers if we wish to remain a world power in science and technology.

There is nothing uniquely white or uniquely male about engineering. We must identify and remove any impediments to the full participation of women, Blacks, and Hispanics if the nation is to be competitive in science and engineering. The situation has gone beyond the issue of social equity to become one of national necessity. Despite all of the attention being given to the issue, engineering and science are losing market share with bright Americans, and we do an even poorer job in reaching bright women and bright minorities.

When not a single Black American received a doctorate in electrical engineering in 1987 and none received a doctorate in mechanical engineering in 1988, you know you are not in the market for bright Black Americans. When, across all degree levels, engineering has a lower percentage of women graduates than any of the sciences, you know you are not in the market for bright American women. When, over an 11-year period, a total of nine Black women received doctorates in engineering, you know you are not in the market for bright Black American women. When more than 50 percent of graduate students are not U.S.-born, you know you are not in the market for bright Americans. When almost two-thirds of the untenured engineering faculty are foreign-born, when less than 1 percent of engineering faculty are Black Americans, when less than 2 percent of engineering faculty are Hispanics, and when only 2 percent of engineering faculty are women, you know the number of role models available is insufficient to attract to faculty positions increasing numbers of those who will constitute the majority of the workforce at the turn of the century.

Before leaving the pipeline issue, I want to focus on the issue of foreign students. Many who should know better are decrying the number of foreign students in our nation's engineering graduate schools. How quickly they forget that this country and its reputation in science and engineering was created largely through immigration. Following World War II, immigrants from Europe, especially Germany, provided the foundation for the nation's space and electronics research programs. The Cambodian and Vietnamese "boat people" are now keeping the nation afloat; if it were not for first- and second-generation Asians, the engineering and science community in this country would be one of the worst among the developed nations. The problem is not that there are too many foreign students in our graduate programs; it is that there are too few Americans attending graduate school.

Many students complain about the difficulty of understanding a graduate teaching assistant or professor whose first language is not English. In the global environment within which engineers must operate, our students must learn to communicate using languages other than Fortran, Pascal, Basic, and other computer languages. There are too many examples of leaders in the American engineering community who are foreign- born for the community to tolerate the narrow, parochial view that we should restrict the number of foreign students attending our graduate schools. Rather than criticizing them, we should do all we can to assist them in assimilating into our culture, including providing intensive language courses.

Providing educational opportunities for the "best and brightest" students from other countries has many positive benefits. Our own graduate students grow from exposure to those from other nations. Some foreign students choose to remain in the United States, elevating our talent pool. Those who return to their country favorably influence future relations between the two countries. This has often been overlooked. However, when someone who has been educated in the United States returns home and becomes an industrial, academic, or political leader, that person can have a significant impact on the relations between the two countries; hence, it is especially important for those individuals to view their U.S. experience positively — to feel wanted, not rejected, by our political system. Our education system can play the role of ambassador if we allow it to do so.

Conclusion. In conclusion, we know that giant oaks grow from little acorns. However, not *all* acorns produce giant oaks, and those that do, do not do so overnight. The "acorn of competitiveness" is research. Just as acorns depend on fertile soil and a supportive environment to produce giant oaks, so does research depend on fertile minds and a supportive environment to produce competitive products and processes.

The National Science Foundation is committed to increasing the number of fertile minds and to ensuring that a supportive environment exists for performing high quality research. Just as predators and disease can destroy acorns and young trees before they mature, so can America's young minds be diverted and subverted from studying science and engineering.

A long-term perspective is needed to produce an oak forest. Likewise, a long-term perspective is needed to restore the nation's competitive position in world trade. The competitive race is not a sprint — it will not be finished quickly or during one election period. It is not a relay — the baton cannot be handed to someone else. The responsibility is ours. The competitive race is a marathon — to be successful we must spend a great deal of time training and a great deal of time running. We must "stay the course."

16

U.S. Government and Productivity: Problems and Prospects

Kevin F.F. Quigley, Council on Foreign Relations, Carnegie Endowment for International Peace

Why is productivity growth important? Rising productivity is the key to economic growth, which in turn provides for a rising standard of living. In the past, our economic strength enabled the United States to advance its economic policy, foreign policy, and national security interests abroad. The relative decline in that strength in recent years has weakened our ability to promote our interests overseas.

Since 1960, U.S. productivity growth has lagged behind all our major competitors, whether measured in terms of percent changes in manufacturing productivity or in the broader measure — domestic product produced per employed person. From 1960 to 1986, U.S. manufacturing productivity increased an average of 2.8 percent, while Japan's increased at a rate 7.9 percent. Domestic product per employed person in Japan increased at 5.5 percent, while the U.S. increase was a paltry 1.2 percent.

This poor productivity performance is reflected in overall economic growth. In the 1960s, the U.S. economy grew 3.8 percent per year; in the 1970s, it grew 2.8 percent. In the 1980s it has slowed even further, to just 2.2 percent. Other countries are growing faster, and unless we become more productive, our children and grandchildren will not be able to enjoy the same standard of living that we enjoy.

Of course, these differences in productivity increases are both inevitable and relative. Many of our competitors — especially the war-ravaged economies of Japan and Germany — started at a much lower base, and inevitably will do a lot of "catching up." However, if U.S. productivity increases continue to lag behind our strongest competitors, we may find ourselves in the situation that the British found themselves in not so long ago. Over the 80-year period from 1870 to 1950, the United Kingdom's productivity growth was on average less that 1 percent lower than that of the United States. This small amount made a big difference. At the start of the period, the United Kingdom was by far the most dynamic economy in the world, but by the end of the period its overall economic output had fallen 40 percent behind ours.

There are numerous explanations for this dramatic reversal. I'm not here to argue those. My point is that growth in productivity matters, and our poor performance vis-á-vis our major competitors is a cause of concern. One area of particular concern is that the United States has clearly lost its lead in productivity in the manufacturing sector.

Let me give you just one example. A recent survey of the automotive industry found that it took on average 19.1 hours to build a car in a Japanese plant, while it took 19.5 hours to build the same car in a Japanese-managed plant in the United States. However, it took almost a third longer — 26.5 hours — to build that car in a U.S.-managed plant in the United States.

Not only are the Japanese building cars faster, but their cars are of higher quality as measured by the number of defects and service complaints. We could easily find other industries, steel and semiconductors for example, that make the point equally well that U.S. productivity in the manufacturing sector has weakened considerably.

This decline in the U.S. productivity lead, which has contributed to the recent decline in our international competitiveness, has generated a vigorous debate over whether the United States is a country in decline. Clearly, other countries are growing faster than we are. And with the increasing recognition that economic power is a critical determinant of a country's strength, what we can do to increase the vitality and productivity of our economy is a critical national question.

U.S. Economic Vulnerabilities. Regardless of whether you support the notion that the United States is in relative decline, there is ample and irrefutable evidence of U.S. economic vulnerabilities. Some of the more obvious evidence includes: growing trade and fiscal deficits; declining share of global economic activity; and continuing systemic weaknesses such as relatively low R&D expenditures, low rates of savings and investment, and an inadequate educational system.

These vulnerabilities are especially worrisome in the global economy in which we live. It used to be said, "When the U.S. sneezes, Europe catches a cold." Now, in our interdependent global economy, if *anybody* sneezes the rest of the world catches a cold. The world has changed dramatically over the past twenty years. Our task is to make sure that the United States is prepared to meet the challenges this new world poses.

The first step toward resolving a problem is recognition of the problem's existence. In Washington there is increasing recognition that we must increase our country's productivity growth. However, very little has been done to address this problem.

No Decisive Action Yet. Despite the lack of any decisive action yet, there are some hopeful signs that Washington is beginning to wake up and take our productivity problem seriously. President Bush's first address to Congress called for the establishment of a federal council on competitiveness to respond to our decline in productivity growth and to improve the international competitiveness of our economy.

President Bush's FY 1990 budget contained numerous proposals to boost productivity. These include increases in science and technology programs such as the National Science Foundation, and making the research experimentation credit permanent. He has also sought to encourage development of science and engineering facilities, strengthen math and science education, and improve training and assistance to displaced workers. All of these steps will help the country be more productive, and therefore more competitive.

Putting Our Fiscal House in Order. Before Washington can successfully address the protracted decline in U.S. productivity, there are a number of major challenges we must face. The most important is putting our fiscal house in order. This will require better management of the trade and fiscal deficits and dramatically improving our national savings rate. Let me touch briefly on these issues before discussing specific proposals to improve productivity.

It has become increasingly apparent that the continued economic expansion over the past seven years has masked some fundamental weaknesses. This peacetime record expansion has been fueled by debt — national debt, trade debt, consumer debt, business debt, and student debt. This expansion has not corrected our economic problems but has further contributed to them. We are living beyond our means, and sooner or later we will have to pay our debts.

From 1982 to 1987, total U.S. debt (including household, corporate, and consumer) doubled; while during this same period the national debt tripled from slightly less that $1 trillion in 1981 to more than $2.6 trillion by the end of 1988. The economy has gone on a consumption boom, financed by debt. Maybe we once could afford this accumulation of debt, but we cannot now.

Servicing the national debt has become a major expenditure in the federal budget. In 1988, interest payments on the national debt were $152 billion. This is the third largest federal expenditure after defense and Social Security. This means that, on average, every American pays $630 per year just to service the national debt. And every dollar we spend to service the national debt is a dollar we could have spent on education, on research and development, or any number of other important national priorities.

Despite the recent economic expansion, the U.S. international position has declined. The precipitous decline in our economic position is truly remarkable. In 1981, we had a current account surplus of $6.9 billion. The current account — the sum total of all exports of goods and services minus all imports — is the clearest indicator of a country's international economic position. In 1982, we had a small current account deficit of $8.7 billion. Yet the current account deficit plunged to $140 billion in 1986, and $160 billion in 1987.

An equally precipitous decline occurred in our international credit position. In 1981, the United States was a net creditor in its international investment position by $141 billion; by 1987, it was a net debtor to the tune of $400 billion. And as you probably have heard, we now have the dubious distinction of being the world's largest debtor — from history's greatest creditor to its largest debtor all in less than a decade.

Reducing the Budget Deficit. This dramatic and precipitous decline in our international accounts suggests that the major economic problem facing Washington is to restore a reasonable fiscal policy. A critical step is reducing the federal budget deficit. During the 1980s, the federal deficit has gotten out of control. The annual budget deficit fluctuated between $50 billion and $75 billion in the Ford and Carter administrations. In 1982, as a consequence of the tax cut and defense buildup, the deficit began to rise rapidly and finally peaked at $221 billion in 1986. It dropped back to $150 billion in 1987, and was modestly higher at $155 billion in 1988. Levels like that are unacceptably high.

Forecasts suggest that this year's deficit will exceed last year's level, absent a strenuous effort to reduce it — which does not appear to be very likely. In April 1989, the White House and Congress reached an agreement on the FY 1990 budget that involves a combination of spending cuts, tax increases, user fees, and dubious economic assumptions to bring the budget just a shade under the Gramm-Rudman-Hollings ceiling of $100 billion. However, I'm afraid that the agreement is just not good enough. What is required is a multiyear agreement that will clearly and convincingly lay out how the deficit will be eliminated over the next few years. Even if the budget is balanced, this does nothing to retire the national debt, which will continue to require interest payments that divert resources from productive economic activity.

Before I mention a number of specific suggestions for getting the budget deficit under control, let me state three principles that I think we should keep in mind during any deficit reduction attempt:

1. All parts of the budget should contribute to deficit reduction, including defense, domestic discretionary, and entitlement programs.
2. Those programs that serve the neediest members of our society should be protected (Aid to Families With Dependent Children, Homeless Assistance, etc.).
3. Whatever budget cuts or tax changes are proposed should be only those that improve economic efficiency by boosting savings or reducing consumption.

I recognize, after working both at the Office of Management and Budget and on Capitol Hill for most of this last decade, that reducing the deficit is not easy. Agreements on program cuts are extremely elusive because of the "not-*my*-program" syndrome. It is always easier to propose cuts in a program critical to some other state or congressional district, and our last two presidents have further complicated the matter by making tax increases politically unacceptable. That leaves us in a perpetual deadlock.

Let me suggest a number of program reductions and tax increases that would restore the economy to fiscal well-being while being consistent to the three principles that I just mentioned. I recognize that many of these proposals are very controversial, and that there are powerful interest groups that can easily criticize any single proposal. However, it is important that we go beyond any single interest and put the national interest first. Here are some proposals that, if jointly enacted, would put our fiscal house in order and improve the prospects for renewing productivity growth:

- Reduce Department of Defense (DOD) expenditures. A one-year freeze on DOD spending (that the President supports) provides $13 billion in savings. However, given the dramatic changes that the Soviets are pursuing by shifting from an offensive strategy to a defensive strategy, coupled with the possibility for increased burden-sharing with our allies, there may be opportunities for further reductions without undermining U.S. national security.
- Change Medicare payments and premiums by increasing copayments and premiums, and developing better cost control mechanisms. This could save $18 billion annually.
- Means-test Social Security. Taxing 85 percent of the benefits would raise nearly $5 billion per year.
- Limit cost-of-living increases for federal military and civilian workers. This is currently pegged to inflation, but if it were half of that, it could save nearly $6 billion annually.
- Reduce agricultural supports to insist on greater reliance on market forces. This could easily save $3 billion per year.
- Introduce some form of a value-added tax (VAT). This consumption tax is a powerful way to raise revenues. In fact, the United States is the only major industrialized country not to have this system. A 5-percent VAT would raise $75 billion per year, and it could be used, as it is in other countries, to promote exports by providing them with preferential treatment.
- Increase the current 9.5-cent gasoline tax. Besides reducing consumption (and therefore lessening our dependence on foreign oil), there is an ecological benefit as well, which Congress and the American people are all too conscious of in the aftermath of the EXXON-Valdez accident. A 10-cent-a-gallon tax increase, which would still leave gas cheaper than a decade ago, would raise nearly $20 billion annually.

- Severely limit the mortgage interest deduction cap. The *Washington Post* recently featured an article on Jay Rockefeller's $15.6 million refinancing of his Washington home. The *Post* calculated that Rockefeller's monthly payments on a standard mortgage would be nearly $250,000 per month, and that his annual tax savings would be over $800,000. A system that provides Jay Rockefeller with a nearly $1 million-a-year subsidy is clearly not serving the purpose it was intended to serve.

If all of these proposals were enacted, the savings would amount to $150 billion per year. This would eliminate the deficit and potentially put the government in surplus in just a few years. This would provide a major boost to U.S. economic strength.

Boosting Productivity Requires Boosting Savings. Besides getting the government budget deficit under control, there are other steps necessary to improve productivity growth. One critical step is to reorient the economy away from consumption to savings. This will have a positive effect because boosting savings is the key to improving productivity.

Efforts to reorient the economy from consumption must begin with the federal government. The government can encourage this reorientation by reducing federal expenditures, which I have discussed, and by changing the structure of the tax system. The federal government can also play a key role in spurring technological innovation and generating new investments in plant and equipment. Critical to this effort will be the government's ability to promote dramatically increased savings. The government must alter the fundamental predisposition of our economy to consume; we must reduce the incentives for consumption and replace them with incentives for savings. This can probably best be done through the tax system.

By appropriately using the two powerful tools of budget and tax policy, the government can provide the incentives necessary to reorient its spending habits and those of businesses and individuals. Of critical importance is reversing the decline in the national savings rate since savings is the key to investment, which is in turn the key to productivity growth.

U.S. net domestic savings was 7.5 percent of the GNP in the 1950s. In the 1970s it slipped to 7 percent, from 1980 to 1986 it was 3 percent, and during the period 1986-87 it dropped to 2 percent. This decline was primarily due to the burgeoning federal deficits, but decreases in state and local surpluses and deterioration in private savings

also contributed. Our savings rate lags far behind our major competitors; Germany and Japan have considerably higher savings rates.

Savings enable us to invest in the new technology and resources
that are critical to future productivity. Without increased savings, the
only way that we can make these needed investments is by borrowing. That only puts us deeper in the hole and delays the eventual day
of reckoning. And besides, after the recent consumption binge we
can't afford it.

The choices we face are actually relatively simple. We must either
consume less, save more, or do a combination of both. Consuming
less will free critically needed funds for productivity-enhancing investments. To restore the economy's underpinning we must increase
savings and discourage the voracious appetite for consumption that
we have all been party to over the past decade. A few changes in the
tax code, such as providing for more favorable treatment of capital
gains, interest and dividend income, restoring IRAs, and tightening
the deductibility of consumer loans through second mortgages could
have powerful results.

Other Steps. Besides the overall effort to reduce the federal deficit
and to reorient the economy toward savings, the federal government
can help boost productivity by prudent use of resources in three program areas:

1. Supporting the nation's scientific and technological base.
2. Strengthening the capabilities of the workforce.
3. Ensuring the viability of our infrastructure.

President Bush has supported some of these initiatives in the
past, but more needs to be done in the future. For example, the
United States should:

- Increase federal funding of our nation's research facilities. President
  Bush's proposed increase in the NSF budget is the first step in the
  right direction.
- Continue to encourage joint research and technological innovation.
  Consortia like SEMATECH, Microelectronics and Computer Technology (MCC), Semiconductors Research Corporation (SRC), and
  others that were formed to take advantage of the National Cooperative Research Act of 1984 should be encouraged.
- Provide additional funding for human resource development and
  education. Human resources are our most precious commodity, but

our people are lacking in some of the skills needed to keep pace in an intensely competitive global economy.
- Develop tax and other incentives that will spur further research and development and technological innovation.

There are some encouraging signs, but much more must be done. However, many of these efforts cannot be undertaken until a blueprint for achievable multiyear deficit reductions has been agreed to.

The Role of the Private Sector. Despite what Uncle Sam can do, the responsibility for getting much of the job done belongs to the private sector. Government sets the stage, but it is business that takes the leading role.

How well has the U.S. government set the economic stage recently? Up to this point, the federal government has not created an environment conducive to increasing the country's productivity. Despite the government's shortcomings, the U.S. private sector also has some limitations that many are intimately familiar with, and these need to be overcome:

- It often takes too long to get an idea from the drawing board to the marketplace. In the United States it generally takes twice as long as it does in Japan, and it involves more engineers.
- The quality of many U.S. products doesn't meet that of the international competition.
- Persistent labor/management antagonisms are unacceptably high and stand in the way of future progress.
- Wall Street's focus on quarterly profits and the threat of corporate takeovers encourages many companies to postpone long-term improvements in favor of short-term profitability.

How well U.S. business addresses these issues will be a critical factor in determining our success in meeting the international challenge.

What Lies Ahead. The single most important task for the federal government is to develop a critically needed plan for long-term structural reduction of the U.S. trade and budget deficit. Reducing the twin deficits will enable us to increase our national savings, which will in turn provide additional funds for much-needed investment in technological innovation and human resource development.

I am not suggesting that a restoration of U.S. productivity and U.S. global economic preeminence is dependent upon massive new federal expenditures; even if it were they would not be available. Rather, it is contingent upon the government setting the appropriate policy environment to provide incentives to boost productivity and savings, and using what limited resources it has to the greatest possible advantage.

At this point, there are some signs that Washington is beginning to take these issues seriously. While the budget agreement that was just reached in 1989 falls short of the requirements, there is still the possibility that the White House and Congress could reach agreement on an appropriate multiyear budget in 1990. As part of these budget discussions, President Bush and Congress should consider committing additional resources to strengthening the scientific base and the capabilities of our workforce. However, these steps may be "too little, too late" unless they are accompanied by a restoration of a sound fiscal policy that reorients our economy toward savings.

At this point, it is clear that Washington will make small incremental changes that will provide some help to restoring productivity growth. However, truly decisive change may require some crisis to energize Washington and force our legislators to seriously address the deficit problems and to realign our economy so that it emphasizes savings rather than encourages consumption. If we can make these changes, either in response to a crisis or out of a recognition of their necessity, they will make America more productive, thus enhancing our international competitiveness. A more productive America will provide for a better standard of living for tomorrow, help promote our interests abroad, and enable America to meet the challenges ahead.

17

Rules for International Productivity

Jack N. Behrman, Professor, University of North Carolina

There are two ways in which to be productive. One way is to play the game very efficiently and well. The other way is to change the rules of the game so you can play it better. For the United States to perform well in the global economy requires the latter method — changing the rules of the game. I want to talk to you this afternoon about which rules are being changed and who is going to set the new rules. The rules for international competitiveness were set by the United States for the twenty-five years from 1945 to 1970. Since then, there really has not been an agreed-upon set of rules. We are kind of playing it by ear. I am going to run through how the rules were established, how they have changed, and what we are probably going to face in the future.

The United States literally ran the world economy from 1945 to 1970. We were the biggest kid on the block. In fact, we were as big as all the other kids on the block put together. We made up half of the world from 1945 to about 1970. World peace was economically dictated by the United States. That stopped in 1970. Since then there has been a cooperative effort to get the world together.

Part of the problem is that the world has successfully accelerated its economic growth. The United States has assisted in developing a new international economy, which is obviously more dominant and larger than any other economy because it is the whole pie. The United States can no longer dominate. On the contrary, our economy is subservient to the world economy. At the same time, we are trying to hold onto disputed governmental policies. It will not work. The situation has changed, and the old rules do not fit anymore, yet we do not have a new set of agreed-upon rules.

One of the problems is that there is no worldwide agreement as to what the criteria for a new set of rules would be. Each of us has our own ideas. We also do not have any process for establishing new rules. Consequently, we are currently unable to establish a new set of workable worldwide rules, as we did in 1945. There are too many participants. In 1945 there were only three or four significant nations who sat down to set the rules. Now there are 140 nations in the United Nations alone. There are just too many of them, with too many different ideas, to get together.

Furthermore, there are new linkages around the world between trade and finance. When I was in graduate school, we only studied trade. Finance was basically an insignificant thing. Now, international finance is much more important than trade. For example, it takes $20 billion a day to carry out the world trade in *real* goods and services. But total transactions around the world using dollars amount to $200 billion a day. So, $180 billion is circulating around for intangible transactions. Finance is much more important in some respects than trade is.

Since the situation is so complicated, the new rules are going to be set in a piecemeal fashion. Little pieces of things are going to be settled one at a time through new rules. This will be done through regional associations, as is happening in Europe. This has not yet happened in the rest of the world, but should and probably will in Asia and in Latin America. Also, arrangements will be made that are oriented toward specific sectors — steel, auto, chemicals, and so on — simply because we will find a way of agreeing on these key industries. We just cannot agree on industry as a whole.

The Changing U.S. Role. The United States has lost its leadership role. Whether or not we will get it back is another discussion. There will be two leaders: transnational (or multinational) enterprises and governments. They will be involved in these regional associations and sectoral agreements. There will need to be agreements of a kind never before seen in U.S. history.

The situation is as follows: From 1945 to 1970 the United States dominated the world. We set the rules as to where economic activity would take place in the world. The rules were that free markets would dictate the flow of trade, and market signals would determine what would be produced. We made adjustments to changes in the world. We made sure that the gains from growth were distributed through foreign aid. We opened our trade and orders to the rest of the world. We gave financial assistance and maintained a strong dollar, high levels of employment, and military strength. Because we did all that, we set the rules.

It worked for 25 years. But by 1970, we were already in trouble. We had provided aid for the rest of world, and they were growing. It's fascinating: we were not prepared for the success of our postwar policies. They *were* successful. We helped get the rest of the world on its feet. We gave aid to Japan and Europe, and they moved out. As they moved out, somehow we did not move with them.

During the 1960s, the United States unwisely pursued two policies under President Johnson — the Vietnam War and the Great Society. I am not saying that we should not have done either of those. That is another argument. But Johnson refused to tax in order to adequately fund those two programs, so he ran up inflation. A dollar surplus was created by a combination of domestic inflation and the sloshing around of dollars to pay for the Vietnam War. When we went off of the gold standard in 1971, the dollar was devalued. Since 1970, 1973 is the only year that we have had a trade surplus. In 1961, when I went into the government, the trade deficit was $2 billion and was a cause of presidential concern. By 1983, it was $62 billion. In 1986, it was $170 billion. After that, from 1986 to 1988, we sharply devalued the dollar. In 1987, the deficit was down to $140 billion. Still, it was close to 40 percent of our export trade. In other words, our country is not in a position of strength. Our position is weak, with a fluctuating dollar. We are not playing the role that we were in the post-World War II era.

As a consequence, the United States insisted on staying in sectors in which there is worldwide overcapacity: autos, chemicals, textiles, and electronics. Fine, these are great industries to be in. The trouble is, the United States has become noncompetitive. This noncompetitive position was showing up in quality and price. We lowered our prices to foreigners by devaluing the dollar by close to 50 percent — over 50 percent in some currencies, such as the Japanese yen. Clearly, it is easy to export goods if you give them away. That is what we have been doing with the devalued dollar. We are paying twice as much as we used to for Japanese imports. We became more competitive, but we fixed it in the wrong way. We fixed it with a weak dollar rather than with higher quality, better goods, better delivery, and better service. The "fix" is, therefore, short-term.

Management, not labor, is responsible for what has happened in the United States. Labor responds to management. The Japanese say that productivity is 85 percent the responsibility of management and 15 percent the responsibility of labor. The U.S. measures productivity by labor, not by management. We have it upside-down. We have a few more problems. Our country has adversarial government/business relationships. The rest of the world has a way of getting business and government together to do things both nationally and internationally.

Management education bears part of the blame. It is about 20 years behind the times. Few of our top 500 business schools are teaching about the international economy and international business. A few courses are offered in most schools, but the curriculum does not address the global economy. We have much to do in human resource management, improving low productivity rates, and so on. These are things we need to correct now.

The World Economy. Changes in the world economy are altering the U.S. role. The world is being shoved together by technology, communications, and transportation. At the same time that the world is being pulled together, nations are trying to pull themselves apart. No one is really trying to adjust to what is going on in the international economy. Second, there are a lot of new players, the newly-industrialized countries (NICs). China and the Soviet Union are coming in and are going to ask to help set the rules.

There is greater global interdependence whether we like it or not. What is fascinating is that we are not psychologically ready for it. We have talked about one world; about the world getting together. But, neither the United States, Europe, nor Japan are really ready to play a major role in an integrated world economy.

We will also have to face new types of adjustment. We have to be ready to make some adjustments in terms of employment, interest rates, growth, distribution of income, and so on, to fit into this new world. The United States, rather than being a leader, is a net debtor to the rest of the world. It is very hard for debtors to lead. It is the people who have money who tend to lead. Of course, Japan particularly has the money. But the trouble with Japan is that it does not want to lead; it is not psychologically attuned to lead, either.

So, we have a situation in which the country that people look to for leadership does not have the economic strength to lead. Not only that, but between now and 1995 to 2000 our international debt is going to get bigger, not smaller. Every time we have a trade deficit, it is paid for in debt. That debt is projected to grow. By the year 1995 we could have an international debt of $1 trillion. It will cost $200 billion a year to service a debt that size and begin to whittle it down. That means that the United States must shift from a $170 billion trade deficit to a $200 billion surplus. That is a swing of $370 billion. It will require major adjustments, not only in the United States but in the rest of the world as well.

Other things are also happening. The world is becoming more similar in many ways. As attitudes become more similar, in some respects adjustments become easier, because we are talking about things at the margin in industrial sectors. We are not talking about giving up autos to other countries. We will be talking about changing where the radiators or hub caps are produced. As a consequence, we will have more specialization within sectors. Everybody wants to produce automobiles. China wants to produce automobiles, and they are going to get in. Korea wanted to get into automobiles; it is now exporting them. Taiwan is exporting automobiles. Yugoslavia, of all countries, is trying to export automobiles. Everybody wants to get into high-tech sectors.

Consumer patterns are beginning to merge. You can find jeans all over the world; you can find T-shirts all over the world; you can find the same kind of running shoes all over the world. Copiers and computers are becoming more similar all over the world. Industrial structures, therefore, are going to begin to merge and look very much alike. The United States is not going to be the exclusive producer of the electronics, chemicals, or optics for the world. Everyone else will be producing them too. Technology has become similar to financial institutions in its integration and rapid spread.

How do we get together, though? How do we find the new set of rules so we know what the game is? The game isn't just a free market out there. The rest of the world does not really possess every market.

I have worked in 46 countries since I left the government. I can assure you that they are not interested in the free market that the United States preaches. They are interested in some aspects of it, but they are going to interfere with it and intervene in it to their advantage if they can. So, we have to find ways to negotiate in setting new rules.

We will face many difficulties. There are too many people with divergent objectives, and existing rules are unacceptable. Another difficulty is the widespread reluctance to adjust. Germany does not want higher unemployment or inflation; it likes things the way they are. Japan does not want to change, except to have a weaker yen so they can export more. They do not want higher unemployment levels, the dreaded inflation, or the loss of an export stimulus. So, the surplus countries are not now willing to adjust as we think they should.

Finally, the world is being pulled together by what is known as cross-national investment. That is, the major transnational companies are investing in each others' countries. I have a friend in Washington who is an agent for Siemens in Germany. He talks about buying several small U.S. companies to facilitate Siemens' penetration of the United States. It is not just Japan. We are investing in exactly the same things that the others are. As a result, complex interlocking patterns of corporate relations evolve. Thirty percent of U.S. auto sales are supplied by Japan, much of it produced in the U.S. itself. If we stimulate the U.S. auto industry, who will benefit — ourselves or Japan? It is very difficult to know what the cost-benefit analysis is for supporting industry when things become so intertwined.

At the same time, we are still concerned as to whether or not Japan is buying us out or if they are getting a bargain in buying America. I was talking to a Texan recently about the Japanese buying some buildings in Houston. I asked if he was worried about it. He said he would like them to try to take one back and see how far they got. These changes are increasing the turbulence, and we do not seem to know how to handle it. However, we are going to face a higher degree of uncertainty in the future.

What do we do about all this? The U.S. government does not seem to know what it is doing, because it does not really understand how interdependent the U.S. economy has become with others. Congress still believes we can be protectionist. That is not possible anymore. The world is too big, moving too rapidly, and there are too many ways of getting around any U.S. protectionism. If the United States chooses to become protectionist, we may well be treated the way Russia was. Russia has now become sensible enough to know it has to move into the world economy, not stay behind.

Setting New Rules. I want to focus on what a new design of the rules would be. My first professional job when I left graduate school was to work on the Bretton Woods Agreements of U.S. post-World War II planning. I have been working on international plans for rules for my entire professional life. The United States is stuck with some old rules. They are 15 to 20 years out of date. We are still looking back to the "golden days" of 1945 to 1970. It won't be like that anymore.

What I am looking for are some criteria for new rules. How would you set the rules? What would be acceptable in setting the rules for the new world economy? The first thing we need to recognize is that no "ideal market" is going to exist, but markets are useful in allocating resources and distributing products. Markets produce efficiently under free trade, and that is what we want — efficiency. But that is not the only rule. The world also seeks an equitable way to balance benefits and opportunities among nations.

Third, a key concept in this decade is participation. Everybody wants to get into the act. Everybody wants to participate. And everybody wants a chance to be creative. Creativity is another key concept of Western civilization. Finally, ecology is being pressed on us, and we need to take care of that.

The concepts of efficiency, equity, participation, creativity, autonomy, stability, and ecology are complex, and it is difficult to make trade-offs among them. Smaller groups of nations will emerge who are willing to find solutions for specific issues. This can be accomplished through regional associations that will look at free trade and economic equity within the region. This is a radical concept, because it is not U.S. policy to support regional associations around the world. We want the world to operate as a single unit.

Another approach is to work through specific sector agreements. That is, we can focus on the problems of the auto industry or the chemical industry and come up with ways to promote free trade and more equity in the apportionment of industry activities. This leads to a concept that I call "structured investment with free trade." I want the government out of the act once it has set the rules. The rules have to do with the location of economic activity, the structure of investments, and the restructuring of investments so that everybody gets to play. We need new leadership — someone who possesses this vision of the world and is able to support it. Unfortunately, I do not see any current leaders capable of enunciating such a vision.

PART V

The Human Resource
Equation

18

The Critical Role of Management Skills in America's Future

Kim S. Cameron, Professor, University of Michigan

For the first time in history, a book on management recently led this country's best-seller list. A host of additional books discussing management principles and organizational success stories continue to sell hundreds of thousands of copies a year. Business services and organizational consulting have become the second most rapidly growing area in the U.S. service sector, lagging only behind health care services. Why has management suddenly become such a hot topic in America? Why has so much attention been focused on the management of American organizations?

In this chapter I first discuss current conditions of American business that illuminate the reason that competent management is so critical right now. Second, I discuss the extent to which effective management education and training are being provided by business schools and other executive training programs. Last, I summarize the characteristics and qualities of successful managers derived from several research studies and present a model that describes how these characteristics and qualities can best be developed.

Current Conditions in American Business. In approximately one decade America has been transformed from the world's undisputed economic leader into the world's largest debtor nation. In the five years from 1981 to 1986 the United States went from a position of trade balance surplus to the largest trade deficit in the history of the world. Until recently, most of that debt resulted from trade deficits in manufactured goods, but the same trend has recently come to characterize services as well. In the service sector, which accounts for 71 percent of America's GNP and 75 percent of its jobs, a trade deficit developed for the first time at the beginning of 1988.

The decline of the U.S. position in the global business environment has been dramatic and rapid. With the exception of nations that have been devastated by war, it is unlikely that any country has ever experienced as extensive and rapid an economic decline as is currently underway in the United States. In 1986, for example, two-thirds of the net investment in the United States for housing, capital equipment, R&D, and plant construction was funded by foreign capital. Our biggest export, by far, has become IOU's.

In every previous decade Americans consumed slightly less than 90 percent of what they produced, but since the beginning of the 1980s we have consumed 235 percent of our domestic production. Only 30 percent of the growth in consumption over the last decade can be accounted for by increases in productivity. The other 70 percent has been funded by cutbacks in domestic investment and foreign debt. Over the course of the 1980s the U.S. investment rate has been the second lowest in the industrialized world, while the growth in output per worker has been the absolute lowest. It took Britain 75 years of productivity growth rates that were only one-half a percentage point below competitor nations to slide from its position as the world's economic leader to virtual second-class status. The U.S. productivity rate as compared to competitor nations is three times lower than Britain's was during its period of economic decline, so the slide is proceeding much more rapidly (Peterson, 1987).

The number of business failures per 10,000 concerns has been at record levels since 1983, eclipsing the levels recorded during the Great Depression of 1929-32. Since 1986, business failure rates have been more than double those experienced during the Depression. Failure rates in the service sector are also at record levels. Bank failures set new all-time records every year. The top 100 banks in the United States have not made a net profit for the past three years, and one bank a day is added to the FDIC's problem-bank list. In the 1970s six of the ten largest banks in the world were American. In 1988 not a single U.S. bank is in the top 25. Seventeen of the 25 largest banks are Japanese. Similarly, in 1979 eight of the largest public firms were American, but in 1987 only two made the list — the other eight are Japanese.

In the past 15 years America has experienced a 25 percent decline in patent applications (innovations). Almost half of the U.S. patents approved in 1986 and 1987 were awarded to foreigners. The results of the U.S. decline in R&D investment is evidenced by a 1988 survey of top scientists. Most estimated that Japan will lead the world in R&D technology in the future with America lagging well behind. Consumers also demonstrate skepticism toward American performance. A recent poll asked American consumers which product they would buy if the only information available was that one brand was made in the United States and the other made in Japan. A majority said they would buy the Japanese product on the assumption that it would be of higher quality than its American counterpart. One result of this skepticism is that America's standard of living, which was rated highest in the world until the mid-1970s, now ranks fifth or below.

Thurow (1984) asserted that the blame for such a decline rests squarely on the shoulders of the managers — not government regulations, not Asian trade barriers, not the stock market.

> America is not experiencing a benevolent second industrial revolution, but a long-run economic decline that will affect its ability to competitively produce goods and services for world markets. If American industry fails, the managers are ultimately accountable. While we cannot fire all of America's managers any more than we can fire the American labor force, there is clearly something wrong with management. That something is going to have to be corrected if America is to compete in world markets.

Roy H. Pollock, recently retired executive vice president of RCA, characterized America's condition this way: "With the exception of the Civil War, it's doubtful that America has ever faced such an awesome trauma. This situation won't be painless. But the alternative is to accept continuing economic decline and the end to America's greatness."

The Role of Management. Even in the face of these dismal indicators of economic performance and the threat of wrenching adjustments that will be required of American businesses, discouragement and resignation are neither appropriate nor predestined. There is reason to be hopeful. One reason for optimism is that there are no secrets regarding how to effectively manage a firm or to turn around ineffective performance. There is no magic to competitiveness. Two scientific studies illustrate this point.

The first study was an investigation of the factors that best accounted for financial success over a five-year span in 40 major manufacturing firms (Hanson, 1986). The five most powerful predictors of success were identified and assessed. They included:

1. Market share (assuming that the higher the market share of a firm, the higher the profitability).
2. Firm capital intensity (assuming that the more a firm is automated and up-to-date in technology and equipment, the more profitable it will be).
3. Size of the firm in assets (assuming that economies of scale and efficiencies can be used in large firms to increase profitability).
4. Industry average return on sales (assuming that firms will reflect the performance of a highly profitable industry).
5. Emphasis on management of human resources (assuming that an emphasis on good people management helps produce profitability).

Statistical analyses revealed that the human resource management factor was three times more powerful than all other factors combined in accounting for financial success over five years. Good people management was more important than any other factor in predicting profitability.

A second study was conducted by the U.S. Office of the Controller of the Currency (1987). It studied the reasons for the failures of national banks in the United States between 1979 and 1987. The total number of national bank failures during that period was 162. Two major factors were found to account for the record number of bank failures during that eight-year period — distressed economic conditions and poor management. However, the relative impact of those two factors was somewhat surprising to the investigators. A total of 89 percent of the failed banks were judged to have poor management. Only 35 percent of the failures experienced depressed economic conditions in the region in which they operated, and in only 7 percent of the cases was a depressed economic condition the sole cause of bank failure. The government research team concluded:

> We found oversight and management deficiencies to be the primary factors that resulted in bank failure. In fact, poor policies, planning, and management were a significant cause of failure in 89 percent of

the banks surveyed. The quality of a bank's board and management depends on the experience, capability, judgment, and integrity of its directors and senior officers. Banks that had directors and managers with significant shortcomings made up a large portion of the banks that we surveyed.

These studies indicate that good management fosters financial success; bad management fosters financial distress. Loss of competitiveness and financial decline are more a product of shoddy management in U.S. firms than of macroeconomic factors or off-shore price advantages.

The argument regarding the importance of the role of good management in organizational success is also supported by practical examples in two separate industries. Two different organizations recently underwent a change in top management, and the results produced by the introduction of a new management approach were dramatic.

The first example comes from the General Motors automobile assembly plant in Fremont, California, built in the 1950s. In the early 1980s, workers were assembling the Chevrolet Nova and the plant had a history of labor and productivity problems. At the end of 1982, annual performance statistics were dismal:

- Absenteeism: 20 percent
- Grievances: 5,000 per year, averaging more than 20 a day with 2,000 unresolved at year's end
- Wildcat strikes: averaging 3 to 4 per year
- Employees: 5,000
- Productivity: worst in the corporation
- Quality: lowest in the corporation
- Costs: 30 percent above its Asian competition

In light of this data, corporate headquarters issued an order to close the plant and lay off the workers at the end of 1982.

In 1985, General Motors agreed to form a joint operating agreement with one of its major competitors, Toyota. Much had been written about the Japanese method of managing, so General Motors asked Toyota to reopen and manage the Fremont plant. Most of the former U.S. auto workers were rehired, but GM agreed to have the plant managed solely by the Japanese. The primary difference between 1982 and 1985 was simply that a new management team was put in place, with essentially the same workforce. At the end of 1986 — in just one year's time — the performance data looked like this:

- Absenteeism: 2 percent
- Grievances: 2 outstanding
- Strikes: none
- Employees: 2,500 (producing 20 percent more cars)
- Productivity: highest in the corporation
- Quality: highest in the corporation
- Costs: equal to those of the competition

The remarkable thing about this turnaround is that it did not take five or 10 years to produce major improvements in productivity, cohesion, and commitment. It occurred in just over a year simply by changing the way workers were managed.

The second example involves a television manufacturing plant near Chicago. It was sold by its American owner to a Japanese company several years ago. All of the American workforce remained, except that half of the white collar employees were let go. In addition, a top management group was brought in from Japan. The plant continued to produce essentially the same product using the same workforce. The only difference was a new top management team. A comparison between performance statistics under American management and Japanese management was dramatic:

	U.S. Management	Japanese Management
Defects per 100 TVs	150	4
Product rejects per 100 TVs	60	3.8
Annual warranty costs	$17 million	$3 million

Table 18.1   A Comparison of Performance Statistics for an American Plant under U.S. and Japanese Management

In addition, productivity per day doubled after the sale of the plant from 1,000 sets per day to 2,000 sets per day under the new management team.

These illustrations point out, as Thurow and others assert, that management is a key predictor of both firm success and firm failure. When excellent management is present, dramatic and rapid improvements can be effected. Surveys of CEOs, executives, and business owners consistently show that the factor most responsible for business failure is "bad management," and the factor most responsible for overcoming business failures is providing better management. Of much less importance are factors such as interest rates, foreign competition, taxes, inflation, and government regulation. When asked the question, "What are the factors that are most important in overcoming business failure?" two answers dominate all other responses: "Provide better managers," and "Train and educate current managers."

By using Japanese comparisons in the example above, I do not intend to suggest that the Japanese management system is superior to the American system. I also do not intend to suggest that Japanese methods should be adopted on a wholesale basis in American firms. In my own interviews with Japanese managers in Japan and in America, many have explained their success this way: "We just practice what you preach." Good management is not the prerogative of any single nationality or culture. Equally dramatic examples of firm and industry turnaround and excellence are prevalent in American firms with American managers (for example, Xerox, IBM, the U.S. steel industry, Ford Motor, and so on). What I mean to point out is that changing the way managers behave in organizations can bring about quick and dramatic improvements. Preachings about how to do that have been around for a long time. Neither the Japanese nor any other culture have discovered many new principles that were not being preached thirty years ago. The difference lies in the practice.

The problem with the examples and research studies discussed above is that they do not make clear exactly what was done by these managers that was so effective. The questions of what constitutes good management and how an individual can learn to be a good manager are still left unaddressed.

Management Education. For the past decade, management education in America has been held culprit in contributing to this country's economic decline. This criticism has most often been pointed at business schools and other management education programs. Over 200 articles have appeared in a wide array of academic and popular publications with titles such as "Managing Our Way to Economic Decline" (1980), "Overhauling America's Business Management" (1981), "The Failure of Business Education" (1982), "The Crisis in Business Education" (1983), "Are Business Schools Doing Their Job?" (1983), and

"Business Schools and Their Critics" (1985). The criticisms are pointed. For example, Peters (1983) asserted: "The business schools ...are doing more harm than good. I no longer flippantly say, as I used to, 'close their doors,' because now I'm beginning to believe that maybe this idea has serious merit." Wrapp (1985) added: "Business schools have done more to ensure the success of the Japanese and West German invasion of America than any one thing I can think of." Steele (1979) stated simply: "Too many schools are now coming up with answers to questions that nobody out there is asking."

Even the American Assembly of Collegiate Schools of Business (1985), the accreditation agency for America's business schools, admitted:

> In recent years, as the U.S. seems to have lost its edge in worldwide industrial competitiveness, nearly every sector of society has criticized U.S. corporate management. Critics say that the U.S. manager is short-term oriented, naively quantitative, averse to risk, self-centered, deficient in ethics and loyalty, impatient for promotion, overpriced, and unconcerned with real productivity. Not all managers fit such descriptions by any means. But enough apparently do to prompt the question, how did they become that way? What kind of managers are the business schools and other management development programs producing?

In a study of career advancement among Harvard MBAs, Livingston (1971) found that "managers are not taught in formal education programs what they most need to know to build successful careers in management. Unless they acquire through their own experience the knowledge and skills that are vital to their effectiveness, they are not likely to advance far up the organizational ladder."

Pfeffer (1981) argued that the main problem in business schools and management education is the type of training provided:

> Management education or performance in management schools does not predict subsequent career success for managers. But why not? It is because of the type of training imparted. Management schools impart both the ideology and skills of analysis... Optimization techniques for the core of current courses... Students emerge from such a program believing that there is an optimal answer or set of answers discoverable through quantitative analysis.

Scientific data support Livingston's and Pfeffer's assertions that performance in school is not predictive of subsequent career success.

Cohen (1984) summarized the results of 108 studies of the relationship between performance in college courses (as measured by grade point average) and subsequent life success. Life success was measured by a variety of factors including job performance, income, promotions, personal satisfaction, eminence, and graduate degrees. The mean correlation between performance in school and performance in life in these 108 studies was 0.18, and in no case did the correlation exceed 0.20. These low correlations suggest that school performance and successful performance in subsequent life activities are only very slightly related.

Why strive hard, then, to achieve in formal education programs? Do grades matter at all? What is the explanation for these dismal results? Should students and executives invest in formal education and training to try to improve their managerial competencies, or can good management be learned only on the job? Obviously, I believe that formal education and management training can positively affect managerial performance. I also believe that there must be a concerted effort to help develop such management talent in order to foster turnaround and excellence in American firms. Those beliefs are not based on blind optimism. Scientific evidence exists that such training can make a difference both to an individual and to the bottom-line performance of a firm. I summarize two studies below that provide support for this contention. First, however, the question, "What constitutes effective management?" must be addressed. Then how one can improve management competencies and the extent to which improvement will affect the performance of an organization can be discussed.

Effective Management. In an effort to identify what constitutes effective management, a colleague and I conducted an investigation in which we identified individuals who were rated as highly effective managers in their own organizations. We contacted organizations in business, health care, education, and state government agencies and asked senior officers to name the most effective managers in their organizations. We then interviewed these people to determine what attributes they associated with managerial effectiveness. We also reviewed studies done by other researchers that attempted to identify the characteristics of effective managers.

In our own study, 402 highly effective managers were identified. We interviewed these individuals and asked them questions in an attempt to try to identify what made them so successful as managers. Among the questions were:

- How have you become so successful in this organization?
- Who fails and who succeeds in this organization and why?
- If you had to train someone to take your place, what knowledge and what skills would you make certain that person possessed?
- If you could design an ideal course or training program to teach you to be a better manager, what would it contain?
- Think of other effective managers you know. What skills do they demonstrate that explains their success?

The results of our analyses produced about 60 characteristics of effective managers. The ten identified most often are listed in Table 18.2. Note that these ten characteristics are all behavioral skills. They are not personality attributes or styles, nor are they generalizations, such as luck or timing. They also are not very surprising. Characteristics of effective management, we concluded, are not a secret.

The attributes derived from our study are similar to those resulting from several other surveys published in the management literature. I have about a dozen such studies in my files, all with fairly consistent results. Regardless of whether respondents are CEOs or first-line supervisors, working in the public sector or the private sector, the skills of effective managers are generally observable and agreed upon

---

- Verbal communication (including listening)

- Managing time and stress

- Managing individual decisions

- Recognizing, defining, and solving problems

- Motivating and influencing others

- Delegating

- Setting goals and articulating a vision

- Self-awareness

- Team building

- Managing conflict

Table 18.2 The Most Frequently Cited Management Skills of Effective Managers

by observers. It is not hard to identify and describe the skills of effective management, and most people know them when they see them.

Two notable characteristics are typical of most of these lists of critical management skills. One characteristic is that the skills are *behavioral*. They are not personality attributes or stylistic tendencies. They consist of an identifiable set of actions that individuals perform which lead to certain outcomes. An important implication, therefore, is that individuals can learn to perform these behaviors, or they can improve their current level of performance. Although individuals with different styles and personalities may approach the skills differently, there are, nevertheless, a core set of observable attributes of effective skill performance that are common across a range of individual differences.

A second characteristic is that the skills in these lists are, in several cases, seemingly *contradictory* or *paradoxical*. For example, they are neither all soft and humanistic in orientation nor hard-driving and directive. They are not exclusively oriented toward either teamwork and interpersonal relations or individualism and entrepreneurship. A variety of types of skills are present.

To illustrate, Cameron and Tschirhart (1988) assessed the skill performance of over 500 mid-level and upper middle managers in more than 150 organizations. Those skills characterize the most effective managers. Through statistical analyses it was discovered that the skills could be grouped together into four main types. One group of skills focused on participative and human relations skills (for example, supportive communication and team building), but another group focused on just the opposite, that is, on competitiveness and control (for example, assertiveness, power, and influence skills). A third group focused on innovativeness and entrepreneurship (for example, creative problem solving), while a fourth group emphasized quite the opposite type of skills, namely, maintaining order and rationality (for example, organizing work and rational decision making).

The second characteristic associated with effective management skills is that the skills are paradoxical. That is, the most effective managers were found to be skilled at being participative and nurturing, and at the same time were hard-driving and competitive. They were able to be flexible and creative while also being controlled, stable, and rational. Effective managers demonstrate well-roundedness as well as diversity in the types of skills they can perform competently.

Improving Management Skills. Successful management, of course, is more than just following a cookbook list of sequential behaviors. Developing highly competent management skills is much more complicated than developing skills such as those associated with a trade, such as welding, or athletics, such as shooting baskets. Management skills are (1) linked to a more complex knowledge base than other types of skills, and (2) inherently connected to interaction with other, frequently unpredictable, individuals. A standardized approach to welding or shooting baskets may be feasible, but no standardized approach to managing human beings would be possible.

On the other hand, what all skills do have in common is the ability to be improved through practice. Any approach to developing management skills, therefore, must involve a heavy dose of practical application. At the same time, practice without the necessary conceptual knowledge is sterile and ignores the need for flexibility and adaptability to different situations. Therefore, developing skill competency is inherently tied to both conceptual learning and behavioral practice.

My good friend and colleague David Whetten and I have written a book, *Developing Management Skills*, to apply this learning model to the improvement of management competency. The method we elaborate in the book, and have found to be most successful in helping individuals develop management skills, is based on social learning theory (Bandura, 1977; Davis and Luthans, 1980). This approach marries rigorous conceptual knowledge with opportunities to practice and apply observable behaviors. Variations on this general approach have been used widely in on-the-job supervisory training programs (Goldstein and Sorcher, 1974), as well as in allied professional education classrooms such as teacher development and social work (Rose, Crayner, and Edleson, 1977; Singleton, Spurgeon, and Strammers, 1980).

This learning model, as originally conceptualized, consists of four steps:

1. The presentation of behavioral principles or action guidelines, generally using traditional instruction methods;
2. The demonstration of the principles to participants by means of cases, films, scripts, or incidents;
3. Opportunities to practice the principles through role plays or exercises; and
4. Feedback on performance from peers, instructors, or experts.

Our own experience in teaching management skills has convinced us that three important modifications are necessary in order for this model to be most effective with these complex skills. First, the behavioral principles must be grounded in social science theory and in reliable research results. Common sense generalizations and panacea-like prescriptions appear regularly in the popular management literature. To assure validity of the behavioral guidelines being prescribed, the learning approach must include scientifically based knowledge about the effects of the management principles being presented.

Second, participants must be aware of their current level of skill competency and be motivated to improve upon that level in order to benefit from the model. Most people receive very little feedback about their current level of competency in skill areas. Most organizations provide some kind of annual or semiannual evaluation (for example, semester grades in school or performance appraisal interviews in firms), but these evaluations are almost always infrequent, rather narrow in scope, and do not assess performance in most critical skill areas. For individuals to understand *what* to improve as well as *why* improvement is needed, therefore, it is necessary to have a preassessment activity as part of the model. In addition, most people find change rather uncomfortable and therefore avoid taking the risk to develop new behavior patterns. A preassessment activity in the learning model also helps foster an attitude of receptivity to change, since strengths and weaknesses are illuminated. A person knows where weaknesses lie and what needs to be improved. Preassessment activities generally take the form of self-evaluation instruments, case studies, or problems that help highlight personal strengths and weaknesses in the designated skill area.

Third, a back-home application component is needed in the learning model. Most management skill training takes place in a classroom setting where feedback is immediate and where it is relatively safe to try out new behaviors and make mistakes. Transferring learning to the job is often problematic. Application exercises are helpful in generalizing and applying classroom learning to the real world of management. These exercises often take the form of an intervention or consulting assignment outside of class, or a problem-centered intervention that is then self-analyzed with regard to its degree of success or failure.

In sum, evidence suggests that a five-step learning model, outlined in Table 18.3, is most effective for helping individuals develop management skills. Step 1 involves the preassessment of current levels of skill competency and knowledge of the behavioral principles. Step 2 consists of the presentation of validated, scientifically based principles and guidelines for effective skill performance. Step 3 is an analysis step in which models or cases are made available in order to analyze the behavioral principles in real organizational settings. This step also helps demonstrate how the behavioral guidelines can be adapted to different personal styles and circumstances. Step 4 consists of practice experiences in which experimentation can occur and immediate feedback can be received in a relatively safe environment. Finally, Step 5 is the transfer and application of the skill to a real-life setting, with follow-up analysis of the success of that application.

Research on the effectiveness of training programs using this learning model has shown that it produces results superior to those based on the traditional lecture/discussion approach. In addition,

Components	Contents	Objectives
Skill Preassessment	Survey Instruments Role Plays	Assess current level of skill competence and knowledge; create readiness to change.
Skill Learning	Written Text Behavioral guidelines	Teach correct principles and present a rationale for behavioral guidelines.
Skill Analysis	Written and video cases ✓	Provide examples of effective and ineffective performance. Analyze behavior principles and why they work.
Skill Practice	Exercises Simulations Role plays	Practice behavioral guidelines. Adapt principles to personal style. Receive feedback and assistance.
Skill Application	Assignments behavioral and written	Transfer classroom learning to real-life situations. Foster ongoing personal development.

Table 18.3 A Model for Developing Management Skills

evidence suggests that management skill training can have significant impact on the bottom-line performance of a firm. For example, a
study was completed a few years ago by the U.S. Postal Service in
which 49 of the largest 100 post offices in America were evaluated. An
important question in the study was, "How can we make post offices
more effective?" Productivity and service quality were both monitored over a period of five years. The two major factors that had impact
on these effectiveness measures were (1) degree of mechanization
(automation) and (2) investment in training. Two kinds of training
were provided: maintenance training (training in operating and
maintaining the equipment) and management training (training in
developing management skills). The overall conclusion of the study
was, "Performance levels in these organizations vary systematically
and predictably as training levels vary. The training-performance
relationship is positive and statistically significant."

More specifically, the study found that providing management
training was more important than providing maintenance training in
optimizing productivity and service effectiveness in these organizations, and that both kinds of management training were more important than having automated or up-to-date equipment in the post
office (mechanization). Low-tech offices outperformed high-tech offices
when managers were provided with management skill training. In
sum, helping employees to develop management skills was the best
predictor of organizational effectiveness over the targeted five-year
period for the U.S. Postal Service.

The point I am emphasizing is that management skill training is
a critical developmental activity for both potential and practicing
managers. There is evidence that many American organizations are
in great danger of losing their competitiveness to foreign competition
as well as their credibility here at home. Moreover, evidence suggests
that it is, to a significant extent, the managers who are at fault. To
improve management, and thereby to improve organizational performance, I suggest that one important activity is developing more
competent managers in critical management skills. Mintzberg (1975)
made a similar point several years ago:

> Management schools will begin the serious training of managers
> when skill training takes its place next to cognitive learning. Cognitive
> learning is detached and informational, like reading a book or listen-
> ing to a lecture. No doubt much important cognitive material must

be assimilated by the manager-to-be. But cognitive learning no more makes a manager than it does a swimmer. The latter will drown the first time he jumps into the water if his coach never takes him out of the lecture hall, gets him wet, and gives him feedback on his performance. Our management schools need to identify the skills managers use, select students who show potential in these skills, put the students into situations where these skills can be practiced, and then give them systematic feedback on their performance.

More recently, Porter and McKibbin (1988) made a similar argument in a study of management education in American business schools sponsored by the American Assembly of Collegiate Schools of Business:

> The challenge of how to develop stronger people skills needs to be faced by both business schools in the education of their degree program students and by corporations and firms in their management development activities.

19

Boeing Culture Change for the Year 2000

Larry G. McKean, Vice President of Corporate Human Resources, Boeing

I want to review with you what we call "culture change" at Boeing; what our status is today, including the change process now in place; and how our future direction regarding strategic change in our human resource systems will address the challenges of the next decade.

In recent years many drivers have been impacting our corporate culture:

- Customer concerns about quality.
- Government regulations about how we conduct business.
- Increased competition in all our markets.
- Our own financial performance, how it is viewed by investors and shareholders, and the internal pressures this creates.
- Our business strategy, which determines which markets we compete for and the risks we will accept.
- The significant impact of computer technology in our products and workplace. As we make the transition from stand-alone computer systems — which automated our old methods of designing, building, and servicing our products — to integrated systems, the way we operate and how we utilize our people will have to change.
- Finally, our people are a major driver of change. A more skilled, highly mobile, career-oriented, involved work force representing more females and minorities has a tremendous impact on our culture.

All of us saw these drivers coming, and we each responded in our own way. Divisions initiated programs of their own making. Functions responded to their own sets of needs, including human resources. Corporate offices initiated programs of their own. So we moved forward independently. We did not wait for a crisis to motivate us or a grand plan to direct us. While we were busy reacting to these external change drivers, our work force itself was changing.

Coping with Skill Dilution. During the past two years we have grown to our highest-ever employment level, 146,000 employees. That represents a seven to eight percent increase each year. That rate might not seem dramatic, but to do it we had to hire 32,000 new employees. That involved replacing 15,000 people, including 5,000 retirements that represented many years of solid Boeing experience. Over 4,000 new supervisors were put out on the line to help manage that new work force, a work force where almost a third of the employees are under age 30. Employee training was more than doubled to get the new people up to speed and provide new skills to other employees.

These adjustments have brought problems. Hourly workers in the factory were increasingly inexperienced, even as production rates were increasing. The number of employees with less than two years of service jumped from 2,900 to almost 10,000. They now represent more than a quarter of our hourly work force, and in some skills and shops the level of inexperience is significantly higher. Similar skill dilution can be seen in engineering and other areas.

We were also taking some of our good, experienced technical people and making them supervisors — too often with inadequate preparation and training. This trend, coupled with the fact that we have added 4,500 *new* supervisors since the start of 1986, means 30 percent of our supervisors have had less than two years of management experience. The inexperience level is even greater if we just look at first-line supervisors. That is also skill dilution!

Incidentally, the payroll where skill dilution has had the most significant impact is the executive payroll, with 50 percent new to these ranks since 1986. It's also a safe bet that a lot of the veterans have been faced with new responsibilities.

To calibrate where we are in this culture change process, we asked employees for their perceptions in a survey last year. We asked them to rate in priority order what should be the most important value to management. Quality and customer satisfaction led the list. There was no doubt that our employees understood what the culture *should* be. Then we asked about what today's realities are at Boeing.

The reality is that our actions seem to be sending a different message than we intend. When employees were asked how important these same issues *are* to management, the perceptions changed. Quality was perceived as about fifth in priority, with *schedule* emerging as "King of the Hill." The real world out there on the factory floor and in the offices was giving very different signals to the employees than the values we wanted to communicate. This is not just a reaction from some uninformed, recently hired workers; the same perception exists with our first-level supervisors!

In a later survey, 75 percent of our employees gave the company a positive rating for quality, yet only 50 percent gave us a positive rating on whether we encouraged innovation, and less than 40 percent gave the productivity environment a positive rating. It appears we are getting mixed signals.

As we reflected on our initial efforts to get employees more involved in the improvement process and tackle the rigidity of our people management practices, it appeared as though we had created a lot of disconnected events, programs, and change initiatives. Like pieces in a disarranged jigsaw puzzle, they just weren't fitting together. That doesn't mean they were bad ideas; they just didn't have a focus or a common sense of direction. We didn't pull some of them off very well, but we learned valuable lessons about managing in the process.

We had been approaching this change process from a perspective of the traditional organization — the classic pyramid — with the people at the top doing the thinking for everybody and an ever-expanding band of controllers across the middle developing regulations, passing information, and overseeing the doers who form the base of the pyramid. Compounding those vertical layers further were the functional walls we built into that pyramid, each function having its own goals and objectives. Most of our managers have climbed up those functional ladders, further embedding a limited view of the whole enterprise. Few Boeing managers had the kind of experiences that tend to develop general management thinking.

And so we reacted in the typical way, adding a program — that is, weight-saving, cost-savings drive, and quality circles — here and there, but not changing our traditional ways of doing business. It's a safe, comfortable way of reacting to change issues. The program can slip away when the fad passes, and life goes on as usual.

We have learned some lessons about cultural change, not only from our own experiences, but from other companies as well. We clearly needed to communicate a vision of where we were going with our people-management practices, and our direction had to be based on principles that we believe in. We needed a process for examining all the elements of the human resources system, a process that involved the key players in building commitment and providing support. And we learned the need to be patient.

Many of you have been involved in the change process. You have experienced the challenge of defining mission statements and articulating a vision of the future. These are not simple tasks in any organization. The size and complexity of our company only made it more challenging.

Guiding Principles for the Cultural Change Process. Through a consensus-building process with our senior executives, we have developed and communicated a set of principles that guide the cultural change process. The words are perhaps not new — they evolved from many decades of Boeing heritage — but they are our principles:

1. Integrity is our way of life.
2. Quality and customer satisfaction are fundamental.
3. Technical excellence will distinguish our products.
4. People are our key resource.

We have developed a long-term vision of an organizational concept that encourages and enables all our people to be involved in the continuous improvement process as an integral part of their everyday job. We believe that a properly structured high-involvement organization

- involves employees in management of the business;
- encourages them to be more skilled, committed, and productive; and
- gives information, knowledge, power, and rewards.

We believe managers need leadership skills to

- build trust and openness;
- develop and communicate a shared vision;
- move decisions to the proper level; and
- empower others

The key is consistency and tightly linked company and individual goals. High involvement organizations can become self-controlling and outperform traditionally designed organizations.

Regardless of what it is called, that kind of organization has certain functional features. Our principles say that people are our key resource. By involving employees in the management of the business, developing their skills, providing them with information and knowledge, rewarding them for improved performance, and tightly linking company and employee goals, we have taken a set of words and turned them into action. Clearly it takes managers with leadership skills to create and sustain this type of organization.

It also takes employees with certain attributes to thrive in this new organization. The ideal employee is

- inquisitive
- committed
- involved
- skilled
- productive
- flexible
- innovative
- self-motivated
- team-oriented

In order to develop and sustain those attributes in employees, the system or the organization must provide nourishment. If we want inquisitive employees, we must be ready to inform and trust them with information about the business. If we want committed and involved people, we must give them commensurate responsibility and recognition. If we want skilled and productive people, we must provide them with training and the time to take it. Innovation is nourished when the behavior and rewards in the organization encourage it. The people and the organizational culture are one and the same. They must reinforce one another.

That's our sense of direction for the long term. Not every organization or division will get there at the same time. Some may be close now. Our task in the near term is to provide ways to get there when opportunity exists.

To help foster these change processes, we established a Human Resource Management Council, which is composed of division and corporate functional executives. It is our sounding board for strategic change issues concerning our people. With similar board oversight, we established the Corporate Quality Council, which provides guidance on corporate-wide quality issues. We utilize a quality improvement team approach, with the stakeholders involved in studying the issues and designing new approaches and solutions for particular issues. Policy issues — such as our recent changes concerning management development — are reviewed with the Executive Council. Implementation is the responsibility of division management.

Certain strategic human resource issues have emerged — strategic in the sense that they are critical to the change process. They play together with strong linkages. Change doesn't happen without management leadership. To develop leadership requires a process of selecting and developing managers who are focused on the attributes we want to promote. Good performance management is the feedback process that assures continuous improvement. Rewards are the glue that reinforces desired outcomes.

Working with the Human Resource Management Council, we've developed a general plan for the change initiatives. For each strategic issue there are either specific tasks to implement what we have committed to do, or studies to evaluate options available to us.

We also recognize that there is a long road ahead of us that will take us into the 1990s. For example, we intend to test some approaches to performance management that provide a pay-or-rewards linkage. We'll introduce them in 1989 and 1990, evaluate the process and results, and then be ready for a pay- linked system for all management by 1991. We know that other unforeseen issues will arise, and we expect some changes as we learn along the way. But we do have a path, a sense of priorities, and the outline of a plan to lead us in the right direction.

Preparing Managers to Lead: The Management Development Process. Let's start with management development. Preparing managers to lead in an ever changing environment is our number one priority. We must shift management behavior to reflect our new emphasis on people management skills. Our approach is based on dealing with management development as a process, not just classroom training or sending someone off to a university for a few weeks. The process was first outlined by the Management Development Study Team, comprising both line and HR professionals. The process starts with selection and how we prepare candidates; it ties what we need organizationally and individually to our resource requirements, and is reinforced by a performance management process. The entire process is based on the value system and the priorities expressed in our principles and in our business plans.

To implement the process we are revising our policy, revising core management development courses, developing new programs for middle- and upper-level managers, improving the management selection and resource planning processes, and instituting performance management.

Fostering Union Cooperation. At the same time we are continuing to improve our relationship with unions. As in most aerospace companies, Boeing has a high degree of union representation. Approximately 88,000 of our 146,000 employees are represented by 12 different unions. In 1983 we agreed to keep the unions advised of the impact of new technology and to cooperate in exploring retaining initiatives for employees.

In 1986 we added a process for pilot projects to explore new concepts in work practices to improve both productivity and quality of work life. Following 1986 negotiations, we initiated a process to encourage pilot projects in each division. The Everett wire shop is involved in combining and enriching jobs — getting away from specialization. Aerospace computer maintenance is insourcing work previously done by outside service vendors. The gear line at Portland is exploring pay-for-knowledge in a manufacturing cell environment. We're looking at owner/operator concepts on several electronics manufacturing processes and the possibility of a nontraditional work week for the Wichita 737 line. These projects are all under the umbrella of a joint company/union committee.

A new $200 million sheet metal facility is being built for our fabrication division. Both IAM and SPEEA are on our advisory committee concerning the sheet metal modernization program at the Auburn site, south of Seattle. We intend to continue fostering the kind of relationship where we can work together with unions in areas of mutual interest.

Much that I have talked about has involved trying to improve our traditional environment. It's a lot more challenging to actually bring in that new culture when you're right in the middle of living with the old culture every day.

Organization redesign involves a major change in our thinking about how we approach managing and doing the work. We are encouraging such initiatives wherever we have targets of opportunity. There are some risks involved, because these are definitely nontraditional approaches. We have to have the right environment and a supportive process with managers ready to lead the change process.

We have a long way to go, but we know where we are headed. We have begun to move beyond generalities to specific actions. We are not all moving at the same pace in the Boeing company, but we are all moving in the same direction — a direction that is both exciting and challenging.

While it is too soon to predict the certainty of success, we believe that Boeing is on the right track to a successful change in culture, which will better equip us to face the challenges we will encounter as we move toward the year 2000 and beyond.

20

1990s: The Work Force of a New Age

Nancy Dreicer, Vice President of Corporate Resources,
American Transtech

The best evidence that the 1990s are here is how hard all of us are trying to recycle the 1960s. There is this growing nostalgia attached to the Summer of Love, the Camelot days of the Kennedy administration, Woodstock, and the romance of a decade that barely qualifies as history at this point.

Part of this reverence for the 1960s is, I believe, a misguided quest to recapture some of the values that were "lost" or transformed throughout the 1980s. It is a counterattack, in a sense, against the materialism and the future shock that have characterized both the business world and society at large over the past ten years.

Going from Woodstock to Wall Street in a span of 20 years was a big cultural stretch. But this sentimental turning toward the recent past, is, in my opinion, an inappropriate launching pad for what faces business — and society — in the 1990s.

The tenor of the 1990s' work force and the problems or opportunities associated with it reflect an entirely new cultural framework. The diminishing importance of manufacturing, the growing strength of service industries, and the high-technology foundation in place for the future are just a few of the changes that make the 1990s a whole new ball game for business.

The changes have occurred faster than anyone could have predicted. A recent article by Peter Drucker underscored this. Drucker pointed out that only 80 years ago, at the outset of World War I, most people in developed countries earned their living in just three occupations:

- In Britain, one-third of the workers were domestic servants;
- In every country except Britain and Belgium, more than half the population were farmers;
- The last major category was blue collar workers, the fastest-growing occupation, and the one that would account for 25 percent of the U.S. labor force by 1925.

In this context, "management" is an integrated approach to bring together people of widely varying skills and knowledge in one organization — with a distinct culture — to maximize productivity.

The 1990s will tax these management skills to the fullest. With most of the skilled baby boomers already in the work force, industry in the 1990s will be faced with a growing labor shortage and the challenges that accompany it. Not only will we see fewer skilled workers, but we'll be dealing with a multicultural work force that is aging — requiring a whole new set of specific demands.

On top of that, we'll be operating under the pressure to "globalize" our businesses, big and small, to provide new levels of top-notch customer service, and to accommodate a speed of doing business never before seen in the world marketplace.

On a point-by-point basis, this is how the scenario stacks up in terms of the 1990s' labor force:

Today, domestic servants have all but disappeared (which may be why everyone talks about how hard it is "to get good help"). Full-time farmers account for less that 5 percent of the working population in non-Communist developed countries. And the blue collar worker is going the way of the carrier pigeon, making up only 18 percent of the current work force. This percentage is expected to drop further — to 10 percent — by the end of the century.

So what are we doing these days? Contrary to what we see on popular television, not everyone in America past the age of 21 is a hot Wall Street broker or a Harvard MBA. Nor are they all doctors, lawyers, interior designers, or TV journalists. Most of them are, in fact, part of a growing work force that has already earned the tag "new collar workers."

The new collar worker is very different from his blue collar predecessor. One generation of new collar workers is now employed and maturing. The typical profile of this worker is someone born after 1946, who grew up with television, who lived in suburbia as opposed to inner-city neighborhoods, and whose life was comfortable in comparison with that of his parents.

These people watched the decline of industry in the United States during the 1970s; some saw their fathers being laid off as a result. This was the era during which steel mills were shut down, auto plant workers were cut back, and political upheavals such as Watergate and the Vietnam War were commonplace.

In a sense, this generation witnessed the fact that the "old" values didn't necessarily pan out — not when it came to job security; not even when it came to the integrity of the Oval Office. These workers bring a whole new set of values into the workplace, which I'll address later.

Another factor that has changed the composition of the work force is the growth of management as a way to increase productivity. As Drucker points out, for the first time in history, through the *management* process, we can employ large numbers of educated, skilled people in productive work. No previous society could do this. Until management came to the fore in business, no one knew how to put people with different skills and knowledge together to achieve common goals on a wide scale.

Today, the United States produces almost 1 million college graduates a year, most of whom have had little trouble finding well-paid employment. What enables us to employ them is management. Knowledge, then, is fast replacing manual labor as a major resource. As factories become computerized, even physical labor is being replaced by mind power. Combine this with the service sector turning toward information processing — PCs, CRTs, and so on — and you can easily see the increases in the number of knowledgeable workers.

A Shortage of Skilled Labor. Bureau of Labor Statistics projects that the overall labor force will grow only 1.2 percent a year between 1986 and 2000, down from the 2.2 percent rate that occurred between 1972 and 1986.

This will be the slowest labor force growth rate since the 1930s, and it is a result of two factors. First, the population growth rate is slowing. Second, the baby boom has matured, leaving a gap in the total number of similarly skilled workers to fill the future needs of a rapidly expanding, services-oriented economy.

As a result, employers will be forced to look to the non-male, non-white, and non-young population for all sorts of workers. There may be a push for non-citizens as well. Much of the minority labor pool may lack the skills necessary for these jobs, which will place greater demands on companies to provide training.

An Older Work Force. By the year 2000, the prime-age work force (aged 25 to 54) will grow by 1.7 percent per year, with a concurrent drop in the youth work force of 0.2 percent a year. By 2000, the median age of the work force will be 38.9 years.

A recent article in *American Demographics* suggests that the maturing of the baby boomers, as well as of the population as a whole, may present problems in productivity growth, since older workers traditionally have been less willing to retrain or move to a different part of the country for a new job.

Our challenge in the 1990s will be to become stronger in training and retraining. Firms that aid in job search and placement, including spouse relocation, will multiply.

The key to managing the work force of the future will be flexibility and the ability to manage cultural diversity.

More Women and Minorities. The Bureau of Labor Statistics projects an annual increase in the women's labor force of 0.8 percent, a growth rate double that of the labor force as a whole.

This growing female contingent in the labor force raises new "societal" issues for business — issues companies must face in order to remain competitive — issues like child care, care for elderly relatives, or (like IBM offers) take-out dinners from the company cafeteria for households with two working parents.

Labor statistics also point to an increase in minority workers. Hispanics are expected to account for 29 percent of all new workers, as the number of Hispanic workers grows by 4.1 percent a year for the rest of the century. By 2000, Hispanics are expected to account for 10 percent of the work force. Asians and other racial groups will account for 11 percent of new workers. Blacks are expected to account for 18 percent of all new workers by the end of the century.

These new numbers of minorities may have less education and, if they are going to be able to take advantage of the job growth in the 1990s, they will need more training. Again, this is a task that will fall increasingly to the private industry sector. All of these changes, from the demographic side to the changing demands of a global market, will place new demands on the organization and on the use of human resources. Peter Drucker's vision of the corporation of the future provides a good example of how I see our business moving.

Drucker sees employees in an information-based company as members of a "symphony" more than of a vertical hierarchy, with everyone responding to one CEO who acts like a conductor to keep everyone on the same beat. This flattened structure reflects a gradual decrease in corporate staffs and dozens of layers of management.

IBM and AT&T are already shifting people out of corporate headquarters and staff positions into sales and marketing.

1990s Organizational Change. The number of people reporting to each manager is increasing, with "spans of control" giving way to Drucker's "spans of communication," or the growing number of people an executive can reach through a good information system.

The flatter corporate structure allows decision making to be pushed down to lower layers, which allows the new collar generation of workers a greater sense of ownership in a company.

Ownership is an important concept these days when it comes to employee motivation. Whether we achieve ownership through profit-sharing or the sense that an employee "counts," the message is clear: the work force of the 1990s wants a voice in the company's future.

New collar workers have value systems that stress the importance of individuality. They value the idea of a quality of life that includes leisure time, meaningful work, and a sense of purpose. They place great significance on personal development inside as well as outside their jobs.

This value system has transformed the traditional roles of employee-employer into a greater sense of cooperation. It has brought about the debut of the "corporate culture," a commonly held value system defining the workplace that is designed around joint employee/ company goals.

These changes were incorporated into American Transtech, where I work, at its inception more than five years ago. As we grow and evolve, we find that the needs of the business — as well as our changing work force — continue to exert changes in our culture.

Quality. The most recent evolution in the corporate value system is our movement to embrace total quality as a way of doing business from here on out.

We are not alone in this push toward quality, which is centered on upgrading customer service. In a recent survey of 2,196 companies by the Hay Group, the movement toward customer focus was evident down the line. Xerox is emphasizing product quality and customer satisfaction. At Ford, "Quality is Job One." Southwest Airlines, CompuTrac, and Chili's, Inc., emphasize workplace "fun" to spur new ideas and help customers *enjoy* the companies' services.

The word "quality", used in the context of organizational goals, is far more than a description of a top-notch product offering. Quality is a concept, a way of thinking that says the customer defines quality specifications. It says that if quality comes first, productivity and profits will follow. It asks an organization to think about everything as a *process* to be measured, controlled, and improved. It also says that workers will perform to the standards of their leaders — that quality starts at the top.

The movement toward quality is what will make the motivating difference to tomorrow's new collar workers. The old way of pushing productivity to achieve profit just doesn't fly with this group. Nor does a paycheck guarantee blind loyalty anymore.

The new collar worker's need to feel ownership in the company translates to a desire to perform against challenging personal standards — not just corporate requirements. Only through a vested personal interest and an understanding of the *process* of company growth will these people produce "to the max."

Making our customers the focal point of our work cultures may be the biggest single challenge and opportunity facing us in the 1990s. Building total quality in our work in a decade full of demographic and social change will be no walk on the beach.

The 1990s can't be easily compared to the past; like every decade, they will be their own frontier. Looking back, maybe that is why everyone is feeling wistful about the 1960s. From where we're standing now, even the 1960s seem like a simpler time. Like the 1960s, the next decade may bring about the social awareness we have been missing. Labor shortages in the future could actually present us with the demand to improve the lot of the poor — for the good of business. Early intervention, through nutrition programs, parenting classes, and education, may help the new workers get a real toehold on the future and thereby fill our demand for a skilled work force. We may find a way to help our retired workers and our elderly acquire the new skills we need, and give them a more productive role once again in the workplace. We may find a way for two-worker households to survive without sacrificing the needs of children.

In summary, the changes, in and of themselves, may pave the way for a healthier and more dynamic nation. It's that aspect of the next ten years that excites me the most — the idea of transforming *social challenges* into *new solutions*. When I think of it, maybe that *does* sound a little like the 1960s. Maybe it will work this time around.

21

Union/Management Teamwork

Donald F. Ephlin, International Vice President,
United Auto Workers

I want to talk about union/management teamwork. The teamwork that is taking place in America in the auto industry, as well as in the steel and communications industries, is very impressive.

We are proud of what has happened in the auto industry. The 1989 Rose Parade included a huge float jointly sponsored by the UAW and General Motors dedicated to technology and teamwork. For the first time, a union and management sponsored a parade float together, and it turned out very well. As a matter of fact, we won a prize for the best depiction of life in the United States — and we thought that was very appropriate.

We have heard from Alan Magazine, the current president of the Presidential Council on Competitiveness, at this conference. When President Reagan initially appointed this panel, it was composed entirely of high-tech management people. The chairman of the Council at that time was John Young, the president of Hewlett-Packard. Most of the other members were from other computer and high-tech installations. That was during the period when people thought, "Who needs the old smokestack industries like auto and steel? We are all going to move to Silicon Valley and make a living out there."

Subsequent to the initial appointments, it was decided to add two union representatives to the Council. Howard Samuel, who heads up the industrial union department of the AFL-CIO, and I were appointed. I used to joke about it — here we had a presidential commission on industrial competitiveness and I was the only representative from the auto industry. Most of the CEOs from the high-tech businesses had never dealt with unions, and some of them were notoriously anti-union.

I invited the commission to visit Detroit to see some of the things we had underway. The Saturn study was going on then with our joint training efforts. As a result, this group of people with no union relationship endorsed the advancement of labor/management relations. This is very significant. I have continued to serve with John Young and others on this council. It has now been expanded to include a few more people from unions and some academics, including the president of the Massachusetts Institute of Technology. This group is very concerned with competitiveness, reducing unemployment, and restoring America to its former greatness.

I have been involved with General Motors and the UAW most of my life. When I accept my pension from General Motors in July, 1989, I will have close to 42 years of service with them. So, I have been in this business all my life, principally with GM. And while I have had a wonderful, exciting career, sometimes my timing has been very bad.

I became a union vice president in 1980 and was assigned to the Ford Department just when the bottom fell out of the auto business. Ford was in terrible shape. In fact, had they not had a profitable European subsidiary they might have been out of business if the situation had continued. Although we had made some progress in changing our working relationship with GM management through our quality of work life efforts and other programs since 1973, progress at Ford was very slow. In 1980 the industry was in crisis. Ford needed relief and we in the union understood that. Some very progressive management people at Ford were quick to join in the effort of making productive changes.

Although the union has made concessions in many areas, we have never negotiated any wage cuts in the auto industry. We did give up a paid personal holiday plan which we had started in an effort to shorten the work week. It was necessary to lower our sights as far as economic gains were concerned for a few years. We retained our cost-of-living increase arrangement and we get raises once in awhile, but these amount to less than they would have in the past. It was essential to bring ourselves in line with what our competition was doing. At that point the Japanese had a decided advantage over us. They were able to build cars in Japan and ship them to America for far less than we could produce them.

In going to work on the problem, we changed some very basic things in our labor/management agreement. For instance, we began to address the issue of outsourcing work, which is critical to retaining jobs in-house. We instituted the first really large-scale joint training program at Ford. Five cents an hour was committed into a worker training fund to be jointly administered by the UAW and Ford. In some cases workers were trained so they could find work elsewhere. We knew the industry was shrinking, and we wanted to help people get jobs.

We negotiated a profit-sharing plan at Ford for the first time in 1982. Ford lost $2 billion that year, so profit sharing was no great issue. However, since then the average Ford worker has received approximately $10,000 in profit-sharing payments. As the UAW director, I was invited to address the Ford board of directors on a regular basis. We instituted a very broad-based employee involvement quality improvement program. A lot of highly qualified people worked hard to broaden these joint programs.

I mentioned that my timing was poor. In 1983 I moved back to General Motors just as they fell on hard times. The 1980-81 crisis had not been too severe at GM, but by 1983 — when Ford was going back up — GM was starting down. I got to GM just as Ford was starting to make profit-sharing pay-outs. Ford workers got $3,500, GM workers got zero, and I almost got killed! I guess that's the way the ball bounces. GM's profits were very bad and their problems were really more basic than those at Ford. GM management was very pleased to have the union participate with them in joint efforts to turn General Motors around.

As we approached the 1984 contract negotiations I met with General Motors' management and said, "You know we want to work together to improve productivity and to make our plants more efficient, but you can't ask workers to make that kind of effort if the end result will lay them off." So a joint committee consisting of my staff and General Motors' staff put together the first outline of a job security program, which was introduced in the 1984 bargaining session. As a result of our negotiations, for the first time in our history we arrived at an agreement with the corporation that provided that no one with one year of seniority would be laid off because of the introduction of new technology, outsourcing, or negotiated productivity improvements. That job security agreement has been critical to our subsequent achievements.

By working together, we have made tremendous improvements at General Motors. We have greatly expanded the joint training effort that we started at Ford. We now have a very large, wonderful building in Arbor Hills, Michigan, called the UAW/GM Human Resource Center. It houses our joint staff, as well as some neutral staff that we jointly hire, who administer the largest privately funded training program in the world. We spend in excess of $200 million a year on training General Motors workers. We offer a great variety of programs to meet the different training needs: for in-house work, to facilitate leaving General Motors to start new careers, high-tech training, interpersonal skills training, and other programs. It has been a very successful and rewarding effort.

Our human resource center was so effective that we decided to set up a training program for union leaders. This is the one area where I had a little trouble with Al Warren, GM vice president. When I told him I wanted to have an intense training program for union leaders, he said, "Why in the name of anything would we want to finance teaching people how to file grievances?" I said, "Al, we already know about filing grievances. I am talking about something far more basic."

Eventually we set up a four-week program called Paid Education Leave. We take groups of 25 people to Detroit, where they visit GM headquarters and the UAW. Instructors from Wayne State University and the University of Michigan teach them about the international auto industry. Then they go to Boston for a week to absorb a little culture back in my home territory. People from M.I.T. and Harvard continue teaching them about the competitive situation we are in, international trade, and the various implications of those things.

After their stay in Boston, the training group travels to Washington, DC, where UAW lobbyists and GM representatives take them around and show them how government works and how regulations impact the auto industry. Then they return to Detroit for another week with University of Michigan and Wayne State people. Our union leaders return from this innovative educational experience with a much better understanding of our competitors' situation, the world in which we live, and a realistic view of the future.

This program has helped impact the decision-making process. I explained this to Phil Callwell at Ford one time and he said, "My goodness, don't the people understand the state we're in?" I replied, "Phil, they don't understand the state you're in because you never told them. When you were making all kinds of money you wouldn't give them any numbers, and now that you are losing money you expect them to understand your problem when you have never taught them anything about the business." Back then we instituted the policy of sharing information. At General Motors, this Paid Education Leave program has helped considerably. We now have reduced it to miniature, one-week, local Paid Education Leaves. In many areas around the country we set up one-week programs using community college people. We now draw our participants from jobs-bank people, individuals who are laid off but are covered by the job security program. We are gradually training the entire work force in this fashion.

Even though this is a great program, we realized we were missing out on educating our people in another area. They still needed to know what market share means, where GM is, and what profits are all about. To address this need we started putting out a joint newspaper at GM's Buick-Oldsmobile-Cadillac (BOC) Division, a practice that has now spread throughout the corporation. Our monthly newspaper is similar in format to *USA Today*, using a lot of visuals. One page in every issue is devoted to huge, colorful graphs that clearly show market share, who's selling and who isn't, our competitive costs, a breakdown of labor and health care costs, and all the other things that go into the big picture. We are trying to give the average union member a better understanding of the corporation and the world in which we live.

In 1987, we initiated a team quality improvement effort. When Bob Stemple became GM president in 1987, he asked me to co-chair a corporate-level quality council. Since then we have been working together very closely in instituting the broadest-based, most uniform quality process that General Motors has ever had. It is based on beliefs and values. To have General Motors management concentrate on our beliefs and values was a major step forward. Bob Stemple and I gave a joint statement to *Fortune* magazine that this is the way we are going to work from now on. Yesterday a speaker at this conference talked about a corporation developing their own code and then talking to the union about it. In our case, the code was developed through a cooperative effort.

I am going to Florida on Sunday. Over a six-week period we will have 2,000 union and management people going through a two-and-half-day training program that will focus on understanding the beliefs, values, and philosophy that underlie GM's union-management relationship. An understanding of the way you're going to live and work together is more important than anything in the agreement. Through the quality network process, we are jointly changing the culture of General Motors in a fashion I would never have believed possible.

Lastly, in the 1987 negotiations we included a provision dealing with changing and improving operational effectiveness in the plants. Very briefly, that provision states that in every plant throughout General Motors the manager and the local union leadership have to sit down together, lay out the problems facing their plant, and come up with a plan for improving operational effectiveness. They are required to report that plan to me and GM Vice President Al Warren. We bring together representatives from several plants in a division. One after another the plant representatives stand up in front of us, union and management together, and tell us what they're going to do to improve the operating effectiveness of their plant.

How have these programs worked? Today GM quality is the best in the domestic industry, and we are making inroads on the imports. In a recent survey of the top ten cars, the only three domestic cars included on the list are Buick, Oldsmobile, and Cadillac.

How did our "attack-and-think" operational effectiveness teamwork approach work? In 1987, all the Wall Street analysts were telling GM to get rid of its components, but today GM is still the most highly integrated of the auto companies. If GM had reduced integration to the same level as Ford, 100,000 jobs would have been lost. We didn't think that was a very good idea. We went to work on that problem together through the "attack-and-think" process, which was really underway before the negotiations formalized it. Today the components divisions of General Motors are among its most profitable. The anchor that was pulling GM down is now leading the way, is very profitable, and is helping facilitate the turnaround at General Motors.

Top management at General Motors not only acknowledges that teamwork has helped turn the company around — they are bragging about it. We are putting advertisements in papers and on TV about the contributions that GM workers and the union are making. Teamwork has been mutually advantageous for all of us. It has helped to enhance job security and is supported very widely by the GM workers. That is teamwork at General Motors today.

22

Employee Involvement Is a Partnership

James J. Whaley, Vice President – Personnel Relations,
Bank of America

In a business, who has the know-how? Who has the experience? Who knows the product best? Who knows the customers best? Who brings it all together to meet a customer's needs and make the company successful? Who knows best what's needed to get the job done? The employee.

The underlying philosophy driving any effort to foster employee involvement and commitment to the success of the company is recognition that the employee is the answer to each of those questions.

By employee, I mean everyone who works for the company — secretaries, salespeople, technicians, staff employees, production people, line managers, senior managers. I mean everybody from the chief executive to the entry-level mail clerk. Having everyone working together as a team, as partners, results in better bottom-line profits and more satisfied customers.

The road to this partnership starts with respect for your employees' contributions to the company; with the understanding that your employees have the know-how, the experience, and the commitment to do their jobs well and the creativity to discover ways to do them better.

Employees must believe that management means what it says and has a genuine interest in their ideas and participation. Employees must believe that the company cares about them and about how successfully they are able to perform their jobs.

Bank of America has a strong commitment to ask for, listen to, and act upon employee concerns and ideas. We have been through challenging times for human resources professionals and staff. Through the trials of downsizing and reorganization, management's commitment to encouraging employee involvement has been justified and strengthened.

One reason for the success of employee involvement at Bank of America is the family of programs that make it possible for the bank's employees to feel personally connected to the objectives of the company. That feeling is present because the bank makes an effort to personally connect with its employees.

The Power of Employee Involvement. One special, short-term program vividly illustrates the power of employee involvement. A year ago, our chairman and CEO, Tom Clausen, asked all employees to make a special effort to bring in one new customer during the first quarter. He asked our employees to think about what an impact each of them could make by introducing one new customer to a bank product or service. A special telephone line was set up and widely publicized. We staffed it with people from our Quality of Service Department to help employees find the right product for their new customer and to give advice on how to get the job done. Tom Clausen asked employees to write to him personally on special postcards to tell him about the new customers they introduced to Bank of America. They responded enthusiastically, both in gaining new customers and in writing Tom about new business they had secured. The postcards revealed the pride employees felt when they succeeded in bringing in a new customer or convincing a business associate or neighbor to switch banks. The "one new customer" program worked because Tom Clausen asked employees to make a difference. He told them how important they were to the bank's recovery. During the program, 18,000 postcards came to Tom Clausen — each representing one new customer. Imagine the revenue this represented for the bank.

Our employees make it possible for us to compete with a growing number of competitors in a lively marketplace throughout California and around the world. They must respond efficiently and quickly to both everyday problems and major crises. To do that, employees in every department, service center, and office must be team players. They must feel like partners in the enterprise.

Maybe at one time a company could ignore unnecessary red tape and roadblocks to quality, but those days are over. This is a competitive world. Lower profitability and sometimes failure wait around the corner for companies who fail to build a partnership with their employees.

Effective employee involvement programs must be genuine, credible, and consistent. The employees' perception of each of these three qualities is tied to the other two. You will need all three if your programs are to work. Effective employee involvement programs view communication as a two-way street. They encourage employees to communicate up to management, and are designed to be responsive from the top down, as well. But remember, employee involvement is a bottom-line, results-oriented attitude; not a squishy, theoretical idea originated by social scientists who have never run a business or met a payroll. Employee involvement reflects the basic understanding that people who feel involved with their jobs and their company do better work day-in and day-out than employees who are treated like cogs in a wheel. Employees repay the concern a company demonstrates for them by caring about their jobs and the company's customers.

If you practice genuine two-way communication with all employees, you're more likely to keep your top performers. Costly turnover and training expenses are minimized. You have more control over overhead costs, which is critical to enhanced profits.

Programs to support employee involvement can create a lively, dynamic, and very human work atmosphere that has a positive effect on the bottom line.

The programs I am responsible for as Director of Personnel Relations are built on principals of upward communication, confidentiality, openness, and action. They all provide ways for employees to be heard and to make a difference — to be partners.

These programs provide communications alternatives that demonstrate the bank's commitment to enhancing quality of work life. They use education and training about work and life issues to prevent problems that can hurt productivity.

The impact of each individual program depends on how committed management is to genuine and consistent follow-through. Where follow-through is weak, results show it.

Employee Opinion Surveys. An employee opinion survey is a good place to start, because it reveals the strengths and weaknesses inside an organization. However, to be credible the survey must result in action. A survey is a huge undertaking in an organization the size of our bank, but it addresses the need to listen and points to what needs to be fixed. A confidential survey measures a variety of employee attitudes and concerns. The process makes managers accountable for addressing the concerns and problems that surface in the survey results.

After the survey results are in, employees and their managers meet in formal feedback sessions to discuss the issues raised and the changes that can or cannot be made. Action plans are developed by managers at all levels of the organization. And at each level the plans focus on what the individual manager can realistically accomplish. The plans define responsibility for action and reveal those situations where managers need to "manage up" to get something done.

Senior executives receive summary reports of the survey results that give them a clear general understanding of employee attitudes and where action is needed. These senior managers then formulate their own action plans to address the global issues that cross unit and division responsibility.

The process exposes problems as well as what is going right. We compare the results of each new survey with those from past surveys. We also exchange survey results with other companies who are members of a professional survey organization consisting of major U.S. companies. In this way, we can see the progress we're making in relation to our own past and in comparison to our peers. We use this information to become a stronger, more responsive organization.

One issue raised in last fall's employee opinion survey is cited in many organizations as a continuing problem: *too much red tape and bureaucracy* blocking employees from doing a good job.

The bank has several good programs to eliminate bureaucracy and build teamwork. These programs are devoted to opening up a two-way dialogue between employees and management, and helping employees perform more productively.

Ideas In Action. Our "Ideas in Action" program is a good example of a long-term employee involvement program with a potent incentive — cash awards to employees whose ideas are implemented.

An employee with a brainstorm that will save money or improve service describes it in writing and sends it to "Ideas in Action." The employee "owns" the idea for one year. If the time isn't right to put it into operation, ownership can be renewed. The idea goes to experts who decide whether the idea is workable and what its potential impact and cost savings may be.

The largest "Ideas in Action" award is $50,000. The size of the award is based on the projected savings it will generate over the first five years of use. If an idea can't be measured in saved dollars but would bring about other improvements, it is evaluated on other criteria, such as better customer service or improved morale. Then a dollar value is assigned.

During the past five years, $2 million has been awarded to 1,200 employees. The bank saved *$30 million* during that time as a direct result of the program.

What's in the Way? Bank of America's newest employee involvement program — called "What's in the Way?" — is another example of using direct, personal, two-way communication to eliminate red tape and inefficiency. It has produced measurable bottom-line results.

Managers ask employees to give their candid views of what stands in the way of productivity, efficiency, and excellent customer service. Employees are asked to get *directly involved* in finding solutions to the roadblocks that are frustrating their efforts.

The emphasis of "What's in the Way?" is action. Managers are required to respond personally to employees concerning what *can* and *will* be done about problems. Solutions are identified and implemented without delay.

Together, managers and employees use "What's in the Way?" to increase productivity and morale and — best of all — to improve customer service.

It is a partnership that works.

Answering Employee Questions. But what if an employee has a question about a procedural or operational matter? What if he doesn't understand a bank policy, or she has a question about a management decision?

The "Open Line" program helps employees get answers to these kinds of questions. "Open Line" began 16 years ago and continues to provide confidential, upward, two-way communication.

Anonymity is assured, because only the program administrator knows who signed the original letter. Because the program makes it safe for employees to be frank, "Open Line" often deals with issues that employees feel deeply about. The most appropriate senior manager is chosen to respond within a strict time frame to each "Open Line" inquiry.

"Open Line" is a valuable conduit for good ideas, serious concerns, and suggestions for change. It gives employees the opportunity to be heard and lets managers clarify and explain the "whys" or the "why nots."

It also provides a forum to explain and respond to questions about the corporation's strategies, goals, and ideals. Questions and answers of general interest from "Open Line" are printed in one of the bank's employee publications, *On Your Behalf*, which we use to share information with our entire work force.

But what if an employee has a specific concern? For example, what if his problem, as he sees it, is his manager or a coworker? We have a channel to help employees deal with these concerns, as well. It's called "Let's Talk."

"Let's Talk" helps resolve work-related problems promptly. Employees are encouraged to go first to their immediate manager about anything that is upsetting them. If the problem is not resolved at that point, it is taken up the management ladder to the most senior level in the division. An executive officer appoints an investigator, who talks with the employee and anybody else involved.

The investigator reports back to the executive, who makes a decision and communicates directly with the employee about it. If the employee isn't satisfied with the decision, an appeal is possible.

Underlying all of these programs is a vital truth: Backing up what you say you will do for your employees with action is critical to success. At Bank of America, our partnership with employees is reinforced with recognition and rewards.

Recognition and Rewards. Our pay philosophy reflects the importance the bank places on open, two-way communication in the partnership between the company and its employees. Our goal is to pay for performance. Performance is built on clear objectives and is evaluated regularly.

The degree to which an employee meets or exceeds his or her objectives determines the size and timing of salary increases — and it can sometimes lead to special bonuses, awards, and recognition.

Exceptional performance awards and the CEO's "Eagle Pin" awards celebrate employees whose special efforts make a difference. This recognition for employees who go beyond the call of duty is important. These awards are presented publicly in front of peers, and the names of "Eagle" winners appear in the weekly newsletter, which is distributed bankwide.

Whether we communicate with newsletters, videotapes, or in person during senior officer "walkarounds," we want to build that sense of partnership and communicate our commitment to a productive work environment that ties individual effort to unit and company goals.

We want to bridge any misunderstandings and explain the company's strategy and objectives. Employees need to know where they fit into the big picture.

And we want to answer — with actions — the question: "Does this company care about me?" We want to make the answer to that question a convincing "Yes!"

Our employee involvement programs also extend into personal and family issues — *life* issues — that affect how productive an employee can be at work.

The bank is committed to ongoing employee assistance programs that enhance not only the quality of the work environment, but also our employees' overall quality of life. Bank of America concerns itself with people — not just as workers with jobs to do, but as human beings who have personal and family needs and problems.

The Role of Personnel Relations Specialists. The personnel relations specialists who work with me are the essential links in these assistance programs. I would describe them and the assistance programs they personify as the heart of Bank of America.

Each division has a personnel relations specialist assigned to it whose job it is to listen and be objective and nonjudgmental, regardless of the particular problem or situation brought to him or her. These personnel specialists offer guidance and compassion. They counsel. They make referrals. They get involved. They follow up.

And they constantly develop new resources and information that can be used to assist employees.

Any employee can contact a personnel relations representative directly for confidential help with:

- Alcohol and chemical dependency,
- A personal crisis or trauma,
- Life-threatening illness, such as AIDS or cancer,
- Child care,
- Elder care,
- Crushing financial difficulties,
- Grief and personal loss,
- Marital or other family problems, and
- Other personal concerns that have a direct impact on how the employee performs in the workplace.

Regardless of why an employee calls us, our aim is to put that employee in touch with the help he or she needs to make it possible to overcome the difficulty and resolve the situation before it negatively affects job performance.

We want to prevent problems. And if we can't prevent them, we want to help solve them before things get any worse. We do this by emphasizing education, confidential communication, and referrals to appropriate outside resources.

Our alcohol and drug program is a good example. Today we know that chemical dependency is an illness that can be treated and controlled successfully with professional help. Some of our country's brightest and most successful people have been affected.

Qualified case management is the key to our program, providing high-quality care outside the company to help our employees overcome their illness. And we share the cost. Nothing is ever recorded in an employee's personnel file and nobody is told about it unless the employee chooses to do so.

Many times employees fear they'll be putting their job at risk by acknowledging their problem, but they quickly find out that using our program will *not* get them fired. We are only interested in helping individuals conquer these problems before they threaten their lives.

Other employee assistance programs address life-threatening illnesses such as cancer and AIDS. The bank has been recognized as a national leader on the issue of AIDS in the workplace. We have demonstrated our commitment to education, counseling, and support services not only for those who have the disease, but also for fellow employees and managers who are unsure about how to deal with the knowledge that a coworker has a life-threatening condition.

We refer employees to agencies and organizations that offer supportive services, and we help clarify the benefits available to assist affected employees with health care costs, leave, and the critical issues they face.

A terrible emotional toll is taken when people grapple with the loss, or potential loss, of a loved one or a coworker. We often refer employees to grief counseling to help them work through it.

Employees also often need help with other kinds of personal and family concerns to enable them to concentrate on their job responsibilities. The bank understands that it is hard to do your best work when you're worried about your children or an elderly parent who needs care, or about an important relationship.

Personnel relations specialists can refer employees to child care and elder care resources. If an employee asks for other types of assistance or counseling, we listen and try to refer them to the most appropriate outside agency or professional.

When an employee needs to change the conditions at work in order to deal more effectively with other areas of their lives, we help the team work together to find solutions. Flexible working hours, job sharing, leaves of absence, transfers to other positions and new locations can often answer an employee's needs. We are willing to accommodate employees as long as business needs continue to be met.

Some may wonder why Bank of America goes to all this trouble. We are deeply committed to employee involvement programs and employee assistance programs for one reason: We know that when employees feel valued, when we show that we *care* about them, when we are willing to listen and respond to their needs, we create a company where all employees work together and our business needs are met.

You can call it by many different names. Enlightened self-interest is one that comes to mind. But providing channels of communication — listening, responding, explaining, and following through, when possible — is the *heart* of employee involvement and the equation for a caring partnership.

PART VI

The Information
Systems Equation

23

Strategic Information Management

Mylle H. Bell, Director of Corporate Planning,
BellSouth

I would like to suggest two ideas to keep in mind about information management — (1) information is a tool and (2) management is a function. The key question is, how do we manage information better to manage a company better?

Today, information management is shifting from being mainly an operations support function to becoming a strategic management function. In an organization, the scope of information use varies from a narrow level — where it only affects a single person or single business unit — to a broader level, where the information facilitates the conducting of business between organizations.

Strategic information management builds on the foundation of earlier evolutionary stages in managing functional or departmental information: paperwork management, management of automated technologies, information resources management, and analysis of information management as it relates to strategic advantage.

The focus of my discussion will be this last stage: the evolution of the strategic management of information as part of the strategic planning for the firm, or what I am terming "strategic information management."

The objective of strategic information management is to integrate information technologies and the management of information resources into the strategic or overall management of the firm. A prerequisite is building a reliable information technology infrastructure. When the value-added processes that naturally evolve from information systems are applied to internal operations and change how the business unit competes, this application can be called strategic.

Businesses need to search for ways to communicate better. The industry that I work for, telecommunications, can play a major role in this. In fact, telecommunications plays a major role in every firm that successfully manages information strategically.

To play the new information technology game, a firm needs at the very least to:

- Assess the strategic information resources of the industry and potential competitors;
- Search systematically for uses of information technology to gain or maintain competitive advantage, or to reduce the edge of a competitor; and
- Be aware of the strategic uses of information technology, including the development of new lines of business.

Let's talk about each of these. First, assess the strategic information resources of your industry and potential competitors. Information technology can affect the structure of an industry by creating barriers to entry, by changing the balance of power between suppliers and buyers, or by introducing new substitute products.

The classic example of this is the airline industry, where the development of sophisticated reservations systems has reduced the level of competition by making it more difficult for smaller airlines, which don't have these systems to compete. The result has been a significant trend toward consolidation and an improvement in the general attractiveness of the industry.

Second, information technology can create a competitive advantage for the firm. What is more, the advantage is likely to be relatively sustainable because of the expense and time involved in developing a strategic information system.

Again, airline reservations systems provide a good example. American and United are profiting from their extensive systems, while those without systems or with smaller systems are suffering.

It is interesting to note in this regard that Texas Air, with the nation's fourth-largest computer system, has just sued both American and United for using their systems unfairly to make it difficult or impossible for travel agents to book flights on Texas Air's Continental and Eastern flights.

Third, new developments in information technology have spawned whole new businesses. American Airlines, for example, now makes more profit from its SABRE information system than it does from flying. Supermarkets can now offer valuable marketing information developed from the bar codes on the products they sell. Financial institutions have used information technology to create a host of new products, like Merrill Lynch's hugely successful cash management account. Even American Express sells its know-how in billing and collections to those who don't have that expertise.

These new revenue sources all grew from areas of existing businesses that, in the past, didn't generate any revenue. Information technology has turned expertise into new lines of business.

Company-Wide Information Technology. Let's look at two examples of companywide information technology at work: two proven winners, Benetton and Wal-Mart.

Both Benetton and Wal-Mart use state-of-the-art computer and telecommunications equipment in their information management systems. How did they become winners in their respective industries? They put together systems that fit the specific needs of their industry. They also simply work harder than anyone else at communicating better. Benetton and Wal-Mart put their internal information power to work, and do it better than anyone else. Information is power.

Benetton. Benetton, the Italian sportswear retailer, owes much of its explosive growth to strategic information management. Benetton manufactures garments quickly and gets them into its stores quickly. Benetton understands the buying preferences of its customers and puts that information to work.

Founded in 1968 with one store, Benetton grew to 1,000 stores in Italy by 1978. It now has over 4,300 retail stores around the world and 700 stores in the United States, Benetton's largest market outside Italy. In only 20 years, the company has become Europe's largest clothing maker. Its U.S. sales alone were just over $1 billion dollars last year.

The jump from a single store to thousands came over a period of 20 years. Those years were spent developing one of the most sophisticated information management systems in the business world. Benetton's computer systems are the nerve center of the company and control all operations from production to shipping to inventory control. The key element is that Benetton's system fits the company's needs and helps the company respond quickly to customer preferences.

Benetton's information management system is integrated into all aspects of the management process. Clothes are designed and cut at the company's computer-aided design center. Computers are used to lay out cutting patterns, reducing wasted material to only 5 percent. Designers use electronic pencils to tap in sweater coordinates on an actual-size matrix, which are then video-checked and sent to the cutting room, where three automatic machines can cut more than 70 sweaters in 8 minutes. Orders are then collated at the information center and sent to fully automated warehouses.

Benetton manufactures no garment until it is ordered. The time it takes from the moment a garment order is processed until the garment arrives in a local store is between 10 and 15 days.

Benetton's data transmission system provides daily updates on sales at the company's stores in 57 countries. Daily updates allow tight control on manufacturing, inventory, and stock cycles. Without the telecommunications to allow quick turnaround times, Benetton's information management system would not work — or at least not work as well in these times, where speeding products to market is essential. Speed to market can make the difference between profit and loss.

Benetton owes much of its explosive growth and success to across-the-board time compression. Time compression — cutting time out of the design and manufacturing process — is integral to its strategic information management process. Information management and telecommunications play major roles in compressing time in the product development cycle.

Time compression at Benetton starts in new product development, where a computer-aided design terminal automatically expands a new design into a full range of sizes, and then transmits these patterns to computer-controlled fabric cutting machines to await orders for the new product. Fabric is inventoried in and then cut and dyed to order. This allows the company to minimize inventory and respond quickly to customer demand. Orders are then sent to a group of just-in-time factories that allow Benetton to restock the retail shelves in its U.S. stores in only 15 days.

Benetton satisfies the ever-changing preferences of its customers by restocking garments quickly through strategic information management. The information management process allows it to bring products to market quickly, and it allows it to cut costs associated with over-production and under-production as well.

Benetton's key strength is that it finds out what its customers want and responds quickly to changing customer demands through information management.

Wal-Mart. The second company that employs strategic information management effectively is Wal-Mart.

Some of you may not be familiar with Wal-Mart, since it has not expanded into Utah yet. But you have probably heard that it is coming. I am sure Sears and K-Mart have heard that it is coming, too.

Wal-Mart, like Benetton, has grown from a single store in the 1960s to the position it enjoys today through strategic information management. Wal-Mart's information management system, along with its other retailing innovations, has allowed the company to overtake all other retailers in sales and to threaten the retailing giants like Sears and K-Mart.

How would a company retail the Wal-Mart way? It would employ extensive inventory tracking and sophisticated computers, all tied together with telecommunications. Wal-Mart uses computer scanners to track sales and monitor supplies on shelves in each store. Individual stores beam orders via satellite to a computer center at Wal-Mart headquarters in Bentonville, Arkansas. Suppliers coordinate shipping to resupply Wal-Mart's needs. The products are shipped to one of Wal-Mart's regional warehouses and shipped to stores in one of Wal-Mart's 6,500 trucks. Within 36 hours of the individual store's order, the new products are available in the store. Wal-Mart then uses its satellite television network to tell its store managers about discounts on new inventory.

All of Wal-Mart's retailing steps save time and money. Wal-Mart, like Benetton, uses technology and telecommunications to compress time and save the customer money. The company has its own distribution and delivery system because of the remote location of many stores. Wal-Mart orders inventory directly from manufacturers and does not use distributors, thus eliminating the middle-man. Orders to suppliers are coordinated with sales and inventory by bar code and are ordered via satellite. All of Wal-Mart's retailing steps that use telecommunications and information management cut time, save money, and assure the customer that Wal-Mart's "everyday low price" policy is a reality.

Wal-Mart's information management system has been compared to that of the Defense Department in its level of sophistication. This is totally unexpected from a company that prides itself on its homespun image. In fact, many people underestimated Wal-Mart in the past, considering them to be the country bumpkins of retailing. Wal-Mart comes off a little like the old country lawyer who seems a little dumb at first until you realize you've lost your case, and then you realize he's pretty sharp after all.

In reality, Wal-Mart has used information management systems for many years. Its saves time and money at every opportunity using information management. Its sophisticated information management system is one of the primary reasons for its incredible revenue numbers and rapid nationwide expansion.

Both Benetton and Wal-Mart have implemented information technology systems that are helping them win their markets by knowing their customers better and satisfying customer needs. Benetton uses information management to manufacture and stock its stores quickly. Wal-Mart uses information management to cut costs and keep prices low. Both companies tailored their systems to serve the needs of the overall company.

However, information technology can create some serious implementation problems for the uninitiated: There are so many options to choose from developed by an entirely separate industry for evaluating hardware and software systems. Since the really revolutionary developments have been unanticipated, most managers have simply been unprepared to exploit them. Usually the information technology, the systems, and the information resources inside the firm develop differently than expected. Sometimes this leads to additional headaches: Whatever system you wind up with may not do what you originally intended it to do, and modification of an existing complex information system is a real nightmare.

Every business must have a realistic picture of its relative strengths and weaknesses in managing and using information resources and technology. Whether the firm is oriented toward cost leadership, product differentiation, or a mix of both, the executives in that firm will need to evaluate the costs of improving their information management strategies along several key dimensions: opportunity costs, financial costs, risk tradeoffs, timing costs, attitudinal and motivational costs, costs for upgrading existing resources, and uncertainty costs, to name a few.

Each of these cost considerations and the corresponding actual or potential benefits must be assessed directly in the context of the firm's business performance and sources of competitive advantage.

What Can Be. We have been talking about "what is." Now let's turn for a moment to "what can be." As the Apple Computer lecturer at this conference, I felt obliged to include a videotape from Apple showing the potential for integrated information management on the personal level. Of course, this type of integrated information management has implications for businesses as well. The tape is called "The Knowledge Navigator."

"The Knowledge Navigator" implements aspects of information technology that businesses have been striving for in their information systems. The device the professor interacts with blends many aspects of life that we are all familiar with into the information system: it is book-shaped, it is voice-driven, it is easy to use. It also performs some secretarial, organizational, and research functions that would make our work life easier. This brings to mind a comparison with information and management.

As I mentioned earlier, information is a tool, and management is a function. Computers and telecommunications equipment are also tools, and our working life is the function they serve.

Technology, as a part of the information management structure, must function efficiently in the entire information management system. The information management system as a whole should not be technology for technology's sake. It must be a better idea: it should be easy to use, it should be convenient, and it should be more efficient.

In other words, financial costs alone should not be the dominant dimension against which information management strategies are evaluated. A business may squander its information resources if it is "penny wise and pound foolish" as surely as when it is lavish in its expenditures on dazzling technologies or new automated databases.

I will conclude with a few cautions:

1. Select an information management strategy that reinforces your firm's overall business performance and competitive advantage.
2. Ensure that the information management strategies of business units and functional units are closely linked.
3. Remember the link between business and world telecommunications.

It is not enough to recognize that there is a connection between technology and strategy. Despite the fact that we spend a lot of time talking about this connection, nothing can be done about making real use of information technologies unless we remove the barriers imposed by existing structures, corporate cultures, management processes, and the skill levels of our work force. We have all seen that the world is indeed a much smaller place today. On 1988's Black Monday, the New York Stock Exchange sent the London and Tokyo markets on a tumble within minutes instead of hours. Telecommunications has the power to link cultures and businesses. A recently opened data link between the Soviet Union and the United States allows scientists and businesses to pass information across borders as never before. Soon we may be able to instantly translate languages.

Telecommunications has the power to merge voice, data, and video into a powerful information stream. And, as we have seen with innovative firms such as Benetton and Wal-Mart, telecommunications can link businesses together for greater efficiency than ever before.

In summary, the one phrase I hope all of you will take home and remember is *information is power.*

24

Implications of the Changing Information Environment

John Diebold, Chairman, The Diebold Group

During the 1990s, changes in the information technology environment outside the corporation will have broad implications for senior management that go far beyond today's MIS or information systems function. Regardless of what companies do with their internal information systems, senior managers must focus on external changes in the information landscape and how those changes will impact the way businesses are organized and managed.

Until recently, information technology played only a fragmented role in most industries, usually as a support or back-office function. That is changing rapidly. Companies are increasingly investing in strategic information systems for competitive positioning. According to the latest government figures, U.S. businesses invested at least one-third of their 1987 capital expenditures investment in information technology.

Information technology will play an even greater role in business in the future. To understand the information environment of the 1990s, imagine a world in which ordinary people with no technical expertise will be continually accessing all kinds of information systems in the course of the day, both at work and at home. Computers will be embedded in automobiles, in appliances — even in the human body.

Information systems will be accessible by more natural means: voice, touch, or even just thinking a command. Advances in superconductivity will change the way we organize information, and the very structure of computing.

Information technology and its applications are increasingly becoming part of societal infrastructure systems that link consumers, businesses, government agencies, and other institutions. As a result of constant exposure to information systems — such as "smart" television sets and automated bank machines — consumers are changing their behavior patterns. Institutional relationships must adjust in response to these societal changes.

The new environment will change the way businesses interrelate with each other at all levels — from suppliers to distributors to customers. Many companies will find that the very nature or definition of their business is being revised. And the new technological options will raise profound questions about the way we organize and staff our businesses, make investment decisions, and plan for the future.

The Changing Information Environment of the 1990s. The challenge for business managers will be to develop the skills and outlook necessary for coping with a very different information environment. To understand what the future impact of information technology will be, it may be useful to look back for a moment at how far we have come in a very short time.

I founded my company in 1954, which was the year that the first computer was installed for business use. During the 1950s the big question was whether a large company could use *one* computer. By the 1960s it became a question of whether a division or subsidiary of the company would use a computer. In the 1970s it became departments. Now, in the 1980s, it is the individual employee. Some of our clients have more personal computers than people in their organizations. Some enterprises have a 3-to-1 ratio of computers to people. An individual may have a machine in the office, a machine in the laboratory, and a machine at home — and sometimes portable versions as well.

The nature of information processing has also changed. In the 1950s and 1960s, information technology was centralized. Today it is highly decentralized. The MIS manager of a company used to be a wholesaler who dealt with a small number of highly specialized "customers." Today he is a retailer: He may have to deal with thousands or tens of thousands of relatively untrained people who are directly utilizing the technology. In more and more organizations the driving force is the users, not the MIS activity.

In today's world an enormous number of public policy issues are concerned with computers. Many of these issues are of direct economic concern to the managers of enterprises, and range from privacy protection to transborder data flow to intellectual property rights. U.S. Commerce Department figures indicate an annual loss of $60 billion in U.S. balance of payments on unenforced intellectual property rights. That represents half our trade deficit!

There has been a vast change in a relatively short period of time in this field.

The information industry is now capable of building systems for handling information to do whatever we want. Through a long succession of technological innovations, we have built ever more complex, ever cheaper systems. There is, I believe, no other industry that has seen such a continuing decline in the cost of technology. That is the key to the improving human-machine interface: the ability to talk with machines and have them talk back, and to have very high-definition video — including 3-D imagery. Interfacing technology with virtually any activity will have been achieved in a very brief time span.

The essence of any human organization is communication. We are changing the information-handling function of organizations, which means we are going to fundamentally change the nature of all of our social organizations and institutions. It is not a question of managing organizations the way they were, but of changing organizations and managing both the process of change and the new form of the organization.

A Conceptual Model. Our firm recently developed an unusual, proprietary conceptual model of the future of the information technology industry. In a period of enormous structural changes in the information environment, we felt it would be useful to develop a model of these changes to guide us in conducting our regular consulting assignments, so that we might base our client recommendations on a common foundation.

This two-year internal study traced the probable evolution of the information technology industry through the 1990s. We put substantial resources into this research, and the results have been most interesting. Surprisingly, our most compelling findings had to do not with the *suppliers* of information technology, but with the *users*.

Let me mention some of the outside environmental changes that will have a major impact on how businesses of all kinds are organized and operated.

New Communication Paths. We are accustomed to thinking of people communicating with other people and with machines, but many other communication paths are possible, including communication from individuals to inanimate objects, or from one inanimate object to another — say, communications from a truck to another truck, or from a mainframe to a truck.

As new communication paths open among people, machines, buildings, and other inanimate objects, new possibilities abound: Buildings will "talk" to other buildings or with delivery vehicles; home appliances will communicate with other appliances; vehicles will talk to roads and to other vehicles, all without human intervention.

As electronic road maps begin to appear on computer screens in automobiles, a new advertising vehicle will be created for restaurants, hotels, and filling stations that want to appear on those maps.

As we go through the 1990s, business relationships will start to subtly change.

Electronic Data Interchange. The saturation level of computers in businesses is at a point where Electronic Data Interchange (EDI) is a reality. Most businesses that can use a computer now have one, and inter-business communication from one computer to another will become ever more common. Organizations will increasingly exchange data, voice, and image transmissions directly. As more and more businesses require suppliers to be part of their EDI system and distribution network, the internal functioning of companies will certainly be affected.

Infrastructure Services. In our conceptual model of the future, infrastructure services represent a large industry segment involving massive projects. In many countries, common carriers and information services will converge and evolve into this segment. These services will be provided by third parties rather than the users, and will facilitate other activities in the economy.

These activities may include basic integrated services digital network (ISDN) services, database services, transaction-based videotex services, maintenance, nonlocalized monitoring and control systems, educational uses, universal security systems, and entertainment. An example would be a highway traffic control and collision avoidance system.

Societal infrastructure services might include medical service delivery to homes — an area of major current research and investment. We may see government-to-business systems: For example, pharmaceutical companies might develop a network linked with government review agencies to shorten the drug-approval process by a year or two. Many kinds of infrastructure systems are developing, and individual companies must decide whether to take part and whether to take a leading role in this development.

New Marketing Processes. Fifty percent of the retail outlets in the United States now have scanning devices to read bar codes on products. These point-of-sale (POS) technologies give retailers and manufacturers a wealth of detailed data on consumer buying habits. The information gathered at store checkout counters is shifting the balance of power from packaged-goods companies to distributors, who can know precisely what combination of things are bought at what moment, in what store, in which area.

One of the outcomes will be a very large shift in advertising expenditures, as packaged-goods manufacturers shift from general advertising to individual store promotion because of information gleaned from the bar code scanners and point-of-sale technology.

As more sophisticated analyses and uses are made of this information, we will see further changes in the marketing process. In addition, compound document processing — allowing the manipulation of image, data, and even voice files on a single computer screen — will expand the marketing channels available to businesses. Electronic kiosks in stores and shopping centers will allow consumers to shop for anything from real estate to furniture and see full-color moving pictures combined with drawings, floor plans, and other data. Home videotex will be another important conduit for new forms of information and transaction-based services. As consumers grow accustomed to this environment, their behavior changes will further influence marketing processes.

Information Systems Users Become Suppliers. Another important development that was clear in our conceptual model is the extent to which the user of information systems is becoming a supplier, to the point of selling information services and even computer hardware and components.

There are a number of interesting examples: SwissAir, Alitalia, British Airways, and KLM, along with USAir in the United States, recently paid half a billion dollars for a 50-percent interest in United Airline's Apollo reservation system. That was certainly much more than an investment in reservations activity; it was a strategic investment. It was a recognition that Apollo has a billion-dollar valuation, not by virtue of its hardware and software components, but because of the value of information and its impact on marketing. Travel agents that use an airline's reservations network are more likely to book customers on that airline, providing a significant competitive edge to the carrier. The airline business has become, in essence, an information business: one-third of the net profit of the American Airlines parent company comes from the sale of information.

McKesson Corporation, a San Francisco-based pharmaceutical distributor, is now supplying hand-held scanners and a wide range of hardware and software packages to client drugstores. It is part of a competitive strategy of locking in customers. McKesson also sells market data gleaned from its computers to industry analysts. The technology is thus changing sales and distribution channels, competitive strategies, and even the very mission of enterprises.

New Consumer Products. A major segment of the information technology industry of the 1990s does not exist today. It will be based on entirely new products that stretch the imagination — from memory enhancers implanted in the human body to new communication devices to all manner of product-embedded computers.

As we progress through the 1990s, these kinds of changes will clearly become larger, more important, more numerous, and much more interesting and dynamic. What are the implications for the user and individual companies?

Managerial Implications of the New Information Environment. The building of an information technology infrastructure is underway throughout the economy. This infrastructure — with integrated systems that allow the sharing of information resources — extends to suppliers, distributors, customers, consumers, and government regulators.

When these external environmental changes are added to substantial internal corporate changes and advances in new technology, the implications for organizing and managing businesses are substantial. The following are specific examples of the implications of these external changes in the information environment:

1. Industries that have traditionally invested little in R&D but that are deeply affected by information technology may need to allocate more funds to technical research.

   The U.S. newspaper industry, which is a very big, profitable industry, reinvests less than two-thousandths of 1 percent of sales in R&D. By contrast, other industries reinvest a much larger percentage of profits in R&D — typically 2 to 4 percent. The newspaper industry's lack of R&D investment is particularly serious, for it is an industry that is being turned upside down by technology. Other industries that have historically put very little into research and development, such as financial services, will also see a big change — not just in terms of budgeting, but in the very role of technology within the business.

2. As more and more information systems are designed to serve multiple organizations, serious questions will be raised internally as to the assignment of responsibility for external systems:
   • Which organization is responsible for developing systems that link two or more organizations?
   • Which organization is responsible for maintaining them?
   • Where within the organization do these development and maintenance responsibilities lie? Is it the job of the MIS director? The marketing director?
   • The decision on whether to participate in an EDI system is a crucial one. If a business or industry chooses not to participate in EDI, what position should it take toward other companies developing such interconnections? Should it support developing an infrastructure that may help its customers but perhaps also its competitors?

3. When use of information technology represents a competitive weapon, companies will need to think hard about which technologies they support — and which will benefit their competitors more than themselves. For example, electronic kiosks in shopping centers may offer important marketing opportunities to some retailers, but the same technology might hurt another type of

retailer whose goods or services might not be seen to the best advantage on such kiosks. Companies offered the opportunity of investing in a system of shopping mall kiosks should ask whether such a move would turn out to be a better strategic weapon for their competition than for themselves.

4. The extent of forward or backward integration of business units may be decreased in some industries because of the capabilities presented by EDI and infrastructure services. Businesses may come to depend more heavily on suppliers and middlemen.

As the number of information loops and subloops increases in the supply and distribution chain, it allows the corporation to reconsider its capital utilization with regard to both forward and backward integration. If better communication channels allow tighter controls over jobbers and suppliers, an enterprise can free up precious capital from vertical integration, thereby easing the constraints of business cycles, and deploy that capital in other areas.

For example, as EDI comes into the automotive industry, the change in the role of suppliers and distributors can have a major economic impact, and this can happen in other industries. This is an important example of the extensive implications of information technology for business strategy.

Recommendations and Questions. These seem to me to be some of the fundamental implications of major changes on the horizon. The new information environment will raise profound questions about the way we organize and staff our organizations, make investment decisions, and plan for the future.

Recommendations.

- Rethink the definition of your business. Consider the example of Du Pont, which abandoned pioneering work on the silicon chip because it did not fit Du Pont's definition of its business. Today information technology is integral to Du Pont's business, as it is to many other industries, and it will continue to challenge the very definition of the mission of enterprises.
- Cultivate human resources for a fast-paced, competitive environment.
- Consider taking an active role in creating an information infrastructure. This might extend from government regulatory bodies to suppliers to developers, and ultimately to consumers.
- Explore new information products. These might include diagnostic software, market analyses drawn from point-of-sale data, and so forth.

- Ask some rather basic questions of yourself — a key element in the strategic planning process. Some of these questions might include the following.

Questions. Changes in the information environment raise serious questions that are not normally thought of as issues to be resolved by MIS. Although they include much broader areas of business, they pose several questions for MIS as well.

- Who should be responsible for tracking how changes in the external information environment affect functions within the organization? Should it be the MIS department? Whether it be MIS or an end-user department, where the responsibility is assigned should be clear.
- Does information technology call for a reexamination of the investment criteria used for making decisions about information systems? Traditional return-on-investment (ROI) criteria may be inappropriate where the technology is a critical part of competitive strategy or where it is used experimentally. For example, if information technology is essential to a company's customer service function, that alone should be an investment criterion. However, once a strategic decision is made, traditional investment guidelines may be helpful in selecting among competing implementation alternatives.
- How should career paths be structured within the organization to develop staff with an understanding of the information environment? This is an important question for both top management and MIS. Businesses still lack an effective bridge between technological and business skills.

  Companies needs information managers with the vision to grasp the opportunities that exist in the technological environment of the 1990s — who can understand not just yesterday's and today's business, but tomorrow's business as well. Where can top managers locate such talent?

  Should senior executives be rotated with MIS managers? Should MIS officers serve on corporate committees for strategy and planning? Should there be a chief information officer in charge of developing information resources?

Questions Specifically for MIS. While the answers to these questions are still evolving, senior management needs to grapple with the problem of developing an understanding of the information environment, and to bridge that with business strategy and management.

- What kind of career paths should be developed for MIS professionals to prepare them for their important new role in meeting strategic business goals?

- What new attitudes and outlooks are necessary, and how can these best be cultivated?
- Does current MIS staff include people with the know-how and potential necessary for a contribution in strategic areas? Do these people have appropriate visibility and incentives?
- How should the information management function be organized to best support end-user computing from laboratory to marketing applications, while ensuring a coordinated approach to corporate strategic opportunities?
- How can MIS contribute properly focused strategic suggestions to senior management with adequate credibility?
- How can information managers develop a consensus on the proper allocation of scarce resources between strategic and operational needs?

Conclusions. Information managers are under increasing pressure to adjust their information system priorities to meet corporate strategic goals and to respond to a changing information environment. MIS directors will be called upon to acquire an understanding of business strategy. There is a strong argument that the MIS activity ought to be part of the formal planning and strategy process of the business.

Meanwhile, a top priority is developing career paths for MIS staffers with business skills. MIS managers will need to develop human resource management skills in order to handle the kind of situations I have been describing. Capable, bright, young people coming up in the organization will need the latitude to be able to respond to the changing information environment.

Beyond MIS, information technology has an enormous impact on the development of human resources throughout a company. It will be increasingly important for line managers to understand technology. After all, much of the technological innovation in your companies will come from end-user departments. It will become necessary to focus much more attention on familiarizing line officers with MIS activities. If not, how does one achieve that crucial crossover between technical and business skills?

These issues are worthy of our most serious attention, and will be an area of continuing study by The Diebold Group.

25

Trends in Information Technology: Human and Business Changes

James R. Metzger, General Manager,
Department of Information Technology, Texaco

I think it is important for all of us to understand the new trends in information technology (IT). When I graduated from Rice University, there was no such thing as a computer science degree or a microcomputer. Opportunities in the area were very restricted. Basically, you normally came into an information group to support the accountants. That is probably the biggest single area that computers grew up in — the ability to account better. We weren't very creative at that point in time. What has happened to us since is a technology explosion.

We need to start thinking, as information technology professionals who have responsibility for the strategies associated with our field, about the tremendous human implications associated with this. There are also tremendous business opportunities associated with it.

I will contend that the basically hierarchical organization of most of our companies is not adequate for the information environment that we are moving toward. If you ask a corporate CEO to list various areas that they think are problems, one of the areas that they are probably going to list for you is communication, whether it is internal communication, communication with their own management team, communication with customers, or communication with other businesses. The hierarchical style of organization makes it very difficult to communicate in the world that we are living in today.

One of the earlier speakers talked about the fact that in hierarchical organizations the people at the next level are there to say no. I call that a bunch of people who have veto power who add nothing of value to the process. Information technology is changing the world so rapidly that we can't afford to continue to be organized that way.

Adjusting to Technological Change. Now, we need to think in terms other than those associated exclusively with computers. How many of you have children under 12 years of age? How many of your kids can tell time? How many of your kids think they need to learn how to tell time? When you can buy a two-dollar digital watch, they have a real problem understanding why you think that they ought to learn how to tell time. That represents a change in technology. It has changed the way we do business. I have a nine-year-old son who literally sees no value in learning how to tie his shoes. Doesn't every shoe have Velcro on it? That is technology.

We need to think in those terms. It's not just computers. We do things differently. Southwest Airlines, which is a little bitty regional airline in Texas, has recognized for years that if you make it possible for somebody to buy a ticket without coming to the counter, you are probably going to get more business. And guess what? You have smaller lines at the counter! So very early on they implemented systems that would take credit cards and print out tickets, and they had very happy customers. The application of that technology is not new; it is just the widespread acceptance of it that is new.

I just moved back recently from five years in the New York area. I was very much involved with people in the banking area in New York. I was involved in a seminar about educational skills and the availability of qualified people in the work force. This was kind of a brainstorming group. Folks got together, and you got to bring a problem to the group on a given night. Then the group would brainstorm it.

One banker's problem was a tremendous turnover rate for counter clerks in his banks. I had a discussion with him and said, "Well, let's think through this. What kind of people do you look at to hire for those jobs? What is the basic skill requirement?" He said,

"Well, it is pretty simple. We want people that can look at numbers on this side when money comes in, make sure that the correct amount of money and correct paperwork is there, and then stamp it. It goes from the left to the right." Their highest priority for filling that job is to find people who are highly detail-oriented. The last thing in the world that they want is for somebody to make a mistake.

I said, "When was the last time that you just sat in the lobby of the bank and watched?" He said, "Well, I go through the lobby of my bank all the time." I said, "I don't mean go through the lobby. When was the last time that you were in the lobby of your bank and sat down and observed what goes on at the counter of the bank?" He said, "Well, I haven't done that." I said, "Well, I will tell you what I think that you will find." (And again I'm not a bank expert, but I understand what automation has done to their world.) "When you see people in line inside the bank today, why do you think that they are there?" He said, "Well, they are there to process transactions."

Well, I don't know about you, but I've got a bank card. The State of New York has been very aggressive with ATMs. I literally can't remember the last time I was physically inside a bank. I *never* go in a bank, except when that stupid machine doesn't work. When that machine doesn't work, the technology has failed. Then I've got to go in the bank. So I go in, I walk up to the counter, and I'm facing a guy whose primary skill in life is getting things from the left side to the right side.

To begin with, the first thing out of that person's mouth is, "The computer is down, and I don't know anything about the computer." You've hired somebody who's detail-oriented and task-oriented, but technology has totally changed the whole business. What you really need behind that counter is the most customer-oriented person you can find; someone who can keep that guy happy and not lose that account. That employee needs to be able to keep the customer satisfied for ten to 15 minutes while somebody in the back room is figuring out what's wrong with the stupid computer to keep his account from being able to give him the money he wants to get. We are hiring people in our IT organizations who are not going to have the skills to survive in the world that we are going to be in down the road.

I'm afraid that I'm upsetting people here. This morning I talked with a group of folks. Basically, they are computer science graduates. This is personal opinion and I can't give you empirical data to support it, but I contend that the professional title of "programmer" is going to be the shortest-lived profession in the history of American business. Yet we are still out hiring programmers. We are still putting an emphasis in colleges on whether or not people are getting Cobol applications. Not that that is not important, but I can tell you right now if you are telling people to train and develop for a career as a programmer, you are not doing them any favors, because the technology of this world has changed.

We put PCs out there, and now everybody in the world thinks that they are a programmer — and most of them are. We'd better understand that what we do affects people and is changing the environment that we live in.

Now having said that, I have 800 people in my corporate IT organization. We are trying to make fundamental changes in our company. We are putting IT professionals in the business units. We think that people ought to be there at the genesis of the problem. If they become involved down the road or downstream from it, they come in and say, "Have I got a technological answer for you!" Half of the time they don't even know what the question is, so how can they know what the answer is? We are saying that you need to be a business professional first and an IT professional second. Well, those IT people are uncomfortable with this: They have been living in an IT vacuum. I will tell you right now that IT people cause more change in our corporations than all of the other departments combined even have the ability to do. We walk into people's offices with a personal computer and say, "Hi. Look what we are putting on your desk." That scares people to death. We change things and we cause changes to happen. We are constantly the catalyst for change. But I also contend that IT people are the most change-resistant people in the world. You think about that. We are. We do it right; why should we change? We are professionals and we understand this. Technology is pushing us out of that.

If we don't learn to accept change, the IT organization is never, ever going to make a payback on the investment. In the last 25 years Texaco has spent literally hundreds of millions of dollars on computers. Now that is an asset, whether it is knowledge that exists in the experience of the people, whether it is physical programs or intellectual properties, whether it is leases we hold on computers, whether it is physical sites, or whatever. That is an asset. And one of the things that we'd better be prepared to do in the future is understand that corporations are looking at the hard bottom line today. If we are not more than just a service, if we are not managing an asset, we are not going to be successful.

I also contend that if we're just in love with technology, we are going to find out that there is more than enough technology available today to solve the business problems of the future. Technology does not constrain us from doing the work that we need to get done. We ourselves are the constraint. We are the constraint because we have not yet grasped that our role is to be part of those business units, to understand the business that we are part of, and to make sure that we are applying technology to solve the business problems that these people are dealing with.

Users Versus Consumers. We have to understand that we no longer deal with users. A user is a captive audience. They have no other choice but to use your service. I don't know about your corporations, but in our corporation back in the late 1970s and early 1980s we had people concerned about all this money being spent on computers. So how did we react to that? The chairman of the board sent out a "Heads of Department" letter, and in our company that letter is right up there with the Ten Commandments. These are not optional things. The crux of it was that the IT department was responsible for all aspects of computing. "You will not buy computers, you will not do programming. They are responsible." And boy, we loved having that. In the name of having that, we created a bunch of elegant systems — technical marvels that did not solve a single business problem. It's just that simple. I guarantee you that if you really talk truthfully about your own organization, if you have not done a project that did not have any business benefit, then you are highly unusual in the world of IT.

We need to get out of that mode. We don't have users; we have customers. That's a real tough thing for people to recognize. You treat a customer differently than you treat a user. To begin with, a customer is somebody you listen to. A customer is somebody who isn't going to use your service if you are not providing value. A user doesn't have that choice. We'd better understand that we have customers.

The biggest focus that most large companies are getting into is, "How can I get more value and competitive advantage out of my IT?"

You've heard a lot of people talking about that. American Airlines is a good example. American Hospital Medical Supplies is an excellent example of somebody who took information technology, had a business reason for doing it, and created a competitive advantage. They did not go out and put terminals on their customers' desks so that they could complete technological solutions. They did it to get a competitive edge, and they did an excellent job of it. But their focus was to meet a customer requirement; it was not to implement technology for the sake of technology.

We'd better get out of that mode. We are the ones that opened Pandora's box. We put PCs on people's desks. We just convinced them that they were computer experts when we gave them one. I don't know about your company, but when my company first got PCs, they did not very lightly give somebody $13,000, which was what we were spending putting PCs on people's desks. Now, the interesting thing about it is that in a lot of cases we had no idea why we were putting that PC on that person's desk; it seemed like the right thing to do.

When you think about that, you wouldn't do that with any other asset. I don't know about your company, but I can tell you right now that Texaco hasn't gone out and built a lot of refineries based on the fact that they liked the technology associated with refineries. Generally speaking, there was some bottom-line business reason to do that. Part of our problem is that we have considered ourselves to be out of the mainstream of business. We are an entity unto ourselves.

I contend that unless you work with IBM, DEC, or any of those other companies, most companies are not computer companies. My company, for instance, is in the oil business. They are not in the computer business. We need to recognize that, and we need to understand that we ought to be dealing with problems that are associated with our business.

Centralized or Decentralized Processing: A Non-Issue. In every seminar or any discussion I have with people, this question comes up: "What's better: centralized or decentralized processing?" I contend that we ought to know the answer, and the answer has nothing to do with technology. When you put a PC out there and start adding tons of disks; and then you have it communicating with somebody; and then suddenly you say, "Okay, let's put two PCs together" — if you think that isn't a mainframe computer, then I don't know what your definition of a mainframe computer is. Believe me, you're going to have all of the same problems that a mainframe computer has. You put that second PC in there and guess what problem you have: shared data. The technology people say, "I understand what that is." We need to understand that we are using technological terms when we should not be. The question of centralization versus decentralization is a non-issue. The only issue is what business problems I am trying to solve with the utilization of technology. The answer to centralization versus decentralization is simply "yes." You should be centralized *and* decentralized.

Earlier speakers have talked about the fact that telecommunications technology is way ahead of the game. On Monday, I was at Bell Laboratories in New Jersey. We meet with them on a fairly regular basis, as we do with other vendors and suppliers, just to discuss technology issues. I can tell you right now that the advances we are going to see in telecommunications are absolutely astronomical.

Our ability to communicate is absolutely unlimited. Now, having said that, why should we be worried if the computer is in Tulsa, Oklahoma, or in Hamburg, Germany? It is a non-issue. What we need to be focusing on and understanding is what business advantage we will get from having a computer in Tulsa, Oklahoma, versus Hamburg, Germany. I will tell you exactly the way we ought to be thinking about that. Tulsa, Oklahoma may give you tax advantages for putting that computer there versus putting it in Germany. The cost of labor in Tulsa, Oklahoma, may be cheaper than it is Hamburg, Germany. Now, we can understand that when we say Japan is building car plants in the United States. People comprehend that. It is very easy to understand; well, sure, they are going to build a manufacturing plant here. The state of Tennessee is giving them all kinds of tax breaks, cheaper labor, and all of these kind of things. Now, why can't we understand that those are the real technological issues? It is not whether it is a DEC, IBM, or any of those things. I guarantee you that if you have a requirement for a DEC to talk to a DataPoint to talk to a VAX to talk to a IBM, there is somebody out there who will put it together for you and it will work. That is a non-issue. We are spending too much time on that and not enough time on the business problems that we need to be solving.

When we go out looking for new hires, we very seldom put great emphasis on a computer science degree. That is just not a high priority for us any longer. We want people who have demonstrated the ability to solve problems, be creative thinkers, and be innovative. We want them to have enough of a technological advantage to understand the process, but they also need to understand that they do not have to invent that process to be able to solve the problems. We need people who can think. We need people who can reason. We really need people who can communicate. I spend most of my time trying to sell senior management in our company on why this project makes the highest and best sense. We spend a tremendous amount of time trying to communicate the strategic values associated with what we are doing. I believe that as time goes on and technology becomes less of an issue, we will need to have people available to us who have basic business skills, who can communicate, and who understand how technology works. If we can do those things, I think all of us will be much more successful.

IT Organizational Issues. The people in Silicon Valley have a very entrepreneurial spirit. They are able to re-create things. People are much more satisfied in an environment where they are allowed to be creative. We as a company are going into team management. We think that in an information-based organization, the best way to cut across business-unit boundaries and to provide resources that solve business problems is to embrace the team management concept. We are calling it our quality concept. We are using the concept of quality to change a cultural problem that we have: People don't feel comfortable being expected to talk about business issues, and so that will be a tremendous change for them. We have people who have spent 10 to 15 years of their lives developing technical expertise. In essence, we are saying that this is not the highest and best value now, nor will it be for the future. And that is different.

The organizational issues that we are creating within the information technology group itself are significant. Farther out from that group is an even bigger problem. Our customers are confused. They definitely don't understand the power that technology can bring them. We call the *Wall Street Journal* a computer rag, because so much of what's in it has to do with computers. Most of our customers read the *WSJ* and see extremely good ideas and wonder why we cannot implement those for them. That is a really valid question. Why *can't* we implement those ideas for them? I contend that one of the reasons that we can't is because we don't have people with the skills to sit down and discuss and communicate with them the power of the technology and translate that business problem into a solution that all of us can implement.

We are spending a lot of time and money on CASE tools. I believe that is only going to make it more difficult for us to make this transition, because what we are doing is automating another big portion of the traditional IT operation. A lot of speakers are very much aware of the value associated with being able to automate analyst-type functions. If you do this — again, what is going to be left for the professionals who remain in an IT organization? Those people are going to be out in those business units. We have done this. We have moved people out there.

We feel that IT people in general tend to have a little broader focus, because they are exposed to a wide variety of things. If you have worked on multiple projects, you will understand — through osmosis, if nothing else — the different operations in the company. You may not understand everything; in our case you may not understand what makes a refinery work or what makes better exploration possible. But those people, in general, have broader exposure.

One of my responsibilities when we push computer professionals out into the field is to ensure that we continue nurturing their overall professional development and career development. I recently met with the chairman of the Texaco Chemical Company, one of our subsidiaries. He came to me and said, "Look, there are two IT people in my organization who, in my view, are ready for a move into the business unit. I don't want them in there for their IT skills. I am going to give them management responsibilities for business units." We at Texaco see that as the full cycle of the way things should go. Basically, we are giving people an opportunity, if they have basic skills, to flow into any area of the company.

Texaco is a lot smaller than it used to be. Its structure is much flatter. Everybody is doing this. It is survival. It is impossible not to do that. You cannot compete if you do not have an efficient organization.

Now, if you think about it, that has tremendous implications for what people are going to be doing in those layers that still exist. Those people need to have information available to them speedily. A lot of the layers that we have cut out have been information filters. Historically, information has flowed from one level through another level through another level. It supposedly finally got to somebody, and they either acted on it or it came back down. But at none of those levels was any value added to the information from where it was initially collected. People were filters; that is all they were doing. I know that must be the case in a lot of areas, because we just had the most profitable year we have had in ten years. I know it cannot have affected us adversely, or we would not have made that kind of money.

So there is a change out there. Previously introduced automation has enabled us to flatten organizations. What we need to do now is take advantage of the good work we have already done. Back to what I said before, we need to look at it as a corporation looks at any other asset. It has not been free. It is not free to automate manufacturing processes. It is not free to build marketing systems. It is not free to build decision support systems. Sooner or later you have got to get a return of value on those things. Our thrust has been to empower people to be business analysts, to be out in those units, and basically to make sure that they are able, on a day-to-day basis, to function in a way that optimizes their productivity.

Business Unit Needs and Collective Needs. Let me define two business needs. One is what we call *business unit needs*. This is the information that is required for a business unit to operate. A manufacturing plant, for instance, needs capacity and volume information. That is very important. It is operational information that is absolutely required for that business unit to be successful.

We used to call the next category *corporate needs*. We found out that if you start putting the word "corporate" in front of anything, people say, "Well, it cannot have anything to do with me, because I do not want anything to do with corporate." So we started calling it *collective needs*. Collective needs are needs for information that cross business units. Now, one of the problems that we have created is that we have put a bunch of PCs out there and have empowered people to create a lot of data. Those people are suddenly finding out that this data needs to participate as part of a collective need. We are having to go through tremendous exercises now, and this comes back to technology issues. Yesterday, I sat in on an electronic mail presentation. People were talking about how to take DECs, Data Generals, IBMs, and all of these different things that have developed over the years, and get that data up to a level that meets this collective need. And believe me, there are collective needs.

Try reporting information to the Internal Revenue Service and telling them that this business unit is separate from that one. It just does not work if you are a corporation. You'd better be able to do that. The SEC wants to see combined collective information. I do not care how independent and entrepreneurial you are about business units. I guarantee you that somewhere in the frame of things you'd better be able to tie all that information together. Now what happens? Suddenly, at the top of the house, the chairman of the board finds out that his accounting information is different from the accounting information out in the field. Why is it different? It is because he has been downloading data and doing a lot of good things with it, but he has not updated that central data base because it is not something he is interested in doing. He has nobody out there with the analytical acumen to explain to him technologically why that is an important thing for him to do. All of us in this room that have anything to with information management are spending a ton of money right now in building black boxes in software trying to solve that problem. I think that we'd better understand that we created the problem. It is an organizational issue. We must address it now by putting people out there who are capable of making sure that in the future we solve business problems, not just local functional problems.

We think business units and collective needs help drive an organization. Again, what happened in that mode is that you have to have a lot of communication. I do not care if you are highly centralized or highly decentralized; to operate in either one of those modes communication is at a premium. We think that one way to facilitate that communication is to have people who are capable and competent human beings. Like I said, the band width and the pipe lines are there. What you need and we need are human beings who can carry on that communication.

And again, in a college campus environment, we really need to understand what we are influencing and what we are asking for. Look at public school systems right now. I have a son who is in the seventh grade in middle school. Texaco would have hired him ten years ago as summer help, because he can program in Fortran. That is the kind of job market we are looking at. Things are different now, but there are a bunch of people that have recruiters and people working in their personnel offices who are still asking the same questions that they asked people ten years ago. They have not recognized that change. All of us need to understand that as we are successful in implementing technology, we are causing changes, and we need to really focus on that. We need to focus on making a skill base available so that five years from now there will be people coming out of the Utah State Universities of the world who are capable of functioning in that environment. I think that is the key issue and the most critical thing that we as information technologists have to face.

Aligning IT Plans with Business Plans. It is also extremely important that we get our information technology plans in sync with the business plans of the corporation. Having a consultant come in and do an information technology plan for you without having a business plan is not going to work. You can have the best information technology plan in the world, but if it is not achieving the business plan, you have not accomplished anything.

We that think that putting people out into those business organizations is a way to more closely align the business plans with the computer plans. We really need to realize that the tail cannot be wagging the dog, because like I said, a lot of us have spent a lot of time implementing very elegant technological systems that do not meet the business requirements.

26

Information Management:
An Executive's Perspective

Charles W. Elliott, Executive Vice President — Administration,
Kellogg Company

Our information needs at Kellogg Company are much different today than they were when Mr. Kellogg started the business in 1906, but I think the change that's going to take place in the future is going to be even greater than what has taken place in the past.

The output from our computer system is very seldom what we need. I believe this is partly attributable to the many myths that have sprung up regarding the way executives view information. Some of these myths are:

- Executives want to do their own analysis.
- Executives love detail.
- Executives demand precision to the umpteenth decimal point.
- Executives equate quality with complexity.
- Executives like more things to watch, rather than fewer.
- Executives don't know or can't tell you what information they need, so why ask?
- Executives need hard copy.

Now, I don't know whether people really believe these myths, but the outputs from most computer systems reflect this kind of thinking.

Now let's talk about some qualities that executives *really* want from their information. Information has four basic qualities that impart value:

- Accessibility
- Timeliness
- Relevance
- Accuracy

Let's briefly review each of these qualities.

Accessibility. I think everyone is familiar with the term information overload. Today we produce more recorded information each year than was produced in the entire 19th century. Systems that worked well at one order of magnitude are now overwhelmed, and the problem is getting worse. Current estimates are that the rate of information accumulation is doubling every four years. Unfortunately, there seems to be no way to make this information easy to access. Some data is important and other data is not. Our challenge is to make the important information more accessible.

Timeliness. In order for any information to be useful, you must get it in time to act on it. Information becomes less valuable the longer you sit on it and the more hands it passes through before it gets to the decision maker. Information that is too old to act upon becomes completely irrelevant, which brings me to my next point: relevance.

Relevance. Data must have a clear link to your business objectives — that is, it must be relevant. Irrelevant information is neither harmless nor benign. As Peter Drucker points out in his book *Management Tasks and Responsibilities*, "Anything beyond that which is truly needed is noise and leads to information overload. It does not enrich, but impoverishes."

Excess data is bad. It not only impedes the user's ability to get to the information he really needs, but it sends misleading signals to subordinates as to what executives consider to be important. I'm always hesitant to ask my staff for something. I don't know how much detail they're going to go into or how much overzealousness is going to be applied. The excess information that I receive in those situations is costly to gather and certainly adds to the noise.

An old adage in business says "that which is monitored is improved." People will pay attention to anything you measure. If you're monitoring the wrong things, the important things will not improve. I want information that allows me to *control* results rather than simply observe them.

Let me offer a simplistic example. If I'm a manager of a business unit, obviously I'm measured on the profits. I might have a tendency to monitor *only* the profits. But profits are the result of sales. Sales are the result of repeat business, which is the result of customer satisfaction. Customer satisfaction results from product quality and service. So if I want to control profits, maybe I should be monitoring product quality, customer satisfaction, final inspection rejects, customer returns, and so forth.

At Kellogg we spend a lot of time worrying about customer complaints. If you *don't* pay attention to these things, you've missed the boat on what's really happening. We *have* to monitor those complaints. Our chairman believes we should get *no* consumer complaints, and every one represents a failure on our part.

We need to focus on the things that count. One of our consultants gave me a good quote. He said, "What you need is enough advance warning to steer around the iceberg. What you have at Kellogg's with your present financial reporting system is the world's best damage report."

The range of information needed by an executive can usually be defined by his activities and responsibilities. Most existing paper reporting systems fail in their attempts to provide this information. An executive's information requirements usually go beyond the traditional internal reports that percolate up through the transactions of a processing system. We need an information environment that includes a variety of relevant information, not just summaries.

Accuracy. Don't confuse accuracy with precision. We really are not interested in numbers to the fourteenth decimal place. What I need to know is if the numbers are a true indication of what's happening. I want the most current numbers I can get. I also want them to be the same numbers that other managers are looking at. One of our biggest problems is that executives argue about whose numbers are right. It's a disaster in any type of situation. Whenever that happens, the system that has produced the numbers is to blame.

When existing information systems are tested against these criteria of accessibility, timeliness, relevance, and accuracy, it is easy to see why most executives are frustrated with them. Executives are frequently stuck with thick printouts of largely irrelevant data that are never current enough. These reports evolve as the cumulative effect of lots of people asking for lots of data over time. A report that attempts to contain all the information that anyone could possibly want sounds nice, but for executives it's excessive and probably too late.

When I ask people why a specific report has been prepared, I'm usually told that the chairman, the president, or I asked for it once, and we *might* ask for it again sometime; therefore, the report has to be available. We have a lot of excess material floating around. My conversations with other companies indicate that we're not unique.

I believe the management of information for strategic competitive advantage will be *the* great challenge facing us for the foreseeable future. Information technology is spreading into more and more parts of the production and marketing processes in both manufacturing and service industries. Information is becoming an integral part of many products in the marketplace. The opportunities to use information and information systems to achieve a competitive edge are enormous. The risks of not keeping up are equally great. Significant resources must be committed in the face of real technical and business uncertainty.

The resources required, the risks to be taken, and the strategic business opportunities being sought mean that executive managers must be involved in the information planning process from now on. In many cases, a successful information strategy will be the key to corporate profitability.

To explore how we might capitalize on this information challenge, I'll begin with an overview of the issues as I see them in managing overall information resources: people, data, and technology. I will then move to some examples of companies that have successfully used information systems to achieve a competitive advantage. This will lead to a presentation of several concepts dealing with thinking strategically about information. I will conclude by describing steps that can lead to an integration of information planning with the business planning process — perhaps the real key to long-term success.

Let's start by tracing the steps of how information systems have evolved over the years. Information systems (IS) started life very low on the organizational totem pole — it's still there in many smaller companies. At Kellogg we have elevated our services to a higher level, although I am not sure that it is high enough yet.

The pervasive use of and need for information technology has raised conflicts between users of information and suppliers of technology. The need for standards and controls is often seen to conflict with the desire for rapid exploitation of new information technology tools.

Any discussion of the evolution of management and information systems is incomplete without addressing the role that emerging technologies have played. The proliferation of information-processing technologies has dramatically increased the need for effective planning to facilitate integrating these technologies into the overall information management process. Four factors make the integration of emerging technologies a complex business issue:

- The differences between vendors competing for the three major technology markets: manufacturing, business systems, and telecommunications. They just don't fit together.
- Relatively weak standards that compromise compatibility among various technical approaches.
- The continuing tremendous upward rate of change in the quality and cost of technical solutions. The cost of processing a piece of information is going down; the cost of solving the problem seems to be going up.
- The need to integrate the technical solution with the physical process to achieve the best results.

Centralization/Decentralization. To further complicate matters, departmental and personal computers are driving a de facto decentralization of computer power. Users are generally demanding more control over computer processing to help them to better use computers to meet their strategic goals. This centralization/decentralization issue is not a simple "either/or" choice. It is a complex set of issues involving the deployment of costly resources:

- The processors and their operations support staff
- Data and the supporting administrative staff
- Systems development staff and their tools
- Systems implementation support staff and their tools, including training aids and information centers.

Centralization/decentralization decisions concerning any of these resources have a strong impact on the company's need for information standards and controls and on the level of investment in technical and support staff.

The location of processing power is basically a technical and economic decision revolving around the location and needs of the users, balance between communications and processing costs, reliability, security needs, economics of scale, and data center operations. Generally, data that must be shared should be centralized. Local use of data should be decentralized if the volume justifies the economics of storing it locally.

At Kellogg, we have not been very successful in trying to share decentralized data bases. System development resources should be centralized in most cases, because a large pool is a lot easier to supervise than a small pool and will provide more flexibility. System implementation and support resources must be accessible to the users. Some of those people will be centrally located and some will be out in the units.

The perception has grown that information systems are not responsive to users' needs. There's a great deal of truth in this perception, because needs have grown much more rapidly than the resources available to serve them. A lengthy process is required to create a high-quality system. Two- to four-year development cycles are common in some of our large systems at Kellogg.

Companies are attempting much more complex integrated applications. As systems age, the maintenance requirements become much, much greater, and you can get yourself in the trap of not being able to develop new systems because all your people are spending time maintaining the old systems.

New development approaches do provide some relief, but the backlog of user demands is still growing faster than gains in productivity. Optimal use of information resource capabilities requires a new division of responsibility with the users.

At Kellogg our information technology group is moving toward a standard-setting and environments-maintenance function. Only major applications with great strategic importance will be developed from scratch. Information centers and fourth-generation languages will provide our users with more direct access to data, reducing the wait for fulfilling simple requests.

We're turning to packaged programs to reduce costs and lead times at the expense of accepting a less than perfect fit to our requirements. Packages are the wave of the future, but installation is very costly. Excessive tailoring of packages is more expensive than custom development. Therefore, we make almost no changes in packages. We try to change the expectations of the users.

Other criticisms that executive management generally associates with their processing group are rapid, uneconomical turnover in computer equipment, sharp increases in telecommunications costs, uncertainty about how to proceed in managing this area, and systems planning quite often does not satisfy the user needs.

Some of these criticisms are valid, but others simply represent a lack of understanding between management and the IS group.

We're becoming increasingly aware of data security, disaster recovery, and premature obsolescence. We've all heard about systems being broken into and viruses being introduced. There is great concern over security. At Kellogg our board of directors is very concerned about this area, and they ask for periodic updates.

Now I would like to turn to the issue that I view as my most important challenge at Kellogg: the strategic use of information resources for competitive advantages. Let me give a couple of examples that I think you're all familiar with.

The Merrill Lynch cash management account was the first of its kind, and moved Merrill Lynch to a higher level of competition. Many people at Merrill Lynch believe it provided them with their greatest growth ever. It was almost a pure information product, and it changed the whole strategic direction of Merrill Lynch when they adopted it.

Another recent development is the American Airlines boarding pass machine. By punching in a number and using a card, customers can obtain their boarding pass without waiting in line. It makes it easier for the customer. American Airlines needs fewer ticket agents, and it appeals to their best customers — frequent fliers. They hope that this will give them a competitive edge.

A competitive system must touch the customer directly, add value to the product or service, benefit the business, or change the whole process.

Systems can be market-focused. You can focus on marketing or sales. You can provide better sales support. You can ease communications. If you can tie customers into your system, you will obviously have a better shot.

Systems can be production-focused. They can increase your flexibility in manufacturing, improve quality, and control costs. They can also provide better vendor interaction.

The use of information and information systems for competitive advantage requires a willingness to think imaginatively. We have to think about what the business is doing and think strategically about the information.

A good management information plan should, at a minimum, specifically address the current role of your information technology. What areas are supported or not supported? What's the quality and timeliness of the current information and information services? What do you have in terms of technical equipment? What are the organizational relationships?

It is also necessary to look at the industry and the competition. What new products are being offered out there? What competitive threats are there? Customers are a good source of information. Our sales force is quick to point out areas where the competition is getting a leg up on us. They hear from their customers on a regular basis if someone else is doing it better.

We also need to determine the customers' needs. We must understand the business. Supermarkets want to carry as little inventory as possible, and they never want to be out of stock. Those are conflicting demands. We need to figure out ways to help them do both. Customer imposed requirements are constantly increasing on electronic interfaces, a key area for us.

You need to decide what your opportunities are and rank them. Set the priorities. You're not going to be able to afford to do everything in the short term. Focus on the potential payback from each one. I'd like to caution you about tying dollars to all of the paybacks. Some paybacks cannot be measured in terms of dollars. You're going to have a hard time tying dollars to competitive advantage.

And finally, you must identify what your resources are and compare those to your needs. When you determine the priorities and the available resources, you will find that there's a real shortage. You will have to determine whether or not you need to increase your resources.

Kellogg is a very lean organization. We're proud of the fact that we have 15 percent fewer employees than we had five years ago, even though our business has grown significantly. We're very reluctant to add staff. We've found that we can temporarily increase staff through the use of contract programmers and consultants. That's the key for us.

At Kellogg, technology is leading us toward major investments, resulting in very high fixed costs. The return on fixed investments must include flexibility to adapt to change. The basic decisions involve very large resource commitments, and must last for decades. We are constantly struggling with how to build flexibility to keep up with our customer needs and how to defend against extra costs being shifted from customers to us. Basically, we believe companies with the best systems have the superior ability to protect their share of the product value stream. Executive involvement, understanding, and commitment are indispensable.

Successful information planning requires true integration with business strategies. We must keep our perspectives straight. How can we increase value to customers through more effective use of information? At Kellogg we believe in quality in all things, including our information processing and strategic planning.

27

Information Strategies for the 1990s

L. William Krause, Chairman and CEO, 3COM Corporation

Information Strategies for the 1990s is a topic of intense interest to me for two reasons. First, as the chairman and chief executive officer of a company that will break the $1 billion mark in the next few years, I am constantly reviewing my company's information strategies and how they can be implemented to maintain and, more importantly, increase our competitiveness. Second, because my company sells information technology products — specifically networking products — I spend a great deal of time talking to customers and I am privy to the concerns of other executives who rely on my company. The notion of using information strategies for a competitive advantage is certainly not a new concept, but I think it is safe to say that it has been misunderstood.

In preparing this paper, I came across an article in the *McKinsey Quarterly* that crisply and, in my view, accurately defines how to apply information technologies. Unlike other articles written on the subject, it does not prescribe a blanket solution for creating a competitive advantage. I think that's a wise approach. After all, if there were just one solution, everyone would have it and no competitive advantage could exist.

The Evolution of Information Technology. Before venturing into the area of how information strategies can be applied to a competitive advantage, let me give you my perspective on how information technology has evolved.

In describing this evolution to customers, we use the three computing millennia model: (1) batch computing on mainframes in the 1960s for corporate applications; (2) time-shared computing with minicomputers in the 1970s for departmental computing; and (3) networked computing, especially personal computers, in the 1980s for workgroup computing.

What, then, is the fourth millennium and when will it begin? My answer is that it will be distributed computing for all applications, and will begin circa 1991-92. In the 1990s, new generations of corporate, departmental, and workgroup applications will emerge based on UNIX and OS/2 operating system environments using a client-server architecture.

This fourth millennium embodies three concepts:

1. Computer architectures will continue to shrink to platforms based on microprocessors.
2. These platforms will be connected.
3. Applications software will run across all platforms.

The three key factors I see driving this structural change toward the fourth millennium are a growing frustration with the seemingly endless applications backlog associated with centralized computing; spiraling MIS/DP costs, with budgets reaching 4 to 5 percent of corporate sales; and the emergence of the technologies necessary to support distributed computing. These key technologies include:

*   Advances in semiconductors as microprocessors, memory, and gate arrays.
*   New operating systems standards, notably UNIX and OS/2.
*   Fiber-based 100 MBPs local area networks with enterprise-wide network management systems based on OSI and SAA.
*   Networked database management systems, both relational and SQL.

The boundaries between the third and fourth millennia are less distinct than those between the first, second, and third. They are driven to a greater extent by customer demand for greater control over computing resources, in addition to the advances in technology. Computer networking is exploding now, and I don't believe the fourth millennium is yet here. What started as a basic interest in sharing peripherals has blossomed into demand for information access on the network.

The next step in 3COM's evolution, we believe, will be toward personal communications to empower people with information, which will change the way we work more dramatically than have the telephone, typewriter, copier, or desktop computer.

These are the key advances in technology that I see coming in the 1990s, but they alone aren't the answer to information strategies for a competitive advantage. For that, the technology must be intelligently applied. That is the topic of the second portion of today's address.

In reading the *McKinsey Quarterly* article, what I found most interesting was how the authors divided information systems strategies into three categories:

1. Stand-alone information systems;
2. Information systems that leverage an existing advantage; and
3. Information systems that create a new advantage through fundamental changes to the business.

These categories do not have distinct boundaries, nor do they necessarily overlap the history of information technology. Instead, they focus on how information strategies and systems are implemented and applied.

Stand-Alone Information Systems. Let's first examine the application of stand-alone information systems. By stand-alone, we are not limited to personal computers or workstations. Rather, we're taking a broad view of the definition. Simply put, it means the use of information systems to automate a singular process. It is based more on the basic capabilities of information systems than on a strategy for using information systems effectively.

Let me give you an example. In the 1960s and 1970s, companies rushed to automate their back offices and administrative staffs. Systems were installed to handle accounting, and word processing stations were given to secretaries. The fundamental reason for these investments was to reduce the cost of these necessary operations. Customers for this equipment reasoned that if prices remained stable, the savings created by automation would improve their profit picture. Often, the automation did reduce costs — significantly so in some cases. But despite lower costs, there was little or no sustainable positive effect on the companies' profits; no competitive advantage was gained. Why not?

The problem was, and is, that stand-alone information systems are easily reproduced. So when company A automated their operations, so did companies B, C, D, and so on. With all companies able and willing to reduce their costs, no competitive advantage can exist.

What went wrong? The problem wasn't with the information systems. It was with expectations. That's not to say, however, that solutions which simply automate existing practices are wrong. In fact, simple automation might be required to avoid losing ground competitively. But managers must understand from the beginning the likelihood and extent to which competitors will adopt a technology and then adopt approaches that will lead to superior execution of their technology strategies.

Leveraging Existing Business Strengths. The second approach cited by the *McKinsey* article is the use of information systems to leverage existing business strengths. This approach assumes that a company already has a competitive advantage in some other area divorced from information systems, such as marketing, distribution, manufacturing, or product development. Information systems can enhance that advantage, although alone they do not create new competitive advantages. Leverage activities are most commonly seen when companies — especially market-share leaders — apply technology to enhance economies of scale.

The most obvious approach is to reduce total costs or improve service through fixed-cost investments. Competitors will be compelled to follow, but market share leaders will maintain their edge, because they can spread the fixed costs over a larger pool of products or services.

A second way to exploit scale is to use information systems to predict demand more effectively. Let's look at a simple example: National distributors of perishable foods often face the problem of distributing enough product to meet volatile consumer demand. The worst thing that can happen is to run a promotion and not be able to fill the demand. As a result, distributors commonly build multiple facilities around the country and overstock them with inventory to avoid being caught short. Obviously such overstocking creates waste, but the fear of losing sales prevents consolidation of distribution networks. Using computers, the distributor can analyze historical data and more accurately predict demand swings under different sets of circumstances. If the system shows predictability, the distributor can safely reduce its inventories and consolidate its distribution network with greater confidence.

A third way of exploiting scale is to use proprietary information to reduce costs and improve services. For example, a credit card company can improve its predictions of credit-worthiness — thereby lowering the cost of bad debt — by focusing on smaller geographic regions. But to do this cost-effectively requires a large, existing pool of data and the systems to manipulate it.

Finally, companies can exploit scale by sharing the cost of technology across businesses. A U.S. company might, for example, create a new building system that can by used in offices around the world.

Aside from scale economies, information systems can be used to leverage existing advantages by strengthening product differentiation. Federal Express, for example, is a master at the use of technology. Simply put, the company is in the delivery business, just like the Post Office and UPS. It picks up a package at point A and delivers it to point B. What's remarkable, however, is the use of information systems that — at any given time — can identify the exact location of a package. The result is the best on-time delivery schedule of any delivery service, which translates into customer confidence and loyalty. The company's impact is so prevalent that their name has become a verb in many companies. You no longer send a package by express delivery — you "fed ex" it. Information systems, however, did not create a new advantage; they enhanced an existing capability.

A final method of enhancing existing advantage is integration of business functions. This is one area of particular interest to my company, because it involves the integration of multiple systems from multiple vendors in multiple locations. Traditionally, large companies — the ones that stand to benefit most from integration — have found it hard to integrate. Part of the problem has been cultural: they are structured around strong organizations defined by product lines, business functions, or geographic customer segments. This partially explains the critical importance of networking as a platform upon which to build competitive advantage.

The other part of the problem is the technology itself. Although organizations within a company may standardize on a particular manufacturer, overall most companies use multiple products from multiple manufacturers in multiple locations. Until recently, these products tended to be based on proprietary technology and architectures, in which systems vendors attempt to lock in customers. As companies seek new ways to enhance their competitiveness, however, both barriers are falling. Forward-looking companies are adjusting their cultures to eliminate parochialism and enhance the sharing of information. Likewise, those responsible for building the information systems are demanding that suppliers adhere to a core of industry standards that make it possible for systems to share resources, including information.

This is 3COM's foundation — to network more systems to more types of systems by adopting industry standards and working to integrate the technologies of different companies. In each of these examples, information systems, when properly applied, can be a powerful ally in strengthening existing competitive advantages.

New Approaches to Business. New competitive advantages, however, require fundamental changes in the way business is conducted. This is the final area discussed in the *McKinsey* article. These advantages are rare and generally occur in industries that must contend with rapid changes in technology, government regulation, and customer needs. Customers who are among the first to understand and use information systems create new sources of competitive advantage and often change the industry structure.

New competitive advantage can be created through new structural advantages or new approaches to business. One of the most obvious structural advantages is the ability to create and sustain switching costs. These types of costs occur when suppliers develop a link with customers that makes the cost of moving to a new supplier more expensive than any incremental benefit that might be gained.

Two good examples are American Hospital Supply's computerized customer links and American Airlines SABRE system. In both cases, the supplier created an automatic interface that makes frequent purchases more convenient and accurate. And in both cases networking is the platform across which that information becomes usable. Over time, these systems have become institutionalized in customers' businesses. Even if a cheaper alternative emerged, switching would require retraining employees and moving vast amounts of data. For an American Hospital Supply customer, savings on items would likely be perceived as small, since they are of low value to begin with.

Another strategy, scale advantages, differs from the economies of scale discussed earlier. In the previous example, the scale economies were created for existing products and services; here we're talking about the creation of a new service. Such opportunities generally occur when a single technology application dominates the business, when minimum efficient scale requires a large market share, and when the application is difficult for competitors to copy. The best examples of these situations occur in transaction-based businesses like credit card processing.

While structural advantages are powerful, they are rare. More common is the creation of a new business opportunity or better approach made possible by technology. This is particularly true of companies that adopt and exploit a technology early and gain superior institutional experience before others identify its potential benefits. For example, computer networks are doing to Federal Express what it did to UPS in the 1970s. Federal Express's technological advantage remains great compared to UPS, but wanes in comparison to networking capabilities.

So far, I have generally defined how technology can be a platform for competitive advantage. Before closing, let me be more specific about the future. As much as we would like to think differently, most companies around the world are still only using technology to automate existing processes instead of changing the way we serve our customers. Coming from Silicon Valley, we often forget that our view of information technology and information systems is jaded and that our vision of the future doesn't travel very far. What might seem quite commonplace to us is foreign and intimidating to others. But that's what makes the potential for technology so great. Our view will be shared — and soon.

Part of the problem today, meanwhile, has been the suppliers of technology, who have promoted technology as a panacea. "Just install it and watch your productivity grow." Today's responsible companies are taking a different approach — one that focuses on customers, not on bells and whistles and technology for the sake of technology. It is a pattern that I see repeating itself in the coming decade.

What does that customer focus mean? It will mean that adherence to the use of open systems that are based on industry standards, which gained momentum in the latter half of the 1980s, will become the prerequisite of the 1990s. It will mean that incompatible systems from different suppliers will no longer be a barrier, because the networking platform will be in place to tie together systems from multiple manufacturers. It will mean that the information systems salesperson will no longer work alone. Instead, he or she will enter your offices with partners who add complementary expertise and knowledge — some of it technical and some of it industry-specific. As a CEO of a technology company, these are the capabilities that I demand from my suppliers and from my people. I strongly suspect that I am not alone.

Let me conclude today by summarizing the two main lessons that I think the *McKinsey* examples teach. First, I find it most interesting that the further you move away from the strategy of automating what we have, the greater the role played by the information and the lesser the role of the technology. That I think is the primary lesson: Information is fundamentally more important than the technology. Information alone is always a powerful asset; not so technology.

And finally, when you hear someone say they want to sell you something that will give you a competitive advantage, don't believe it. No one can sell you that advantage — it must come from inside. What they *can* sell you, however, are the tools you will need to create that advantage. Make sure your vendors know the difference; and if they don't, buy from a company who does.

PART VII

The Equation
for the Future

28

Strategic Design:
Key to Profit in the 21st Century

Spencer Hutchens, Jr., Senior Vice President,
Intertek Services Corporation,
and President, American Society for Quality Control

To many people, the term *research and development* suggests excitement, glamor, or pure scientific research. These perceptions may be true within the university laboratory or in the public sector, but in business, research and development activities are undertaken for only one reason: pursuit of profit.

Returning continuous profit is becoming harder in today's global economy, and the onus is increasingly being placed on R&D's back. Strategic planning, the traditional executive activity, is now being funneled into specific areas such as strategic design.

A recent *Harvard Business Review* article, "Manufacturing by Design," reads:

> Design is a strategic activity, whether by intention or default. It influences product quality and reliability, efficiency of manufacturing, and flexibility of sales strategies. It may well be responsible for the company's future viability.

Defining "strategic design" is simple. It means aligning the customer's needs — quality, reliability, value, and timely delivery — with the company's goals: productivity and earning a profit.

289

But *achieving* strategic design is *not* so easy. One key to successful implementation of strategic design is business focus. A *Sloan Management Review* article, "The Art of High Technology Management," concluded that highly successful firms are narrowly focused. Most of their revenue is derived from a single product line or from closely related product lines. Examples were cited:

> IBM, Boeing, Intel, and Genentech confine themselves almost entirely to computer products, commercial aircraft, integrated circuits, and genetic engineering, respectively. Companies who have taken the opposite path have not fared well. Two of yesterday's leaders, ITT and RCA, have paid dearly for diversifying away from their core strengths.

Obviously, a company's R&D efforts must be concentrated on those strengths or activities most likely to return consistent profits, and this requires focusing attention on four important areas of concern.

The Big Picture Orientation. The first is big picture orientation. Unfortunately, many R&D specialists tend to perceive themselves as members of a field rather than a business: Their first loyalty is to their professional discipline. As a result, their primary orientation is toward science rather than profit.

R&D team members should always have a big-picture orientation and be cognizant of the company's strategic plan. They should routinely be apprised of the company's market share, revenue, and profit goals. They should also be aware of competitors' activities and the role that the R&D function is expected to play in maintaining or improving the status quo.

Focusing on the Customer. The next concern is market focus. The customer's needs must drive every design effort. Although this seems obvious, the R&D function has been a virtual cliché in many American corporations: a collection of bright tinkerers sequestered in an isolated "think tank." The customer is an abstract element in the grand scheme.

During National Quality Month, John Akers, chairman of IBM, candidly admitted:

> We were spending more than $5 billion a year on R&D, but we weren't communicating with our customers very well. We didn't use their perspective as well as we should in bending and shaping our development

efforts. When we regularly began sitting down with our customers, we learned they expected us to be not simply a supplier but a genuine partner in their businesses.

R&D team members must always start from the customer's needs and work backwards. Information on social and economic trends should be routinely sought by design specialists. Direct customer contact is essential. The overriding question should be, "Where are our opportunities?"

Regis McKenna, a leading marketing expert, cites Apple Computer's experience with desktop publishing:

> Apple's MacIntosh computer initially offered good graphics and easy-to-use features. But desktop publishing didn't even exist then, and no one had predicted its emergence. Apple's customers made it happen. Newspapers and research organizations began tapping MacIntosh's unique graphics capability to create primitive charts and graphs. By visiting and talking to customers, the MacIntosh R&D team recognized desktop publishing's potential and quickly exploited it.

Close interaction between R&D and the customer is critical in determining product reliability standards. Reliability, or lifetime product cost, is the primary factor in customer satisfaction. This issue was addressed in the *Sloan Management Review* article, "How Service Needs Influence Product Strategy." Extensive customer research identified the four basic product design strategies:

1. *Disposable.* An example product is the ten-dollar watch. The customer seeks high reliability for a year or so, then low replacement cost. The designer's primary concerns thus become short-term reliability and low production costs.
2. *Reparable.* Typical products include automobiles and major appliances. The customer seeks high reliability for several years, then moderate repair costs. The designer's concerns for this strategy are high reliability plus simplicity, affording low-cost or "do-it-yourself" repairs.
3. *Rapid response.* Typical products include office and farm equipment. The customer's key concern is minimizing downtime costs. The designer's concern is fast reparability in the field through modular, easily interchangeable components.
4. *Never fail.* Typical products include airplanes and life-support equipment. The customer demands protection against failure. The designer's concerns are tolerance of environmental extremes and built-in redundancy.

More Effective R&D through Cross-Functional Teamwork. The third concern is recognition that R&D is a *function* rather than a *department*. Teamwork is mandatory for success, yet American corporations tend to place R&D professionals on a pedestal, which fosters an elitist attitude.

As a result, communication between designers and other critical functions like sales, accounting, and service can be very poor. Communication with key outsiders such as suppliers, distributors, and retailers can also suffer, causing disappointing results in the marketplace.

A recent *Harvard Business Review* article, "Organizing for Manufacturable Design," said this:

> Designers generally enjoy higher status and pay than manufacturing engineers. They are considered something akin to creative artists and are often rewarded for ingenuity that has little to do with bottom-line results. Pragmatic manufacturing people, whatever their background, often bear the stigma of less well-educated people.

Job rotation can broaden horizons. The promising American engineering graduate is often recruited to spend the rest of his career in a "think tank," and becomes myopic. His Japanese counterpart spends several years each in R&D, production, and marketing. As a result, Japanese organizations are highly flexible and able to adapt quickly to external threats. Political "turfs" are virtually nonexistent in Japanese corporations, and the R&D function is viewed as part of an entire organism, which is seeking perpetual financial health. A recent *Harvard Business Review* article said:

> Managers who cross functional lines during their development thoroughly understand the activities, concerns, and values of their sister functions. Many outstanding managers have risen this way, often by chance. In the future, job rotation should be an essential element of the executive development program, and the primary technique for resolving interfunctional conflict.

R&D must be viewed as a companywide function. An elitist attitude is an expensive luxury. People from all departments and organizational levels can offer valuable insight into product viability and bottom-line profit. Many companies now assemble multidisciplinary R&D teams to insure that products are strategically designed to please the customer while meeting the company's profit objectives.

One approach pioneered by 3M simply asks employees: "Is anyone interested in working on this idea?" This is the first critical test of a proposed product's validity. Using this technique, IBM received over 5,000 applications for the 50 positions in its proposed PC unit. They knew they were on the right track!

Teamwork must also be encouraged between the R&D function and the company's "partners in profit" — suppliers, distributors, and retailers — who can offer valuable, specialized knowledge. The U.S. auto industry has learned this well. Parts suppliers used to bid only after receiving a request for a proposal. They now help set vehicle objectives, design parts and processes, and assist in other aspects of product development. This teamwork has reduced the number of industry suppliers by two-thirds. Automakers are enjoying improved supplier responsiveness and better product quality at lower cost. Chrysler has cut its engineering costs in half and has achieved a quality breakpoint in product design through increased teamwork with suppliers.

Teamwork with distributors and retailers is also critical in today's rapidly changing world. Tremendous innovation and distribution channels exist in nearly every industry.

Teamwork must continue long after a new product has been introduced. The R&D team must receive continuous-loop feedback on its performance. They should be continually apprised of insider information such as customer opinion survey results, sales figures, reliability data, and cost accounting analyses. Outsider information should also be constantly solicited. Problems perceived by suppliers, distributors, and retailers often represent lucrative product opportunities.

Managing Resources. The fourth concern is astute management of resources. R&D must be held accountable for the company's investment in its activities.

Dr. Peter Drucker, a respected educator and management consultant, acknowledged that R&D can be an ambiguous process, yet he says of Thomas Edison:

> Edison, perhaps the most prolific inventor of the 19th century, applied a systematic method to make inventive work productive. He always started out with a clear definition of the end product. He then broke down the process into constituent parts and worked out their relationship and sequence. He set specific controls for key points, and laid down the standards.

Obviously, Thomas Edison was an efficient R&D manager. If only he could share his expertise with us today.

People are our most valuable resource. Sound human resource management policies are critical to maximizing R&D talent. It is wise to foster permanent employment among technical professionals. This encourages a company or business perspective over an exclusively technical orientation. Tying compensation to performance is an effective way to achieve this.

It is also important to tolerate and even encourage failure. Significant technological gains are few and far between. Personal recognition should be based on perseverance in adhering to the process for success. Thus, the "spectator fizzle" should be as much cause for celebration as the breakthrough. Tom Peters and Robert Waterman's book, *In Search of Excellence*, speaks of profitable companies who routinely set off cannons or raise flags in honor of "grand failures."

Capital is another major resource. The R&D function must not only return the investment made in its activities but is also ultimately responsible for maximizing the company's plant and direct labor investments. Employing cost-efficient design techniques is an obvious responsibility.

Post-project appraisals are cost-efficient. A recent *Harvard Business Review* article said: "Few companies examine their completed projects in depth. Most audits are narrowly focused to assure proper controls are in place during a project's process." A post-project appraisal takes a much broader view and asks the big questions:

- Why was the project started in the first place?
- Is product demand at the forecasted level?
- Did our suppliers deliver what they promised?
- Is the product returning its investment?

The R&D function should investigate and recommend cost-efficient process designs and production tools. These might include telecommunication systems, robotics, and flexible manufacturing equipment.

It all boils down to this: *Research and development means business.* Getting technology into corporate strategy and getting business strategy into technical effort are the essential management tasks for the 21st century.

Strategic design represents a total approach to doing business. It can include changes in the pace of design, the identity of the players, and the sequence of decisions. It forces managers, designers, and operations people to cross organizational boundaries and challenges old power structures.

The survival and growth of U.S. corporations will depend increasingly on their ability to manage the R&D function as they do other company functions. R&D must be charged with specific, measurable, and time-bound goals and held accountable for the resources entrusted to it.

29

Intrapreneuring and Innovation

Gifford Pinchot III, Founder and Chairman, Pinchot & Company

The vigor of the entrepreneurial spirit is America's greatest business treasure. We are still something of a pioneer society, not naturally drawn to climbing the ladder in vast hierarchical organizations; our dreams are of making a difference personally. The free enterprise system has given us one way to do this: you can go out and become an entrepreneur; but entrepreneuring is not enough. We can't return to being a nation of tiny proprietorships, because too many of today's tasks are done better by large organizations. Consider building space shuttles, making cars, or even selling soap. There are people who want to make a difference in large organizations, where the bulk of us still work.

To take advantage of the entrepreneurial spirit, we have to combine the advantages of both bigness and smallness: the flexibility of smallness and all the resources of a large organization. I want to talk about a different way to make a difference as part of a large organization without having to leave to become a entrepreneur — a way that is now called *intrapreneuring:* acting like an entrepreneur inside a large organization.

Why is intrapreneuring essential for large organizations that wish to survive? Who are these intrapreneurs anyway? What do they do, what motivates them, how do you become an intrapreneur, and how does management create an environment that will foster innovation and intrapreneuring — the kind of environment that is needed for any large company to survive in the coming years?

I'm not using the word "survive" lightly. The age of big, hierarchical organizations has passed. The Fortune 500 have, on balance, lost jobs since 1965, with all the growth taking place in small firms. This is not just a U.S. trend; it is true throughout Europe, Japan, and the advanced world. The big companies are shrinking, as far as employment is concerned. The small companies are growing, and that's not good news if you are part of a large company and hoping to climb the corporate ladder. The problem is that, on average, big companies are not innovating enough to create new jobs to replace those they eliminate by becoming more efficient. Companies that don't make major changes in the way they manage will find themselves in increasing difficulty. The companies that survive will be a new kind of corporation, with a flowering of productivity and creativity.

The Innovation Age. The renaissance corporation that will evolve is going to be based on individual freedom, independence of mind and action, and the use of new ideas. Corporations have to change because society is changing. We've been through major changes before. Years and years ago we were hunter-gatherers. Then we entered the rather stable agricultural age, stopped being nomads, and settled down. Then we passed the agricultural age and went into the industrial age. People say, "What's next?" Perhaps the information age, but I don't think so. I think calling it the information age is confusing. What we are really entering is the innovation age. For a while, business prophets claimed we were going to become a nation of clerks shuffling ever more papers. This really is a dismal bureaucratic future, in which we all sit around doing nothing but shuffling paper. I do not believe that will happen. The United States will not cease to be an industrial power by ceding all brutish businesses to the Third World — how could we possibly manage the balance of payments? The United States didn't cease to be an agricultural power with the coming of the industrial age; instead, we practiced agriculture by industrial means with tractors, diesel fuel, chemical fertilizers, and so forth. More and more agricultural productivity was based on industry.

As we enter the innovation age, more and more of our productivity will be coming from innovative people. What's left for you and me is to do things in new ways; to meet customers' needs in ways that nobody has thought of. In fact, big companies are on an innovation treadmill, innovating faster and faster and more and more cost-effectively just to keep up with their increasingly aggressive competitors — foreign, entrepreneurial, and now, God forbid, intrapreneurial — who are segmenting our market and attacking our monolithic positions bit by bit, taking away what we have the way the Japanese took apart the U.S. auto industry.

There is only one answer for dealing with that threat. We have to find new ways to contact customers, new internal interfaces, new ways to manage manufacturing processes, and new ways to innovate, as well as new products.

Innovation does not just mean being creative; innovation also means *doing* something about it. You might think the problems in big companies is generating ideas. You may say, "We're good at implementing, we have a lot of MBAs, and we have management talents, so if we had an idea we could do something with it — but maybe we don't have the right new ideas." My experience wandering around corporate America is that this is not true. There are a lot of people with wonderful ideas, but somehow our system of implementation is not what it should be. Inspection, auditing, and control drives out the implementors and leaves people who can manage what already exists. What is missing are the passionate champions — the intrapreneurs.

Texas Instruments did a study of 50 new products. All of the ones that failed had the same problem: They lacked a passionate champion. In our own studies of case history after case history, we have yet to find a significant innovation without someone who was very much an intrapreneur. The greatest threat, therefore, to America's large firms is not just the growing number of sophisticated new competitors; it is the possibility that the best employees will leave to become entrepreneurs. If that happens we are in big trouble.

In the innovation age, most employees are either innovators or deadwood. If the innovators leave, then the company consists of the walking dead, who are waiting to be gobbled up by competitive entrepreneurs who were once fellow employees. The major challenge of our time is keeping the intrapreneurs inside our companies.

Who are these people? It is hard to imagine who intrapreneurs could be. When I first started thinking about this idea, I thought it was a contradiction in terms — someone who behaves like an entrepreneur inside a large organization. Surely the system works against them and ejects them; surely they cannot be exceptions to the rule. Consider, for example, the way we plan. You set goals, you work for a long time planning, and you get it exactly right. That is very important, because when you put it into action the variances have to be small. That's how we judge a good manager, and yet it has nothing to do with the way innovation actually works.

The way innovation actually works is that you start out with an inspiration, you plan, you fool around, you make mistakes, you do something, you have a failure, you get reinspired, and finally you end up doing something entirely different, which may lead to success.

Consider the birth of one product with which you are all familiar. It started out as a method for insulating railroad cars. There was fiberglass insulation in the walls of the railroad cars. An intrapreneur wanted to wrap cellophane around it and seal it with a tape. When that failed completely, he decided to wrap lettuce in the grocery stores and seal it with his new tape. That also failed when DuPont came up with the idea of heat-sealing cellophane. Now, here we have a good idea, but its market failed, and the technology lost its reason for being, but the intrapreneur didn't give up. He decided to use his tape to replace string for sealing packages in department stores, but that failed because the store clerks would pull it off the roll, cut it with scissors, paste it down, and then spend the next half hour trying to pry up the end of the roll with the scissors. A salesman figured out the kind of dispenser that was needed and built it at home in his basement. The result was Scotch tape. Innovation never happens as planned.

The way we have to manage in a situation where innovation does not happen as planned is very different from what we are used to. The key is to choose people to trust, and then let them respond to change. Let me explain how hard that is going to be.

If you are going to choose people to trust, you have to choose other people *not* to trust as much. You have to think about the venture capitalists — perhaps the best and most cold-hearted manager of innovation. They say, "I would rather have a class A entrepreneur with a class B idea than a class A idea with a class B entrepreneur." They're saying that what matters is the people who are going to carry out the plan, not the plan itself, because the plan may never work. If the plan doesn't work, we have to trust the people. If we have to trust the people, we have to choose between people in the same way we choose between plans. That means George comes up to you and says, "I've got this great idea." You look at the idea and think it's terrific. However, you say, "That is a great idea, George, but we're not going to do it," because basically you don't trust him. Then Susan comes up to you with an idea that you can't understand, but you still say, "Susan, that sounds terrific, let's go for it," because her last four ideas succeeded.

Implied is a whole new system of control, which is based on whether or not people get things done and whether or not they can make something out of their ideas — because that is the missing piece. I have never seen a venture capitalist who will invest in a class C idea even with a class A+ entrepreneur, so there is a limit on what we can take, but what I am trying to suggest is that the balance has to shift.

The reason we are having so many problems with innovation is because of the roles we have set out for innovators. Have you ever been frustrated? You think somehow you are going to come up with an idea, you are going to give it to someone, and they are going to know what to do with it. You are fooling yourself. If *you* don't do something with that idea, if *you* don't become the passionate champion of that idea, you can be pretty sure that no one else will.

Intrapreneurs: The Dreamers Who Do. Intrapreneurs are unusual people, because they are the dreamers who do: not just dreamers, not just doers, but people who do both. We say to workers, "I don't want your dreams, I don't want your ideas, just do what you're told." The workers begin doing less and less work and are on their way back to doing nothing at all. They go home at night and become dreamers, or they dream on the job; but they're not dreaming dreams of how to make the organization a better place, they are dreaming dreams of revenge. We make the same mistake in trying to separate the planner and the line manager.

According to executives, the dreamers are up top, when they are really down with the workers. What is an executive but someone who executes somebody else's dreams, one way or the other? And yet we all know that being an executive is not like that anymore. In a world of constant change, nobody can give you a clear enough picture of what you are supposed to accomplish, so you have to begin making it up or dreaming it up for yourself.

Let's think about the real dreamers — the artists, the inventors. Consider Beethoven. When Beethoven went deaf, all of Europe mourned the loss of the greatest artist of their time, and yet Beethoven went on to write the Ninth Symphony. Now, how is it possible for a deaf man to write a symphony, never hearing a note of it? He heard it in his mind. To be a great composer, you have to have the ability to imagine and hold a picture of something that is not yet there.

Inventors do the same thing. They can build a model of a new machine in their mind. Nicolas Tesla, a great inventor of electric power technology — including the way we make three-phase current — used to build a model of a machine in his mind and set it running. Once he had the machine running, he pushed it into the background of his mind and left it running for three weeks while he went about his business. Then he would drag it back into the foreground of his mind, tear the machine down, and check the bearings for wear.

Imagination is the most concrete mental ability people can possibly have. It is far more concrete that all the numbers and all the formulas and all the analytical tools that we are trained to use in business school. It is seeing something that is not yet there as it's actually going to be, as well as you possibly can. If we're going to have intrapreneurs, we have to go on developing this type of vision. The vision of the intrapreneur, however, is not like the vision of the inventor. The inventor tends to see the product as a finished thing in the hands of the customer and imagine how much the customer is enjoying it.

What they don't see is how we are going to get from here to there. The entrepreneur, while driving a car or standing in the shower, is constantly saying, "Let's see, I can move this ahead a little bit if I walk out in this direction and try to get George to join my team. No, that won't work, George doesn't like this. Well, maybe Phil." He is trying out all the different ways this idea can move forward. He is building a branching network of ways to move toward the goal, until he finally finds a pathway that looks like a winner. Since nothing ever turns out as planned, of course he's wrong, but it is his best guess, so he moves down that path until the world teaches him differently.

After the vision comes the doing part. This is the other hard part of intrapreneuring. I asked one great manager of intrapreneurs how he picks them out. He said, "They are people who are good, *but*. You just go to the personnel department and you say, "Tell me all the people who are good, *but*. They seem to do their jobs well, but there's a good reason not to promote them." Often those people are the intrapreneurs, because they are in trouble for doing things they weren't supposed to do. These are dreamers who *do*, and the organization resists doing new things. I don't care what organization it is, it the nature of a big organization to tend toward stability. It resists the new, but the intrapreneur does it anyway.

To be an intrapreneur, you have to carry your "doing" into all sorts of areas that go outside your job description. One great intrapreneur was Michael Phillips, a market researcher at the Bank of California from 1966 to 1970. As Director of Market Research, he held a position of nothingness, because in banking, marketing does not amount to much; that was particularly true in the 1960s. From this position Michael succeeded in introducing Master Charge, consumer Certificates of Deposit, simplified checking accounts for consumers, and customer training programs to the world. All these things came from one unimportant person. I said to myself, "I've got to meet this man. I've got to find out how he did it."

Now let me give you one example of what he did. Take the idea of consumer Certificates of Deposit. Michael knew that there were a lot of little old ladies out there who had a lot of money that they kept in 5 percent passbook accounts. He wanted to get that money out of other banks and into his bank. He was running focus groups at this time. He learned that there was an instrument called a Certificate of Deposit. People in his focus groups had heard of CDs, but considered them to be only for sophisticated investors.

He said, "I'll simplify it; I'll make it easy." Now there was no actual certificate in a Certificate of Deposit. It was an electronic transfer. That was one of the reasons people wouldn't use them. So he drew up a certificate. Now, how could he get it past the legal department? It had to be in simple English. He walked down, showed it to one person — the youngest lawyer he could find — and said, "Hi, I'm doing a little market test and I have to get this thing to the printer in 15 minutes. Could you just put your initials here? Thank you very much." Then he rushed out. Notice that he was doing the lawyer's job, the copywriter's job, and so forth.

Then he came to his biggest problem: How was he going to train the bank branches to process this new instrument when it came in? He wrote an operations manual and pulled the same trick — I will never know how — on the Vice President of Operations: "We're not really doing anything important here, just a little market test. If anything comes of it, we'll let you know and you can write a real manual. But meanwhile we need this for the one branch we're trying this in." Then he went to all the branches and talked them out of most of their advertising budget for the year; maybe I am exaggerating slightly. In the first six weeks he sold $35 million worth of Certificates of Deposit. Now, was that a market test or a rollout? *This* is an intrapreneur.

How to Be a Sponsor. I want to talk to you now about how to be a sponsor; how to support your local intrapreneurs. The role of managers in the future is going to be much less to inspect, audit, and control, and much more to be a sponsor. There are really two kinds of sponsors. We call them sponsors and protectors, just to be confusing. The first is the direct sponsor — the person who provides the intrapreneur with one-stop shopping for "yes."

How tiresome it is to have to climb through the ranks getting permission here and permission there. Sometimes we spend 65 percent of our time trying to get approval for something, and then have almost no time left over to actually do it. What is needed is a courageous new breed of manager who says, "Okay, I don't formally have the right to give you permission to do this, but what I'm going to do is say, 'Yes.' Now you worry about getting it done, and I will worry about working my way through the old boy's network to get the necessary approvals."

This means that the sponsor has to trust that intrapreneur, not just the idea. I want to tell you, sponsoring is a time-consuming business. You cannot sponsor 20 people; you do not have time for that many mavericks. You probably cannot sponsor more than three or four people at any one time and really give them the kind of service that an intrapreneur needs to get a new idea through the system — maybe only two.

To pick those people carefully you have to play the devil's advocate as well as a supporter. You have to say, "Now explain that to me again. I don't understand why that will work." You need to go at it with the idea that it is okay to ask the questions and still leave the intrapreneur with the right to make the final decision. That's tough, isn't it? It is tough because we are used to the habit of making the final decision if we are the senior person in the room, once we begin boring into an issue. But the sponsor has to be more of a coach, more of a mentor — working with the intrapreneur, asking the tough questions, and giving the intrapreneur the benefit of all his or her experience and opinions, yet saying in the end, "It's your shot to call," and then going back and blocking the opponents who are trying to get in the way.

We are really saying that there are four roles in innovation: inventor, intrapreneur, sponsor, and protector. And we have to support all of them. Top management has to set a vision of the future. If there is not a clear vision of where the company is trying to go, then the intrapreneurs go off in all directions and there is no advantage in being part of a larger company. On the other hand, if the vision is too restrictive, there is no room for innovation. So this is one of the great tasks of leadership — how to inspire people to all go more or less in the same direction while using their own individual styles in coming up with new ways to make it happen. You have to have a management that is open not just to ideas but to trusting the intrapreneurs, because without the intrapreneurs the ideas are sterile. You have to simplify the control systems and build new control systems that are based on knowing whom to trust. It is absolutely foolish to put the same controls on a salesman who for 20 years has been producing tremendous results as you put on someone who is new and right out of the box. We tend to have a broad brush system and say, "I'm sorry. We've got to do it this way, because what would happen to the others?"

No, that's not food enough for the innovation age. If somebody has proven themselves, then treat them differently. There is no egalitarian system that is going to produce enough innovation to help a large company make it through in good health to the 21st century.

Obviously, this means thinking about new career paths. If you really have an innovator — somebody who has a passion for doing things hands-on and moving new ideas forward, and you tell him or her that the forthcoming reward will be a promotion (you know, getting to manage people who are doing routine jobs as part of a mature business), a lot of intrapreneurs are going to say, "Me? A desk job? Doing nothing? I don't think so." And yet what other choice do they have? There simply isn't an adequate career path for innovators in most large organizations. That career path must have large amounts of freedom as a reward in it, because the thing that really matters to the innovator is the right to take his dream forward and make it happen. A really good innovator is entitled to more and more access to corporate resources to try new things.

Innovation age leaders are going to have to at least partially replace their over-reliance on analytical tools with reliance on intuition and trust. They will have the very difficult task of having a bunch of people, who may at first seem to be out of control, each trying their own ideas. How do you integrate this into something that gains the benefit from being part of the larger whole? A great challenge, and yet it can be done. Finally, we must balance the needs of the corporation with the needs of the intrapreneur.

30

Turning Ideas into Products*

Ralph E. Gomory, Senior Vice President for Science and Technology, IBM

Events of the past 40 years have demonstrated in unforgettable ways that science, in addition to being a stimulating intellectual pursuit, has enormous practical power. This power has been made evident to everyone.

It was evident first in the stunningly sudden appearance of the atomic bomb — the practical result of the gradual buildup of knowledge about the atomic structure and the nucleus over the previous 40 years.

A second example of the practical power of science was the appearance and rapid evolution of the transistor — again, the result of a steady buildup of scientific knowledge (this time, about quantum mechanics and solid-state physics) since the 1920s. Today this development, in the form of silicon chips, is rapidly transforming the world around us.

A more recent example is the spectacular scientific success of molecular biology and its practical ramification — biotechnology — which seems well on the way to affecting living beings themselves in a profound and transforming fashion.

Scientific versus Product Dominance. Since World War II, the United States has been the dominant scientific power of the world. But, to the surprise of many, automobiles, steel, and semiconductor memories have shown us that dominant science does not automatically mean dominant industry — even in the most high-technology areas. But we should realize that it never did. Long before, as well as after, World War II — before the world was devastated and the other industrial nations were weakened — the United States was the dominant industrial power of the world. In the 1920s, for example, the United States produced more than twice as much iron, steel, and electricity as France, Germany, and Britain combined (and also more than twice as much per capita). It was on this kind of massive and efficient industrial base that the overwhelming air and sea armadas of World War II were built. All of this was done on a negligible U.S. science base. Europe was the capital of science in the early 1900s. One could say with some truth that we were the "Japan" of that period.

To understand why dominance in science does not necessarily mean dominance in products — and how the United States today can continue to excel in generating new scientific ideas, but not so much in generating competitive products — we need to think more concretely about the connection between science and products. We need to realize that the dominance of science and scientists in creating the atomic bomb, the transistor, and biotechnology provides an example or paradigm for the introduction of radically new technology, but not a paradigm for the more ordinary process of product improvement.

Two Different Development Processes. The radical process I have been talking about so far (that produces, for example, a transistor), I call the "ladder" process. It is the step-by-step reduction of a new idea to practice. With that new idea being dominant, the product forms itself around the new idea or new technology. Those who understand this idea or technology (often scientists) play the dominant role. However, there is another much more common process of innovation, which I call the "cyclic development" process, or the process of repeated incremental improvement. In this type of improvement process, an *existing* product gets better and develops new features year after year. Although that may sound dull, the cumulative effect of these incremental changes can be profound.

It is this process of incremental improvement that has given us larger and better computer memories every year. In the past 20 years of incremental improvement, we have come from putting one bit on a chip to 1 million bits. Incremental improvement is also the process that gives us higher-resolution display screens, quieter and better-quality printers, and so on each year. This process of gradual improvement is enormously important. Most products sold today were here in slightly inferior form last year, and most competition is between variants of the same product. Competition is usually my auto against your auto, not my auto against your helicopter. In areas where the United States has not been competitive, it has, insofar as technical factors are concerned, usually lost out not to radical new technology but to better refinements, better manufacturing technology, or better quality in an existing product.

Characteristics of Cyclic Development. One important point to realize is that the world of incremental product development is, by definition, a world built around the existing product — not, as in the ladder process, around a new idea. The people who know the existing product best, and who decide what happens next, are the ones already involved with it. And what they can do to improve the product is strongly affected by what it already is.

A second point to be aware of is the cyclic nature of the process. In the world of computers, printers, and displays, while the current version of a product is in manufacturing, a development team is working on the next product generation. For example, manufacturing could be making a 256-kilobit (K) memory chip, while development is working on the process, other refinements, and the design for a 1-megabit chip. When they are ready, the megabit chip is introduced into manufacturing, which gradually builds up production and phases out the 256K chip. Then the development process starts over again on a 4-megabit chip. A similar cycle of product improvement and production applies to most products in my industry, and to the products of many other industries as well.

Speed is Crucial. One consequence of this cyclic process is that the speed of the development and manufacturing cycle is crucial. If one company has a three-year cycle and one has a two-year cycle, the company with the two-year cycle will have its process and design into production and in the marketplace one year before the other. The company with the shorter cycle will appear to have newer products with newer technologies. But, in fact, both companies will be working from the same storehouse of technology. It is the speed of the development and manufacturing cycle that appears as technical innovation or leadership. It takes only a few turns of that cycle to build a commanding product lead.

A key factor in the speed of the cycle, as well as in its quality and cost, is the relationship between development and manufacturing. Design for manufacturability results in a rapid start-up of production. Likewise, close ties between manufacturing and development translate into early knowledge of technical problems, speed of introduction, and quality. The lack of these ties does the opposite. Another common feature of this development and manufacturing cycle is its relative imperviousness to outside ideas.

Getting Ideas into the Cycle. There is a right moment for getting new ideas into the cycle from the outside. You need to propose them at the beginning of the cycle; halfway through is too late. If you propose a better print-head one year into a two-year printer development and manufacturing cycle, the proposal is useless. Furthermore, even when the new concept is available at the start of the cycle, it will need to be pretty well fleshed out and tested so that the development team can finish their work on the idea in time. Another complication is the fact that the product is often too complicated, or uses processes that are too complex, to be understood completely. Examples are electroplating baths of unknown composition or effects, reactions of ions in a plasma with surfaces, or even the vibrations and other factors affecting the flight of a read-write head over a magnetic disk.

In development and manufacturing, you often do not know exactly how something works, but you know that it worked last time. In this situation, small, evolutionary changes are clearly more acceptable than large, radical changes. All these things are manifestations of the fact that the existing product is there and is being refined by new ideas. The product, its complexities, what the development and manufacturing teams know or do not know — these are the factors that often dominate. And these factors often are understood only by the development teams themselves. This is nothing like the transistor ladder paradigm, where a whole new device is built around a new idea. All of these facts weigh heavily against ideas from the outside, and even more against ideas at a university level of development.

Keeping Well Informed. If new ideas are difficult to get into the cycle from the outside, then those people who are part of the cycle and who understand the present state of affairs in detail must themselves be the bearers of new ideas. This means that the product engineers themselves must be well informed on the relevant science and technology, for they are often the only route in for new ideas. If they are not up to date about what is happening technically in other companies or in universities, a high level of technology in the infrastructure will go to waste — or, more likely, will be seized upon by a competitor. The travel-to-meetings budget, reading the technical literature, being a part of the overall engineering community — all of this is not a grill, nor is it an indulgence to the professional ambitions of the engineer. It is a necessity if we are to compete with those who do make these efforts, and thus are better able to incorporate change into their own complex product worlds.

Factors in Effective Competition. Our most effective foreign competition to date has been characterized by the following:

- Tight ties between manufacturing and development.
- An emphasis on quality.
- The rapid introduction of incremental improvements often known to all in the development cycle of a preexisting product.
- A tremendous effort, by those actually in the product cycle, to be educated on the relevant technologies, on the competition's products, and on what is going on in the world.

These are the things at which the United States, too, must excel. Much of what needs to be done in U.S. industry emerges from a better understanding of the cyclic development process: closer ties to manufacturing, design for manufacturability, a rapid design cycle, and ensuring the technical up-to-dateness of the engineers themselves. Another thing that emerges from this picture is the self-contained nature of the product development world, and the factors that make this world relatively hard to affect from outside itself.

What about Outside Factors? Nevertheless, let us look briefly at several elements outside the development and manufacturing cycle. The first is the important area of the company's own in-house research organization.

An organization for research (as opposed to development) in industry must be closely tied to the product improvement cycle if it is to succeed. Only through close ties to development and manufacturing can it understand the progress of the cycle, present new steps at the appropriate time, and have them fleshed out enough to be acceptable. Familiarity at a personal level also helps to build this acceptability. All of this is much harder from government laboratories as they are now constituted.

Second, cooperative intercompany research (not development and manufacturing) can sometimes help — especially if it is performed by temporary groups made up of people who afterward return to their home companies with new knowledge. Further considerations include reform of the educational system, strengthening the national science base, and so on. These things are all good and help build a strong foundation and infrastructure. But they are unlikely to affect the development and manufacturing cycle itself in the short run. Their effect will be less direct and more long term. Indeed, it may be that governmental policies in this area need to be formulated with the properties of the development and manufacturing cycle in mind.

The United States has been very successful at the science-and scientist-dominated "ladder" type of innovation, where a wholly new idea moves from research into a wholly new product. But there is no escaping the fact that we must also learn to succeed in the rapid, cyclical, engineer-dominated process of incremental product improvement. Neither process is a substitute for the other. We need both.

31

A Framework for Defining Smart Design and Technology Protection in the 1990s

Terril N. Hurst, Visiting Scholar, Stanford Science Center, Hewlett-Packard Laboratories

The drive for competitiveness in a global environment has led companies to develop products that require diverse, distributed engineering. Multidisciplinary development teams located oceans and continents apart must collaborate to create products and systems within ever-decreasing time frames and cost envelopes. The cry for increased productivity is deafening. But what is really needed is increased effectiveness, which means doing the right things as well as doing things right.

An *effectiveness framework* has been developed. By linking strategic concerns with the tools and technologies of the trade, this framework allows organizations to define smart design and technology protection in the broadest possible context: one that addresses the need for organizational continuity amidst change and the wisest possible investment of intellectual capital. While apparently very general in nature, the effectiveness framework illustrates the difficulty of identifying smart design and technology protection if the organizational context as a whole is not considered. Other organizations will find the effectiveness framework useful in posing questions regarding the strategic value of design, technology, and the increasingly large investments of intellectual capital.

Background and Introduction. For the past several years, my associates and I have been involved in Hewlett-Packard's efforts to improve R&D productivity. One result of these efforts is the HP R&D Productivity Network. This network consists of people from HP's product divisions who work together in councils to plan, execute, and review corporate productivity initiatives. The network originated in a bottom-up fashion, as engineers and managers within the divisions realized that new tools and methods would be effective only if properly supported and linked across division boundaries. As HP's "productivity managers" received top management support for their efforts, the way was opened for strategic and operational plans to be integrated within a single planning process. The R&D Productivity Network was formally organized in 1987. Since then, both productivity managers and upper-level managers have increased their proactive involvement within each other's traditional domain. Productivity managers are moving beyond issues of tool and methods to more strategic concerns, and upper management's involvement in issues beyond the purely strategic has increased. This synergy is crucial if new change mechanisms (such as the R&D Productivity Network) are to succeed.

In the 1990s, the value of intellectual capital will increase dramatically. How organizations choose to deal with this change will affect their ability to prosper in a world that is becoming more tightly coupled by global realities.

The Effectiveness Framework. Figure 31.1 depicts the major components of R&D productivity and the relationships between them. "Doing the Right Things" consists of two categories: Business Issues and System Strategy Issues. Business Issues include external elements such as the market, customer needs, competition, and so on. The focus of System Strategy Issues is on internal elements such as standards, integration, and architectures. Methods and Tools Issues include elements of execution, or "Doing Things Right."

All three issue sets are driven by Management Processes. These Management Processes also influence people's engineering and management skills, capabilities, and motivations. Although productivity improvements can be proposed and designed by others, it is the project and management teams who must implement them in order to have an impact. In other words, people can't simply be ordered to be

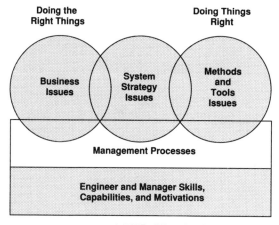

Doing the
Right Things

Doing Things
Right

Business
Issues

System
Strategy
Issues

Methods
and
Tools
Issues

Management Processes

Engineer and Manager Skills,
Capabilities, and Motivations

© 1989 Terril Hurst, Nick Copping, T.W. Cook

Figure 31.1 The Simple View of R&D Productivity

productive; they must be in control of their own environment and participate in any decisions that alter it. Accommodating this participation in planning, executing, and reviewing productivity efforts requires a regularized process that fosters doing, not just talking.

HP's R&D Productivity Network evolved in response to this need to accommodate engineers' participation in the productivity game. Questions such as the following are now being asked: "Where shall we make productivity investments in order to achieve maximal impact?" More specifically, for example, "Which investment will yield more productivity gains for fewer dollars: equipping our mechanical engineers with PC-based finite element modeling (FEM) tools or creating a central analysis group? Or, will it be more productive to the overall product division to improve its rapid prototyping facilities?" Questions such as these require a deep understanding of the organizations and people affected by the decisions. Something more detailed than Figure 31.1 is necessary in order to look for valid solutions.

Figure 31.2 depicts the effectiveness framework. In this model, Business Issues are connected through several layers to basic tools and technologies of the trade. Each layer of the model is now explained.

Theodore Levitt, in his book *The Marketing Imagination* (Free Press, 1986) differentiates between hard technologies (or tools) and

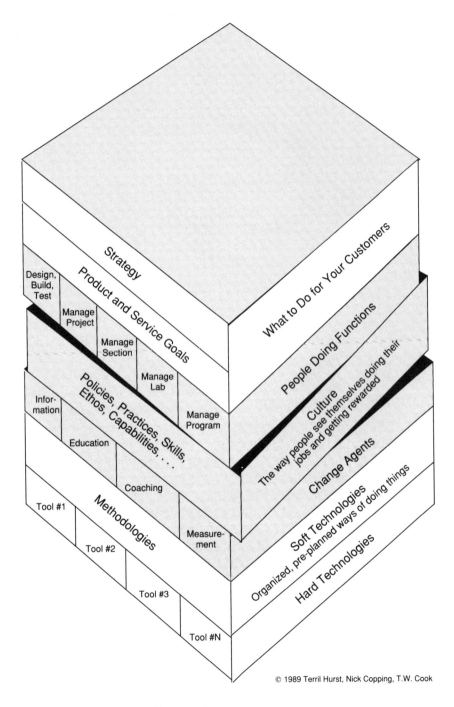

© 1989 Terril Hurst, Nick Copping, T.W. Cook

Figure 31.2 Effectiveness Framework

soft technologies (or methods). CAD systems, software code libraries, and device specifications are all examples of hard technologies. Each can be reused for multiple development projects if made properly accessible. Using them is no guarantee of productivity improvement unless they are properly connected within a sound methodology (an organized, preplanned way of doing things).

Examples of soft technologies (methods) are Structured Analysis and Structured Design, Geometric Dimensioning and Tolerancing, and printed circuit design rule checking. Design paradigms that promise to improve productivity are continually surfacing. However, as Figure 31.3 illustrates, the relationship between tools and methods is a recursive one. Tools (in all their imperfection) both enable and limit the use of idealized methods, which in turn suggest new tools to be developed for their support.

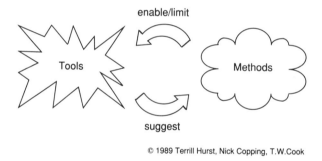

© 1989 Terrill Hurst, Nick Copping, T.W.Cook

Figure 31.3 Interplay between Tools and Methods

Together, tools and methods can amplify existing skills, but they are no substitute for "smart design." It is often possible to create unmanufacturable (albeit precisely documented) designs with leading edge tools, or to create outstanding designs using older, less automated methods.

Neither hard nor soft technologies are of value unless they are accessible to the people for whom they are intended. Whether people use or abandon tools or methods is a function of change agents. Examples of the most powerful change agents include education, coaching, and performance measurement. These change agents can only exist if supported by the organizational culture.

Culture is defined as the way in which people see themselves doing their jobs and being rewarded. For example, an organization that expects people to take a specified number of job-related classes reflects a commitment to continual learning. If properly supported by measurement, coaching, and other change agents, this commitment to learning will improve the organization's effectiveness (as well as the individual's continued employability).

At the next level in the framework, people are actually performing the job functions for which they were hired. Typical job functions include designing, building, and testing things; or managing a project, program, or R&D department. It is only when people perform these functions that product and service goals can be met, which in turn are necessary to provide value to customers and accomplish the company's long-term strategy. The company's strategy and product or service goals are only viable if they competitively respond to customer needs. This usually means the adoption of new technologies and tools. Hence, the framework returns full-circle upon itself.

Smart Design. Most engineering graduates leave campus feeling confident that they are well-equipped to contribute to the companies that hire them. This is often true from the perspective of technical competence. However, as the effectiveness framework illustrates, technical competence represents only a fraction of the knowledge required for engineers to make significant contributions on the job.

Additionally, several job changes are in store for the engineering graduate entering the job market of the 1990s. One pervasive example of these changes in the electronics industry is the "re-treading" of electrical engineers as software developers. Since growth rates in the industry have slowed from the previous 30 percent levels to 10 percent levels, organizations can no longer depend on an infusion of "new thinking" from universities alone to keep them at the leading edge. Current employees must be given a larger share of the opportunity and responsibility to innovate within the effectiveness framework.

Design automation tools are credited with shortening the half-life of an engineer's usable technical knowledge base; however, a more subtle effect of the technology explosion is the rapidity with which leading-edge capabilities permeate the global engineering community. A company's success depends not just on getting the best people to produce the best products for customers but also on doing this for a competitive cost in a responsive time frame.

Figure 31.4 describes the dynamics of knowledge and flexibility during a development project. At inception, relatively little knowledge exists regarding the device or system being developed. As the design process continues, knowledge increases rapidly but then asymptotically approaches a limit. Simultaneously, the organization's flexibility (that is, the ability to react to new knowledge) decays as a result of the increasing costs associated with changes late in the design cycle. Paradoxically, the time at which the most is known about the device or system is the same time at which the least can be done in response to this knowledge!

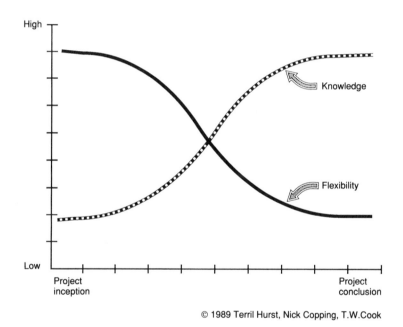

© 1989 Terril Hurst, Nick Copping, T.W.Cook

Figure 31.4 The Real-World Design Paradox

Improving on this paradox can only be achieved with an understanding of the organizational framework described above. Knowledge must be made more reusable (without leading to overly conservative projects). Processes must remain flexible longer during development. In other words, smart design is more than defining and creating fancy devices faster. Smart design is the development of products, systems, and processes that can be responsively integrated within the organization's context.

Smart Technology Protection. Paul Strassman, in his book *Information Payoff: The Transformation of Work in the Electronic Age* (Free Press, 1985), asserts that over two-thirds of all working days in the United States are devoted to "information work," (versus working with actual physical devices). Information work reflects relationships between people who must collaborate to provide goods or services to customers. This predominant form of work produces and consumes enormous amounts of intellectual capital.

Unlike other forms of wealth, technical knowledge often decreases in value with time. Its strategic value often is realized only when it is shared. Sharing technical knowledge with competitors is sometimes the best way to gain value from it, if in so doing the playing field is redefined in terms more compatible with the company's effectiveness framework. Patents and security measures are important tools for managing intellectual capital; however, many other tools must be used in order to maximize the company's return on intellectual investments. In other words, smart technology protection is the acquisition and nurturing of intellectual assets to assure their maximal contribution to the organization's effectiveness.

Companies must remember that people are their most valuable asset, possessing enormous amounts of technical and organizational knowledge. Efforts must continue to develop and maintain the corporate memory. But the corporate memory is only of value as the knowledge it embodies is communicated. Mark Stefik, in the book *The Ecology of Computation* (Elsevier Science Publishers, 1988), foresees major changes coming as a result of the now-pervasive electronic networks. Within Hewlett-Packard, for example, the HP-Internet connects more than 12,000 workstations and 50 sites worldwide. The capability of delivering mail in seconds from Palo Alto, California, to Boblingen, West Germany, qualitatively alters the way people work. It is only a matter of time before customers connect to networks such as these to define product requirements. Any organizational framework that cannot respond to such direct access will be short-lived.

Conclusion. The effectiveness framework described here was developed to cope with the complexities of managing innovation. A dynamic tension will always exist between the need to innovate and the need to provide continuity amidst change. The effectiveness framework is a thinking tool to allow people to fully consider tradeoffs between these two forces. As we move into the 1990s, tools such as this will increase in importance, for change will only continue to accelerate.

I especially thank my two associates, Nick Copping and T.W. Cook, for their contributions in creating the model discussed in this chapter.

32

The Quality and Productivity Equation for the Future

Ross E. Robson and Karen S. Richards

The seriousness and immediacy of the global challenge has caused U.S. government and business to identify and begin to use the components of the quality and productivity equation to enhance America's competitive posture. Considerable attention has been devoted to this challenge by the Council on Competitiveness, the Cuomo Commission, the M.I.T. Commission, and other groups, as is evidenced by the numerous studies and books which have addressed competitive global issues (see Bibliography). Nevertheless, there appears to be considerable room for further improvement. Only a small number of Baldridge, NASA, and Shingo awards — which recognize companies that have successfully applied the equation to their quality and productivity efforts — have been given in the few years since they were inaugurated.

Part of the problem may be the predominant American philosophy of: "If it's not broken, don't fix it," which contrasts dramatically with a reported Japanese philosophy of: "If it isn't perfect, make it better." Thus, the first step in meeting the challenges which confront U.S. business may be to internalize the goal of achieving perfection in quality and productivity. As Alan Magazine notes: "JIT is necessary and we must keep moving, must keep shooting higher and increase the rate of productivity growth."

The contributions of the essays in this book can be summarized into five sections which warrant attention by business and government in using the constants and variables of the quality and productivity equation to respond to the challenges of the future.

The Global Challenge. The United States is clearly confronted with declining economic growth. The U.S. share of the world economy has declined markedly. America has shifted from being the world's largest creditor nation to its largest debtor nation in just a few years. The prospect of such a decline was unimaginable in the recent past. In fact, rapid change seems to be the order of the day on the global front. While Malcolm Forbes, at the time of his address in January 1989, called attention to the prospect of significant change in the very near future, no one could have foreseen at that time the incredible changes in Eastern bloc countries that would occur by the end of 1989. Changes occurring in the political and economic relationships between the Eastern and Western blocs, the Pacific Rim, and Third World countries pose real challenges. Mr. Forbes is very optimistic that U.S. "know-how" provides tremendous advantages in responding to these challenges. The present American economic decline, however, — for which there are two possible explanations — is still very real.

One explanation is offered by Paul Allaire: "We became arrogant and complacent." The three themes outlined below can be explained, at least in part, by this arrogance and complacency. We lost sight of the changing national and world environment and failed to respond.

The second broad explanation for the current U.S. economic position is that world competition — particularly in the Pacific rim — evolved at a phenomenal and totally unexpected rate, and the United States failed to adapt by not working both smarter and harder to meet the challenge. Kim Cameron points out what Japanese managers have consistently reported: "We just practice what you preach." Whatever the explanation of the decline, many chapters acknowledge it and clearly imply that U.S. pre-eminence cannot be attained in either the short term or the long term, but that the decline can be halted if we attend to quality and productivity.

The three themes evolving from this book in response to the global challenge are: (1) the need for technological adaptation; (2) the necessity for innovation and change; and (3) the importance of human resources in being competitive in both quality and productivity.

The Need for Technological Adaptation. Technological adaptation is multifaceted. On one hand is the view that global competition is driven by technology, and that we lost sight of the necessity for continual technological improvement in order to remain competitive. A short-term orientation, reduced spending (or failure to increase spending) for research and development, and reduced emphasis on scientific development have been identified as U.S. shortcomings over the past ten to 15 years. Key to these issues are appropriate roles/relationships between business and government. There appears to be a general belief that dynamic and farsighted national leadership is sorely needed in steering our country to renewed strength in scientific research and development.

The second perspective outlined addresses the need for further development of computer-integrated manufacturing designed for continuous improvement, with total quality control as the goal. Related concerns involve the elimination of waste, inventory reduction, and using networking to ensure that businesses and/or suppliers do what they can do *best* in adding value to business endeavors.

Lastly, the technological revolution has required adapting information systems to the quality and productivity equation. The need for strategic information management which is integrated with all business functions is widely acknowledged. Situational, fully integrated implementation of information technology within a company can result in competitive advantage.

The importance of technology is not generally viewed as the ultimate answer to the quality and productivity equation, but rather as one important element which should be subsumed under the necessity for innovation and change.

The Necessity for Innovation and Change. Rapid change — beyond virtually all predictions by futurists — is a given as we enter the 1990s. Thus, it goes without saying that organizations must be flexible and open to change. Nevertheless, the emphasis given to the necessity for innovation and change by conference participants was remarkable; many implied that U.S. business firms are not well-prepared.

First is widespread acknowledgement that "old rules" won't work in the future. The rules of the past in terms of business/government, employee or union/management, and producer/customer relations must change to meet new expectations.

A second theme is the call for organizational change, development, and role clarification aimed at insuring the existence of a responsive structure. This call includes a move toward flatter, less hierarchical structures, and is closely related to the organization and management of human resources. Bureaucratic organizations are generally incapable of fast responses. However, bringing about change in an organization's culture clearly requires a long-term orientation.

Manufacturing is the third area requiring change and innovation. Whereas many preached the doomsday message of "manufacturing death" during the early 1980s, not a single essay in this book argues anything but the potential for a resurgence in manufacturing in the years ahead. A call for innovation and change is outlined based upon the importance of value-added manufacturing in contributing to the wealth and well-being both of employees and businesses. The theme of "doing what you do best" and networking businesses prevails.

The last and possibly most important call for innovation and change concerns the overall focus of this book — quality and productivity improvement. Emphasis is given to a continuous and simultaneous approach to ensuring total quality control to satisfy increasing customer expectations. Both quality and productivity are necessary to ensure a competitive edge in the global marketplace.

In sum, maintaining a competitive edge demands that innovation and change be built into the corporate culture of a business and be customized to its particular product(s) and/or service(s).

Importance of Human Resources. The human resource factor has drawn considerable attention during the decade of the 1980s, and will undoubtedly continue to be a major focus in the 1990s for corporate leaders who are convinced that quality and productivity are necessary to achieve and maintain a competitive advantage in a global economy. Two human resource themes prevail throughout the chapters of this book:

1. Organizational adaptation to the changing workforce; individual role clarification to ensure fast response; and structural adjustments that emphasize teams and teamwork.
2. The importance of education, training, and re-training.

The importance of organizational and individual adaptation to the human resource aspects of business is strongly emphasized in many chapters. Individual adaptation is required in two ways:

1. Role clarification aimed at organizing people to simultaneously achieve both personal and organizational goals and objectives through flexible and rapid response.
2. Effective team organization is based upon the premises that employees know the answers to problems, and solutions will emerge when a climate conducive to cooperation and "brainstorming" with fellow employees prevails. For most organizations, this sharing of power and influence requires significant cultural change.

Organizational re-design has been addressed by several individuals. Less hierarchy, flatter organizational structures, and increased decentralization are continually pointed to as necessities for insuring competitive advantage in the future. The increasingly heterogeneous and untrained workforce described in "Workforce 2000" make the challenges of re-design even more apparent. President Bush and the 50 governors have recognized education as a vital ingredient of competitive advantage, but its successful implementation appears uncertain based upon existing data and social conditions.

The second primary human resources theme addresses the need for effective management skills training. The evidence suggests that successful managers share characteristics and qualities that can be taught via experiential learning activities that emphasize skill building rather than cognitive learning. The emphasis in training must be on process, such as teamwork activities. Recognition of the value-added dimension of continual training and re-training is also a prevalent theme in a number of chapters. As Tom Peters has suggested, it would be warranted to tax credits for training equivalent to tax credits currently granted for hardware. The empirical evidence regarding the benefits that training offers in terms of quality and productivity continues to grow.

The human factor, including increased emphasis on corporate ethics, is an essential ingredient in spurring and maintaining improvement in quality and productivity in the 1990s and beyond.

The Ethical Dimension. Two chapters of this volume directly address the question of business ethics. Anthony Burns persuasively argues that business ethics is *not* an oxymoron, but simply the foundation of good business practice. Good customers demand business relationships that are based upon firm and positive ethical values. The Partners in Business program is pleased to participate in furthering the practice of high business ethics with annual M. Anthony Burns Lectures on Business Ethics.

The story of the Johnson & Johnson Credo documents the value of serving the public first and the stockholder last. The assumption is that if the public is well served, thus ensuring competitive advantage, the stockholder will ultimately benefit as well. Johnson & Johnson mince few words in arguing that the trust that resulted from following the Credo and their related corporate culture saved the day following the Tylenol tampering cases.

Conclusion. Although the quality and productivity equation is difficult to quantify, the sharing of best practices clearly documents its most important variables. This compilation acknowledges and defines the global challenge for business in the 1990s. Four strategies emerge as prevailing themes throughout the chapters in this volume. Whether these strategies represent all the variables necessary to ensure quality and productivity may be argued, but what is clear is that the values discussed — technological adaptation, innovation and change, creative human resources management, and ethics — are key ingredients of the quality and productivity equation. In many cases the United States needs to rebuild trust that was lost due to the production of goods of inferior quality. Productivity improvement is equally necessary to ensure competitive advantage in a global market. It is toward these ends that this book is aimed.

Selected Bibliography

Baily, Martin Neil, and Alok K. Chakrabarti. *Innovation and the Productivity Crisis*. Washington DC: The Brookings Institution, 1988.

Bain, David. *The Productivity Prescription: The Manager's Guide to Improving Productivity and Profits*. New York: McGraw-Hill, 1986.

Basu, A.P. *Reliability and Quality Control*. New York: Elsevier, 1986.

Bluestone, Barry, and Bennett Harrison. *The Deindustrialization of America*. New York: Basic Books, 1982.

Business Roundtable. *American Excellence in a World Economy*. New York: The Business Roundtable, 1987.

Council on Competitiveness. *America's Competitive Crisis: Confronting the New Reality*. Washington DC: Council on Competitiveness, 1987.

Crosby, Philip B. *Quality Without Tears: The Art of Hassle-Free Management*. New York: McGraw-Hill, 1984.

The Cuomo Commission on Trade and Competitiveness. *The Cuomo Commission Report*. New York: Simon and Schuster, 1988.

Deming, W. Edwards. *Quality, Productivity, and Competitive Position*. Cambridge MA: MIT Press, 1982.

_____ . *Out of the Crisis*. Cambridge MA: M.I.T. Center for Advanced Engineering Study, 1986.

Dertouzos, Michael L., Richard K. Lester, Robert M. Solow, and The M.I.T. Commission on Industrial Productivity. *Made in America: Regaining the Competitive Edge*. Cambridge MA: M.I.T. Press, 1989.

Dornbusch, Rudiger, James Poterba, and Lawrence Summers. *The Case for Manufacturing in America's Future* (Revised). Rochester NY: Eastman Kodak, 1988.

Gitlow, Howard S., and Shelly J. Gitlow. *The Deming Guide to Quality and Competitive Position*. Englewood Cliffs NJ: Prentice-Hall, 1987.

Goldberg, Joel A. *A Manager's Guide to Productivity Improvement*. New York: Praeger, 1986.

Griffith, Gary. *Quality Technician's Handbook*. New York: Wiley, 1986.

Harrington, James H. *The Improvement Process: How America's Leading Companies Improve Quality.* New York: McGraw-Hill, 1987.

Hayes, Robert H., and Steven C. Wheelwright. *Restoring Our Competitive Edge Through Manufacturing.* New York: John Wiley, 1984.

Juran, Joseph M. *Quality Control Handbook.* New York: McGraw-Hill, 1974.

Kanter, Rosabeth Moss. *The Change Master: How People and Companies Succeed Through Innovation in the New Corporate Era.* New York: Simon & Schuster, 1983.

Kendrick, John W. *International Comparisons of Productivity and Causes of the Slowdown.* Cambridge MA: Ballinger, 1984.

Lawrence, Robert Z. *Can America Compete?* Washington DC: The Brookings Institution, 1984.

Levering, Robert, Milton Moskowitz, and Michail Katz. *The 100 Best Companies to Work for in America.* Reading MA: Addison-Wesley, 1984.

Link, Albert N., and Gregory Tassey. *Strategies for Technology-Based Competition: Meeting the New Global Challenge.* Lexington MA: Lexington Books, 1987.

Naisbitt, John. *Reinventing the Corporation.* New York: Warner, 1985.

National Academy of Engineering. *The Technological Dimensions of International Competitiveness.* A Report to the Council of the National Academy of Engineering prepared by the Committee on Technology Issues that Impact International Competitiveness. Washington DC: National Academy of Engineering, 1988.

Ouchi, William. *The M-Form Society.* Reading MA: Addison-Wesley, 1984.

Peters, Tom. *Thriving on Chaos.* New York: Harper and Row, 1987.

Peters, Thomas J., and Robert H. Waterman, Jr. *In Search of Excellence: Lessons from America's Best-Run Companies.* New York: Harper and Row, 1982.

Pinchot, Gifford, III. *Intrapreneuring.* New York: Harper and Row, 1985.

President's Commission on Industrial Competitiveness. *Global Competition: The New Reality.* Vol. 1 and 2. Washington DC: U.S. Government Printing Office, 1985.

Schonberger, Richard J. *Japanese Manufacturing Techniques: Nine Hidden Lessons in Simplicity.* New York: The Free Press, 1982.

———. *World Class Manufacturing.* New York: The Free Press, 1986.

Sepehri, Mehran, ed. *Quest for Quality: Managing the Total System.* Technology Park, Atlanta: Industrial Engineering and Management Press, 1987.

Shetty, Y.K., and Vernon M. Buehler, eds. *Competing Through Quality and Productivity.* Cambridge MA: Productivity Press, 1988.

Shingo, Shigeo. *A Study of the Toyota Production System from an Industrial Engineering Viewpoint* (Revised). Cambridge MA: Productivity Press, 1989.

_____ . *Non-Stock Production: The Shingo System for Continuous Improvement*. Cambridge MA: Productivity Press, 1988.

_____ . *A Revolution in Manufacturing: The SMED System*. Cambridge MA: Productivity Press, 1985.

_____ . *Zero Quality Control: Inspection and the Poka-Yoke System*. Cambridge MA: Productivity Press, 1986.

Sinha, Madhav H., and W.O. Willborn. *Essentials of Quality Assurance Management*. New York: John Wiley, 1986.

Stebbing, Lionel. *Quality Assurance: The Route to Efficiency and Competitiveness*. New York: Halsted Press, 1986.

Thurow, Lester C. *The Zero-Sum Solution*. New York: Simon and Schuster, 1985.

Townsend, Patrick L. *Commit to Quality*. New York: John Wiley, 1986.

Twiss, Brian. *Managing Technological Innovation*. White Plains NY: Longman, 1986.

Wadsworth, Harrison M., et al. *Modern Methods for Quality Control and Improvement*. New York: John Wiley, 1986.

Werther, William B., Jr., et al. *Productivity Through People*. New York: West Publishing, 1986.

White House Conference on Productivity. *Productivity Growth: A Better Life for America*. Report to the President of the United States. Washington DC: U.S. Department of Commerce, National Technical Information Service, 1984.

Young, John A. "Technology and Competitiveness." *Science* 241 (1988): 313-316.

Biographical Notes

Paul A. Allaire is the president and a member of the board of directors of Xerox Corporation, where he directs the business products and systems divisions. Mr. Allaire previously was managing director of Rank Xerox, Xerox's European business. He graduated from Worcester Polytechnic Institute with a B.S. in electrical engineering and earned an M.S. in industrial administration from Carnegie-Mellon University.

Jack N. Behrman is the Luther Hodges distinguished professor and associate dean at the University of North Carolina Graduate School of Business Administration, where he has taught international business, ethics, and comparative management. He holds an M.A. from the University of North Carolina and a Ph.D. from Princeton University, and has published over 100 articles and 40 books on economics and business.

Mylle H. Bell is the director of corporate planning at BellSouth Corporation, Atlanta, Georgia. Ms. Bell is a graduate of Emory University. After her graduation she taught gifted children in the North Syracuse, New York, school system until 1972. Prior to joining Bell South she spent 12 years with General Electric. Ms. Bell has also served as the president of BellSouth International.

James E. Burke was chairman and CEO of Johnson & Johnson, the world's most diversified health-care company, for more than 12 years. Under his leadership, annual worldwide sales grew from $2.5 billion to $9 billion. Mr. Burke joined Johnson & Johnson in 1953 and was named director of new products in 1955. He was elected a director and member of the executive committee in 1965, and became president of the corporation in 1973. He stepped down as chairman in April 1989.

M. Anthony Burns is the chairman, president, and CEO of Ryder System, Inc., Miami, Florida. He joined Ryder System in 1974 as director of corporate planning and treasurer. He was elected president in 1979, CEO in 1983, and chairman in 1985. Before joining Ryder System, he spent nine years as a manager and controller for Mobil Oil. He holds a B.S. from Brigham Young University and an M.B.A. from UC-Berkeley. Mr. Burns serves on the boards of Pfizer, J.C. Penney, Southeast Banking Corporation, and Southeast Bank. A recipient of numerous awards, he is a former chairman of the National Urban League and serves on the boards of the University of Miami and the U.S. Chamber of Commerce.

Kim S. Cameron is an associate professor of organizational behavior, human resources management, and higher education at the University of Michigan. He also serves as the co-director of the IBM Organizational Studies Center. He holds B.S. and M.S. degrees from Brigham Young University and an M.A. and Ph.D. from Yale. He has authored numerous articles and five books on subjects such as organizational effectiveness, adaptation to turbulence and decline, organizational downsizing, and developing management skills.

Joe C. Collier, Jr. became president and CEO of Central Maine Power Company on July 1, 1989. At the time of the presentation included in this book, he was a senior vice president at Florida Power & Light, where he was responsible for corporate planning and regulation. While at FPL, he was part of the management team that developed the corporate quality program that resulted in Florida Power & Light winning the prestigious Deming Award.

William E. Conway is the founder and president of Conway Quality, Inc. and the former president and chairman of Nashua Corporation. He is an advocate of using statistical methods as well as human relations, the principles of work, and imagineering to make dramatic improvements in quality and productivity of all work. In 1984 he received the prestigious Edwards Medal from the American Society for Quality Control.

John Diebold is the chairman and founder of The Diebold Group, Inc., the international firm of management consultants. He is a pioneer in the field of automation; he coined the word in its present meaning and did much to introduce it to general usage. He wrote his first book, *Automation*, at the age of 26 and originated many of the concepts which are accepted today as basic in the fields of both automation and management.

Nancy Dreicer is vice president of corporate resources for American Transtech, Inc., an AT&T company headquartered in Jacksonville, Florida. Prior to joining American Transtech, she held various management positions with AT&T which focused on managing large groups through transition. She has extensive experience in human resources, organizational development, and training.

Charles W. Elliott joined Kellogg Company as executive vice president–administration in February 1987. Previously, he held various executive positions during his 30-year career with Price Waterhouse. He most recently served as partner-in-charge of their

Chicago Tax Department and as a member of the Price Waterhouse Policy Board (Board of Directors). He is a graduate of the University of Illinois and a Certified Public Accountant.

Donald F. Ephlin has been the international vice president of the United Auto Workers since 1980. He is also director of the UAW's General Motors Department, which has a membership of 400,000. He is a pioneer in union negotiations in the areas of job security, profit sharing, and worker participation in the corporate decision-making process. He is widely recognized as an authority in joint labor-management problem-solving.

Malcolm S. Forbes, chairman and editor-in-chief of *Forbes Magazine*, Inc., graduated from Princeton University in 1941. He entered the newspaper business two days after graduation. Following service in WWII, he joined the staff of the business publication founded by his father. He became a vice president of Forbes, Inc. in 1947 and served as associate publisher of *Forbes*. On the death of his father in 1954, he was elected editor and publisher of *Forbes*.

Jay R. Galbraith is a professor of management and organization and a member of the Center of Effective Organizations at the University of Southern California. His area of specialization is organizational design, change, and development. Dr. Galbraith has extensive consulting experience in the U.S., Europe, and South America on the design of corporate structures, international organization, project and product management systems, internal new ventures, and major organizational changes.

Ralph E. Gomory was the senior vice president of science and technology for IBM when he gave this presentation. He led the company's worldwide research division, as well as its science and technology assessment and university relations functions. He is a member of the University Council for the Graduate School at Yale University and a trustee of Princeton University. Dr. Gomory holds six honorary doctorates and was a member of the White House Science Council from 1986 to 1988. He is a recipient of the National Medal of Science and the current president of the Alfred P. Sloan Foundation.

Terril N. Hurst is currently a Visiting Scholar at Stanford University serving as a member of Hewlett-Packard's Science Center Program, where he is collaborating to improve the electro-mechanical design process through the application of artificial intelligence. Dr. Hurst has previously served as chairman of Hewlett-Packard's Mechanical Design Technology Council. He received a Ph.D. from Brigham Young University.

Spencer Hutchens, Jr., is a senior vice president of Intertek Services Corporation. He is also the 1989 national president of the American Society for Quality Control. Prior to joining Intertek in 1979, he held a number of positions with the federal government, including the post of deputy director of quality assurance for the Defense Contracts Administration Services Region, Los Angeles, California. Mr. Hutchens has received numerous awards and honors.

Sidney L. Jones is a professor of public policy at Georgetown University and an associate faculty member at the Center for Public Policy Education at the Brookings Institution. Dr. Jones has had six presidential appointments, including Assistant Secretary of the Treasury and staff of the Council of Economic Advisors. He received a B.S. in economics from Utah State University and an M.B.A. and Ph.D. from Stanford.

L. William Krause is the chairman and CEO of 3COM Corporation, Santa Clara, California. He joined 3COM as president in 1981, and was elected chairman in 1987. 3COM is computer networking company which provides local and wide-area network solutions worldwide. From 1967 to 1981 he was employed by Hewlett-Packard as general manager of the general systems division. Mr. Krause holds a B.S. in electrical engineering from The Citadel.

Richard L. Lesher assumed the post of president of the U.S. Chamber of Commerce in 1975. Since then he has been instrumental in spurring tremendous growth in all areas of the Chamber and has emerged as a leading national and international spokesman on economic issues. Since taking the helm of the Chamber, Dr. Lesher has drawn on his top-level management experience in business and at NASA to transform a respected but passive association into one of the most powerful and effective volunteer organizations in Washington.

Alan H. Magazine is the president of the Council on Competitiveness. He works with leaders from business, labor, and higher education to increase public awareness and understanding of the competitiveness problems and facilitate implementation of far-reaching solutions. Dr. Magazine has a B.A. degree from Monmouth College, an M.P.A. from Kent State, and Ph.D. from the University of Maryland in public administration.

Larry G. McKean is vice president of corporate human resources at The Boeing Company. Since 1953 he has progressed through various assignments at Boeing, including senior manager of personnel and director of personnel. His current assignments include facilitating union negotiations at the various Boeing subsidiaries throughout the U.S. and Canada. He was appointed to his present position in March of 1987.

James R. Metzger was named general manager of the information technology department at Texaco, Inc., Houston, Texas, in 1988. He graduated from Rice University in 1969 with a bachelor of commerce degree and joined Texaco as a programmer trainee. He subsequently held various positions in the computer services department.

Edward H. Northrop is the chairman of Xicom, Inc., a Tuxedo, New York-based management consulting firm specializing in organizational development and training for business, industry, the health profession, and government. He has had considerable experience working with organizations on the management of conflict and the use of power. A graduate of Dartmouth College, he also holds an M.B.A. from the University of Virginia.

Gifford Pinchot III is the founder and chairman of Pinchot & Company, and is an author, speaker, and consultant on innovation management. His best-selling book on "intrapreneuring" defined the ground rules for an emerging field of enterprise: the pursuit of new ideas in established organizations. He graduated with honors in economics from Harvard.

Kevin F.F. Quigley, currently the director of public policy at The Pew Charitable Trusts, wrote this article while he was a Council on Foreign Relations International Affairs Fellow working as a resident associate at The Carnegie Endowment for International Peace. Formerly the legislative director to Senator John Heinz, he was also a senior budget examiner at the Office of Management and Budget, specializing in international trade and finance.

Karen S. Richards, a freelance copy and rewrite editor, is completing a master's degree in human resource administration at Utah State University. Her major areas of interest include interviewing, recruiting, and training. Ms. Richards is currently conducting research on the costs and benefits of on-site child-care facilities. She holds a B.A. degree from Brigham Young University.

Ross E. Robson is associate dean for business relations and director of the Partners in Business programs of the College of Business, Utah State University, and executive director of The Shigeo Shingo Prizes for Excellence in Manufacturing. At Utah State since 1979, he is an associate professor of management and human resources, and was the first coordinator of the Master's degree program in Human Resources Administration. Dr. Robson previously taught at the University of Tennessee and University of Georgia, and received a Ph.D. from the University of Maryland. He has extensive consulting experience with both business and government in the U.S. and abroad, including numerous publications, contracts, and grants regarding management and human resources.

Wickham Skinner is the James E. Robison Professor of Business Administration Emeritus at the Harvard Business School. He holds a B.S. in engineering from Yale and an M.B.A. and a D.B.A from Harvard. Dr. Skinner joined Harvard, where he subsequently became associate dean, after 10 years with Honeywell Corporation. He has lectured worldwide on production management, manufacturing, and operations. He received the McKinsey Prize, which is awarded for the best article in the *Harvard Business Review* for 1986.

Martin K. Starr is a professor at Columbia University's Graduate School of Business and the director of the Center of Operations. He earned his M.S. at MIT and his M.S. and Ph.D. at Columbia. He is past president of the Institute of Management Sciences and former editor-in-chief of *Management Science* journal. He is also appointed to the faculty of Columbia's School of Engineering and Applied Sciences.

James J. Whaley is vice president–personnel relations at Bank of America. He holds a degree in psychology and has been involved in human resource functions in the past with Crocker National Bank, Shaklee Corporation, and Firemans Fund Insurance Companies.

John A. White is the assistant director for engineering at the National Science Foundation. A member of the National Academy of Engineering, he is the past president of the Institute of Industrial Engineers and past chairman of the American Association of Engineering Societies. In addition, he has co-authored five textbooks and numerous articles.

Also From Productivity Press

Productivity Press publishes and distributes materials on continuous improvement in productivity, quality, customer service, and the creative involvement of all employees. Many of our products are direct source materials from Japan that have been translated into English for the first time and are available exclusively from Productivity. Supplemental products and services include newsletters, conferences, seminars, in-house training and consulting, audio-visual training programs, and industrial study missions. Send for our free book catalog.

Competing Through Productivity and Quality
edited by Vernon M. Buehler and Y.K. Shetty

Fifty authorities from American industry, labor, and higher education share their most up-to-date strategies and policies for productivity and quality improvement. Inspiring, insightful, and practical guidance from such people as David Halberstam, Shigeo Shingo, C. Jackson Grayson, Lynn Williams, and John Young. This book provides the information necessary to ensure the long-term economic health of the U.S.
ISBN 0-915299-43-7/576 pages/$39.95/Order code COMP-BK

1992
Strategies for the Single Market
by James W. Dudley

In 1992 the European community will unify to create the second largest market worldwide. Published in England, here is the first comprehensive guide for action for anyone who wants to take advantage of the opportunities, and overcome the threats, that this major changes to the world's economic structure holds. It examines financial structures, marketing programs, political strategies, and much more.
ISBN 1-85091-240-8/400 pages/$24.95/Order code 1998-BK

Today and Tomorrow
by Henry Ford

The inspiration for Just-In-Time and so many other "modern" business practices. Originally published in 1926, this autobiography by the world's most famous automaker has been long out of print. Yet Ford's ideas have never stopped having an impact, and this book provides direct access to the thinking that changed industry forever. Here is the man who doubled wages, cut the price of a car in half, and produced over 2 million units a year. Time has not diminished the progressiveness of his business philosophy, or his profound influence on worldwide industry. You will be enlightened by what you read, and intrigued by the words of this colorful and remarkable man.
ISBN 0-915299-36-4/286 pages/$24.95/Order code FORD-BK

Productivity Press, Inc., Dept. BK, P.O. Box 3007, Cambridge, MA 02140 1-800-274-9911

Tough Words for American Industry

by Hajime Karatsu

Let's stop "Japan bashing" and take a good close look at ourselves instead! Here is an analysis of the friction caused by recent trade imbalances between the United States and Japan — from the Japanese point of view. Written by one of Japan's most respected economic spokesmen, this insightful and provocative book outlines the problems and the solutions that Karatsu thinks the U.S. should consider as we face the critical challenge of our economic future. For anyone involved in manufacturing or interested in economic policy, this is a rare opportunity to find out what "the other side" thinks.
ISBN 0-915299-25-9/178 pages/$24.95/Order code TOUGH-BK

Better Makes Us Best

by John Psarouthakis

A powerful and highly practical guide to performance improvement for any business or individual. Focusing on incremental progress toward clear goals is the key — you become "better" day by day. It's a realistic, personally fulfilling, action-oriented, and dynamic philosophy that has made Psarouthakis's own company a member of the Fortune 500 in just ten years. Let it work for you.
ISBN 0-915299-56-9/1989/112 pages/$16.95/Order code BMUB-BK

The Eternal Venture Spirit
An Executive's Practical Philosophy

by Kazuma Tateisi

Like human health, organizational health depends on discovering the causes of symptoms that indicate an imbalance in the system. Tateisi, founder and CEO of Omron Industries, one of Japan's leading electronics companies, analyzes the signals of "big business disease" and how to respond to them so that technological innovation and entrepreneurial spirit can thrive as the organization grows and the market changes. An outstanding book on long-term strategic management.
ISBN 0-915299-55-0/208 pages/$24.95/Order code EVS-BK

Productivity Press, Inc., Dept. BK, P.O. Box 3007, Cambridge, MA 02140 1-800-274-9911

BOOKS AVAILABLE FROM PRODUCTIVITY PRESS

Buehler, Vernon M. and Y.K. Shetty (eds.). **Competing Through Productivity and Quality**
ISBN 0-915299-43-7/1989/576 pages/$39.95/order code COMP

Christopher, William F. **Productivity Measurement Handbook**
ISBN 0-915299-05-4/1985/680 pages/$137.95/order code PMH

Ford, Henry. **Today and Tomorrow**
ISBN 0-915299-36-4/1988/286 pages/$24.95/order code FORD

Fukuda, Ryuji. **Managerial Engineering: Techniques for Improving Quality and Productivity in the Workplace**
ISBN 0-915299-09-7/1984/206 pages/$34.95/order code ME

Hatakeyama, Yoshio. **Manager Revolution! A Guide to Survival in Today's Changing Workplace**
ISBN 0-915299-10-0/1985/208 pages/$24.95/order code MREV

Hirano, Hiroyuki. **JIT Factory Revolution: A Pictorial Guide to Factory Design of the Future**
ISBN 0-915299-44-5/1989/218 pages/$49.95/order code JITFAC

Japan Human Relations Association (ed.). **The Idea Book: Improvement Through TEI (Total Employee Involvement)**
ISBN 0-915299-22-4/1988/232 pages/$49.95/order code IDEA

Japan Management Association (ed.). **Kanban and Just-In-Time at Toyota: Management Begins at the Workplace** (Revised Ed.), Translated by David J. Lu
ISBN 0-915299-48-8/1989/224 pages/$34.95/order code KAN

Japan Management Association and Constance E. Dyer. **The Canon Production System: Creative Involvement of the Total Workforce**
ISBN 0-915299-06-2/1987/251 pages/$36.95/order code CAN

Karatsu, Hajime. **Tough Words For American Industry**
ISBN 0-915299-25-9/1988/178 pages/$24.95/order code TOUGH

Karatsu, Hajime. **TQC Wisdom of Japan: Managing for Total Quality Control**, Translated by David J. Lu
ISBN 0-915299-18-6/1988/136 pages/$34.95/order code WISD

Lu, David J. **Inside Corporate Japan: The Art of Fumble-Free Management**
ISBN 0-915299-16-X/1987/278 pages/$24.95/order code ICJ

Mizuno, Shigeru (ed.). **Management for Quality Improvement: The 7 New QC Tools**
ISBN 0-915299-29-1/1988/318 pages/$59.95/order code 7QC

Monden, Yashuhiro and Sakurai, Michiharu. **Japanese Management Accounting: A World Class Approach to Profit Management**
ISBN 0-915299-50-X/1989/512 pages/$49.95/order code JMACT

Nakajima, Seiichi. **Introduction to TPM: Total Productive Maintenance**
ISBN 0-915299-23-2/1988/149 pages/$39.95/order code ITPM

Nakajima, Seiichi. **TPM Development Program: Implementing Total Productive Maintenance**
ISBN 0-915299-37-2/1989/528 pages/$85.00/order code DTPM

Productivity Press, Inc., Dept. BK, P.O. Box 3007, Cambridge, MA 02140 1-800-274-9911

Nikkan Kogyo Shimbun, Ltd./Factory Magazine (ed.). **Poka-yoke: Improving Product Quality by Preventing Defects**
ISBN 0-915299-31-3/1989/288 pages/$59.95/order code IPOKA

Ohno, Taiichi. **Toyota Production System: Beyond Large-Scale Production**
ISBN 0-915299-14-3/1988/163 pages/$39.95/order code OTPS

Ohno, Taiichi. **Workplace Management**
ISBN 0-915299-19-4/1988/165 pages/$34.95/order code WPM

Ohno, Taiichi and Setsuo Mito. **Just-In-Time for Today and Tomorrow: A Total Management System**
ISBN 0-915299-20-8/1988/208 pages/$34.95/order code OMJIT

Psarouthakis, John. **Better Makes Us Best**
ISBN 0-915299-56-9/1989/112 pages/$16.95/order code BMUB

Shingo, Shigeo. **Non-Stock Production: The Shingo System for Continuous Improvement**
ISBN 0-915299-30-5/1988/480 pages/$75.00/order code NON

Shingo, Shigeo. **A Revolution In Manufacturing: The SMED System**, Translated by Andrew P. Dillon
ISBN 0-915299-03-8/1985/383 pages/$65.00/order code SMED

Shingo, Shigeo. **The Sayings of Shigeo Shingo: Key Strategies for Plant Improvement**, Translated by Andrew P. Dillon
ISBN 0-915299-15-1/1987/208 pages/$36.95/order code SAY

Shingo, Shigeo. **A Study of the Toyota Production System from an Industrial Engineering Viewpoint** (Revised Ed.)
ISBN 0-915299-17-8/1989/352 pages/$39.95/order code STREV

Shingo, Shigeo. **Zero Quality Control: Source Inspection and the Poka-yoke System**, Translated by Andrew P. Dillon
ISBN 0-915299-07-0/1986/328 pages/$65.00/order code ZQC

Shinohara, Isao (ed.). **New Production System: JIT Crossing Industry Boundaries**
ISBN 0-915299-21-6/1988/224 pages/$34.95/order code NPS

Sugiyama, Tomō. **The Improvement Book: Creating the Problem-free Workplace**
ISBN 0-915299-47-X/1989/320 pages/$49.95/order code IB

Tateisi, Kazuma. **The Eternal Venture Spirit: An Executive's Practical Philosophy**
ISBN 0-915299-55-0/1989/208 pages/$19.95/order code EVS

Productivity Press, Inc., Dept. BK, P.O. Box 3007, Cambridge, MA 02140 1-800-274-9911

AUDIO-VISUAL PROGRAMS

Japan Management Association. **Total Productive Maintenance: Maximizing Productivity and Quality**
ISBN 0-915299-46-1/167 slides/1989/$749.00/order code STPM
ISBN 0-915299-49-6/2 videos/1989/$749.00/order code VTPM

Shingo, Shigeo. **The SMED System**, Translated by Andrew P. Dillon
ISBN 0-915299-11-9/181 slides/1986/$749.00/order code S5
ISBN 0-915299-27-5/2 videos/1987/$749.00/order code V5

Shingo, Shigeo. **The Poka-yoke System**, Translated by Andrew P. Dillon
ISBN 0-915299-13-5/235 slides/1987/$749.00/order code S6
ISBN 0-915299-28-3/2 videos/1987/$749.00/order code V6

TO ORDER: Write, phone, or fax Productivity Press, Dept. BK, P.O. Box 3007,

Cambridge, MA 02140, phone 1-800-274-9911, fax 617-868-3524. Send check or charge to your credit card (American Express, Visa, MasterCard accepted).

U.S. ORDERS: Add $4 shipping for first book, $2 each additional. CT residents add 7.5% and MA residents 5% sales tax.

FOREIGN ORDERS: Payment must be made in U.S. dollars (checks must be drawn on U.S. banks). For Canadian orders, add $10 shipping for first book, $2 each additional. For orders to other countries write, phone, or fax for quote and indicate shipping method desired.

NOTE: Prices subject to change without notice.